Roma:

celts, caesars and catastrophes

Sam Wise

Badger & Seal

Published in 2020 by Badger & Seal
Copyright © Sam Wise 2020
All rights reserved

Paperback ISBN: 978-1-8381442-0-3

E-Book ISBN: 978-1-8381442-1-0

Contents

Introduction
3
Britain Before The Romans
5
The Romans Before Britain
13
Not A History Of The World
29
Julius Invades Twice
34
Civil Wars & Triumvirates
53
The Nabataean Kingdom
68
Britain After Julius Caesar
70
Clever, Apathetic Yet Brutal, and Mad
80
Ancient Egypt
89
Claudius Invades
91
Claudius - A Very Mixed Bag
104
Nam Viet
110
Scapula, Suetonius & The Brigantes
112
Nero
129
Nubia
142

Boudicca Loses It
145
The Roman Army
158
Han China
163
Britain After Boudicca
166
The Year Of The Four Emperors
175
The Parthian Empire
183
Agricola - The Beginning Of Roman Ruler Proper
186
Flavians
198
Teotihuacán
209
Hadrian Knocks Up A Wall
212
From Nerva To Hadrian
226
Ireland
237
Antoninus – Two Walls Are Better than One
240
Antoninus & Aurelius
251
The Kushan Empire
258
Romans In Britain Go Mad & Join In With Wizard Wars
260
Commodus & Three To Five Other Emperors
271
The Year of The Five Emperors - Severus Wins Wizard Wars
276
Samarkand
283
Severus Visits Britain
285

The Severan Dynasty
296
Nazca
303
The Gallic Empire
305
The Crisis Of The Third Century
315
The Nok Culture
323
A British Empire
325
From Crisis To Calm
337
The Hopewell Culture
348
What A Load Of Cs - Constantius Chlorus and Constantine
350
Tetrarchy Civil War
359
Christianity
367
The Great Barbarian Conspiracy
370
The Collapsing Empire
381
Huns, Goths & Vandals
390
The End Of Roman Britain
393
The End Of The Roman Empire (Sort Of)
400

Introduction

The Romans were involved in Britain from 55 BC, when Julius Caesar turned up with a load of his mates, all the way to 410 AD, when the whole Western Roman Empire was collapsing. That's about 20% of recorded history in Britain. That feels important, so we decided it was worth knowing about. Hence, the book. However, figuring out what was going on in Britain while the Romans were in charge is surprisingly hard. That's because a lot of the excitement was happening elsewhere in the empire. So, we decided that, for every chapter on the goings-on in Britain, we would follow it with a chapter on the rest of the Roman Empire. These chapters are handy for context, but it's also a perfect excuse to really dig into the behaviour of the madder emperors. A lot of this book is about the horrible people running things.

There is a stereotype that the British don't have a clue about the history of the rest of the world. That's a stereotype, which probably isn't too far off the mark, but it's hard to get too upset about that, as the world is big, and history is long. However, having a vague idea about what was going on in the places not connected to our island is probably a good idea. If only for pub quizzes. We would like to say that it was in response to this sort of high-minded, drive for self-improvement, that we have also added in 'rest of world history' chapters for every point in our story. Really, it's just because of a short-attention-span.

Hopefully, you will enjoy our telling of the story of how

history started on our little island.

Go on, get to the good bit.

Britain Before The Romans

The start date for 'British history' is when things in Britain started getting written down. That begins when the Romans turned up on our little island, meaning one of two dates, 55 BC or 43 BC. It depends on who you ask, but we like the 55 BC date. Unsurprisingly there was a bit more to it than that, and we can't really ignore everything that came before that. Homo sapiens (modern humans) were knocking about in Africa around 315,000 years ago. 315,000 years is a long time, but we didn't make it to what is now Britain until 40,000 years ago, so we were a bit late to the game. We are just a late bloomer, as my mam would say. Nevertheless, even just the 40,000 years gives us a bit of a gap to fill, so here is a really, really quick tour of Britain before the Romans.

As a bonus fact for all you non-Latin speakers out there, the name Homo sapien comes from the Latin for 'wise man' - we called that too early as far as I can see.

Before Britain Was A Sceptred Isle

Let's start with some proof that humans have been knocking about in Britain for ages. The oldest physical evidence of humans in Britain is a jawbone. It even has some teeth still attached. It was found in Kent's Cavern down in Devon, and how old it actually is can be a bit controversial. So the jaw bone is somewhere between 31000 and 45000 years old. Either way, it was from a while back.

Probably slightly younger than that is 'The Red Lady of Paviland.' This is a more complete skeleton, with quite a few of the bones found together, in a cave near Swansea, South Wales. They are dated at about 33,000 years old. The remains were found in 1823, by a Victorian archaeologist called Rev. William Buckland. Being a Victorian gent, and a Reverend, he wasn't a massive fan of the idea of evolution. Which is probably why he identified the skeleton as a Roman-era prostitute who had worked in a nearby Roman settlement. So he was only out by 31,000 years. As well as being millennia out, the skeleton also belonged to a man - a man who became known as The Red Lady. You would think after 33,000 years, you would be able to avoid social embarrassment, but apparently, it's not a given. To be fair to the Victorians, we don't definitely know that the man wasn't a sex worker.

We don't want to be accused of being speciesist, so it's worth pointing out that we are just talking about modern humans here (Homo sapiens), and there is evidence of human's ancestors living in what is now Britain. For example, a 480,000-year-old shin bone was found in Boxgrove Surrey - the dating on that is also a bit controversial, but, whatever the actual age, we are talking about something that is unimaginably old. This particular bit of shin belonged to a Homo heidelbergensis, a species of humans that died out about 200,000 years ago.

To up the ante on that, we also have the 800-900,000-year-old footprints in Happisburgh, Norfolk. Sediment and sand had preserved them until they were found in 2013. These footprints are believed to belong to a member of the species called, homo antecessor, who knocked about from 1.2 million to 800,000 years ago. That is some old feet.

It's worth mentioning that there haven't been people and their ancestors in Britain for the whole of those 900,000 years. Not continuously anyway. Ice ages meant that humans and animals came and went with the weather. For much the same reasons that Whitby is busier in July than it is in February. Archaeologists reckon that the modern humans made their peace with the bad weather around 12,000 years ago, and have stayed here permanently since then. Even at this point, Britain wasn't Britain as you know it. These fair-weather Britons were able to come and go as they please due to a lax approach to border control and the fact that our island wasn't an island. That's because we were attached to the continent by an area between Britain and Denmark, called Doggerland. Around 6000 years ago, in the original Brexit, this land bridge ended up underwater, and we became the island we know and love. Although the house prices on the now soggy Doggerland probably took a bit of a dip.

Since we can't really cope with the idea of a 6000-year-old English/Danish Atlantis, let alone an 800,000-year-old footprint, let's have a look at a more reasonable time scale.

Bronze Age

The Bronze Age in Britain saw a new group of people show up in about 2500 BC. They came from one of the dominant groups in Europe, who was called the Beaker Bell People (a.k.a the Beaker People). They were named, unsurprisingly, after their beakers, which look like an upside-down bell. This group was big on the continent, around central Europe and the Iberian Peninsula (Spain/Portugal). How these Beaker People made it to Britain is a bit of an unknown. There is a problem with tracking the movement of big groups of people in a time before written records. We don't know if these Beaker Bell People moved into Britain and replaced the people who were there before. The alternative to that is that the people in Britain during the

Beaker Bell period, were the same as before, but they had just adopted the use of the beakers. Maybe they just thought they had cool cups. That's a bit complicated, but a simple way of explaining it would be using a modern example: A lot of 21st-century British houses have a Playstation in them, but that doesn't mean we have been invaded by the Japanese.

Fancy beakers may not seem mind-blowing, but the Beaker People coincided with a pretty big advance in technology. Metalworking. More specifically making bronze, which is a metal made from copper, which had been the big thing before, mixed with tin, which made the copper stronger and more durable a.k.a bronze. Handily for our little island, there were tin mines up and running in the South West, so we could go big into the new metal.

This is the bit of our story, which made us realise that we have completely underestimated the people of the Bronze Age. Devon and Cornwall had mines, where they could extract the minerals to have tin. They could then turn this into bronze, an alloy metal. Not only that, but ports were set up to trade these materials with the continent. It's a sad day when you realise that if you were sent back thousands of years into the past, you still wouldn't be of any use to people. We certainly don't know how to make metal alloys. We even had to search 'alloy' to make sure we were remembering it right from GCSE science.

One interesting archaeological find from this period was the Amesbury Archer, who was alive around 2300 years ago when the Beaker People were running the place. He is known as the Amsbury Archer because he was found buried, in Amsbury, Wiltshire, with some nice stuff, including some arrowheads.

It's already quite cool that we have a well-preserved skeleton of a bloke from 2300 years ago, but how's this for a fact: He wasn't local. Using some sort of science involving analysing his teeth, we know that he grew up on the continent, probably near the Alps. So now we would not only be of little use to the Beaker People if we get sent back in time, but we aren't even as well travelled as some of them.

Britain sacked off using Beakers about 500 years later in around 1800 BC. It's a shame that we really don't know much about them because we don't have anything written down. But saying that, you are familiar with some of their work. They helped to make Stonehenge. Contrary to what people think, the world-famous henge wasn't built by Celtic Druids. They wouldn't appear on the island until well after Stonehenge was finished. It was started before the Bronze Age in around 3000 BC, by people we call The Windmill People. They didn't have windmills, but they are named after a nearby hill, called Windmill Hill. Archaeologists are clearly intelligent people, but we are starting to doubt their creativity when it comes to the naming of things they find. It seems they tend to go for word association when picking names.

When the Beaker People (See. Word association) moved into the area, possibly kicking out the Windmill People, they decided to re-decorate and made loads of changes to Stonehenge, like adding in the bigger Sarsen stones. It was finished off by a group called the Wessex People in about 1600 BC, meaning it took about 1400 years to build. That puts into perspective how long it took to rebuild Wembley, so leave the FA alone.

The Wessex People were just one of the groups knocking about on the island during this period. It's estimated that the population of the island was around 300,000 which would put Bronze Age Britain at about the size of Preston. And we don't see the people of Preston building monuments. Pull your finger out Prestonites, all you have is a mad bus station.

Iron Is The New Bronze

The next big thing in metalwork was iron. This arrival in Britain coincided with a new dominant group across Western Europe. The Celts, who were the biggest group in Britain before the Romans turned up. Although that isn't uncontroversial. Like with the Beaker People, we don't know if Britain became Celtic because they took control through invasion, cultural appropriation or a mixture. It's the Playstation issue again. Generally, people are happy with calling the people of Britain, Celts, and that's what we are going with.

As with the Wessex, Beaker and Windmill peoples, Celtic Britain wasn't one country like we would expect to see today. Bigger cultural groups were split down into smaller tribes. Which isn't too hard to understand. For example, a Yorkshireman is a Yorkshireman, but the people of Rotherham aren't the same as them in York. Not even close.

Despite the island being split up into these smaller tribes, the majority of the island was made up of Brythonic Celts. They spoke Common Brythonic, which was a type of Celtic language, but a version which developed separately from the language spoken on the continent. For that reason, this type of Celtic is called Insular Celtic. If you want to get a bit of a taste of what the language was like go and find someone who can speak Welsh, as that's where the Welsh language originally comes from. Not that the whole island would have sounded the same. It's possible that up in the North of Scotland, people spoke their own thing, which had no relation to what anyone else was saying. Again we struggle with not having anything written down by them, and most historians err on the side of those Scottish tribes actually speaking a form of Celtic.

We might not know a lot about some of them, but we actually know the names and rough locations of a lot of these tribes, because the Romans will spend a few hundred odd years writing about fighting with them initially re going to meet them as we go through our story. However, it wasn't from the Romans we get our first mention in the written records. That prize goes to a Greek man called Pytheas. He visited the island in about 325 BC and mapped out the geography of the island as well as meeting some of the people.

It's impressive to hear of a Greek man in Britain in the 3rd-century BC. However, we aren't too sure he got everything properly correct. There is a map, drawn in the 15th century, which is supposed to originally have been drawn by someone using Pytheas' work. And it doesn't look much like Britain. It's all bent over. Still, it's probably a decent go considering they were making it more than 2000 years ago.

He is also credited with being the first person to record the name Britain (or at least where we get the modern word Britain from), which he probably picked up chatting to folk around what is now Wales.

A theme of Pytheas' writing was how connected to the continent we were, with lots of trade across the channel. He particularly talks about the tin trade between Cornwall and France through the River Rhone. It wasn't just about trade relationships, and it looks like there were very close cross channel ties. There was a Belgic tribe (from around Belgium), the Atrebates, who had a branch in Southern England. Further north in Yorkshire we have the Parisi, who share a name with a group who lived around what is now Paris, and there is some evidence that they are linked. That one blows our mind.

In fact, in the decades before the Romans turned up in Britain, there was a big influx of people from the continent. The Romans were conquering Gaul, and our island was a nice safe place for the Celts of Gaul to hideout. It's estimated that the population of Britain at the end of the iron age, when the Romans turned up, was about one million. That would make it a bit bigger than Liverpool. That makes it sound very empty, but as the Romans are about to find out, it was certainly full enough.

So what have we learnt? Well, the weather used to be a lot worse in Britain. Holidays to Denmark used to be a lot easier. Parisians and Yorkshiremen have a lot more in common than the Parisians would care to admit.

The Romans Before Britain

The start of the Romans getting properly involved in Britain was 55 BC. And as a Brit I can confidently say that, realistically, everything to do with the Romans that came before that is completely irrelevant. However, apparently that sort of world view is frowned upon, so if we are going to start out the history of Roman Britain and Rome, we should probably have an idea of what happened before 55 BC. Since, the 'official' date of Rome's founding is the 21st April 753 BC, there is a lot to cover, so here is a whistle stop view.

The Founding

First let's address the unbelievable specific start date for the founding of Rome. That's definitely bollocks and does smell a bit of someone deciding if they make it as specific as possible it will sound believable. At least they stopped short of giving it time as well.

Either way, there are a couple of founding myths for the city. One of them weirdly bits it as part of the story of Ancient Greece, specifically as a sort of sequel from Homer's Odyssey. At the end of the war between Trojans and Greeks one of the less important Trojans, Aeneas, ran off. Rome's founding myth filled in the gaps and had him going on adventures before settling in Rome. The Greeks being the important culture in that part of the world before them, maybe the Romans wanted a link to a heroic past. Or maybe it was the Greeks being important enough to claim everything as their own achievement including a new city miles away.

Which is all very nice, but the myth you have probably heard before is far more fun. The good founding myth starts a bit standard. In the Italian town of Alba their king, Numitor, was deposed by his brother Amulius. Numitors daughter, Rhea Silvia, was a threat so he sent her off to be a Vestal Virgin (a priestess, who crucially wasn't going to have kids who might be keen on taking the throne back for their mam). Unfortunately for Amulius and Rhea, and this is where it gets proper Roman, the Roman God of War, Mars, found Rhea Silvia and raped her. The resulting two brothers born of this were thrown in the river by Amulius. For some reason they were lobbed into the water in a basket, which washed up on the shore of the river. An amateur move from Amulius there.

The twin brothers, called Romulus and Remus, were rescued by a wolf (more mad Roman stuff) and then taken in to be raised by a shepherd. They eventually learnt of their origins, got together an army, and put their granddaddy back on the throne of Alba. That's Amulius not Mars back on the throne, although we could see why there would be some confusion. They then went on to found a city nearby. The final twist in the tale explains why we are talking about the Roman Empire and not the Reman Empire. The brothers had a falling out when Remus laughed at the small walls Romulus had built, which led to Romulus slightly overreacting and killing him. Which to be fair, set the tone. Or it would have if it wasn't a load of old bollocks. Still, it says a lot about a people, when their own founding myth claims they came from a rape followed by fratricide.

Monarchy - The Painful Early Years

    We would call the people of Rome Italians these days, but Italian wasn't a thing back in the 8th century BC. The name for Italy, or Italia, if you are that persuasion, comes from the Greek word for the bottom quarter or so of the Italian Peninsula. It seems like the folk of the peninsula took that on, and by the time the Romans got involved with Britain it was the name for most of what is now called Italy.

    Since they weren't living in Italia in the 8th-century BC the Romans must have been something else. Rome is in a region that was called Latium and they were part of a group of people, or tribe, who made up the Latins. While you might have heard of the Roman Republic and the Roman Empire, from the 'official' start in 753 BC to 509 BC it was actually the Roman Kingdom. We don't know much about the period, because a. It was two and a half thousand years ago, and b. The records of the period were likely lost when Celts sacked Rome in the 4th-century BC. The traditional story, as told by later Romans, was that there were seven Roman kings during the period. That would mean an average reign of 35 years, which seems like quite a while for an ancient king, but that's what we have.

    If you will allow us to skip over 200 years or so of history, we won't deal too much with the myths, but two events are worth bringing up.

    The first comes from the very start of the kingdom, when Romulus was still king. It is called the rape of the Sabine women. The Sabines were a group in Italy, south of Rome and were an early enemy of the city. Romulus organised a festival for the city's neighbours and during that he kidnapped a group of Sabine women, the number of women varies from about 30 to nearly 700. When he wouldn't return them there was a war, unsurprisingly. What really happened is anyone's guess, but, again, it tells you a lot about the Romans when their early history involves a fratricide founder who sneakily kidnapped hundreds of women to be the wives of the Roman men. He doesn't sound like a nice bloke. I blame the parents. You just can't trust gods, princesses, and wolves to properly bring up a child.

The other Roman Kingdom thing we should probably mention is how a monarchy became a republic. According to later Roman sources that is because the seventh named king was an absolute arsehole. This king was the very oddly named Lucius Tarquinius Superbus - Superbus was being Latin for proud, as in arrogant. Lucius got to be king when he teamed up with his wife to murder her dad, the previous king. He was very much channelling the spirit of Romulus from the start there. Lucius carried on at a pace, putting to death senators who he felt were not loyal to him, and reducing the powers of the Senate generally.

It's worth pointing out the obvious there, that even through there was a monarch, the Roman Kingdom still had a senate. This meant Roman people had some power in some sort of parliament type arrangement. This Senate will be a thing throughout all our Roman history, but how important it changes a lot.

Lucius then went on to fight wars with some of Rome's neighbours with the help of some of the other Latin cities in the region. He must have carried on being an arsehole because it wasn't long before the people of Rome took the opportunity to get rid of him. The excuse was given to them by Lucius' son, Sextus. He raped the daughter of an important man, and she committed suicide as a result. Now that's an apple that dropped directly down.

The angry Romans beat their ex-king and established themselves as a republic in 509 BC, although Lucius, with the help of another group in Italy, the Etruscans, was still trying to regain his throne until his death in 495. As with most of what we know about the Roman Kingdom, this revolt can be classed as 'semi-mythical,' it could just be another generic internal posh people revolt, followed by the winners making the losers look bad by fudging the history books a bit. Either way, the Romans were now a republic.

The Roman Republic - What Was It?

Most of us have a gauge idea of what a republic is, but for those of us who didn't fancy school on the day they covered that - a republic is a country run by the public, either directly or through representatives. That means no monarchs or emperors. Current republics included Germany, Mexico and Iran and loads of others. Britain is not a republic, because we have The Queen.

For the Romans, they replaced their monarchs with their version of a president or chancellor. They were called consuls and what made them different was that they were two of them at the same time. Consuls were elected by the Senate, which was made up of, in the early republic at least, members of the posh families of Rome. The Senate advised the consuls and held the purse strings. Other, less posh Romans were represented in the Legislative Assemblies. This was made up of the rest of the Roman Citizens who had full voting rights (unsurprisingly this didn't include women). They voted in 'tribes' that were set up geographically like constituencies, but they didn't make all that many laws, or elect too many officials, as a lot of the important jobs went to the Senate.

Like with any political system, it was pretty complicated, and that was just a 'My First Big Book of Roman Politics' type explanation. It's made more complicated by the fact that over the period of the Roman Republic, the constitution changed to suit the situations they found themselves in, and to reflect who was on top in the inevitable struggles between the groups that made up the Republic. We put this in to show how surprisingly modern the set up was, considering all this was happening more than 2000 years ago. Also, because it is an opportunity to introduce a quick chat on a topic that comes up a lot in Roman history. There were two big conflicts that happened a lot throughout the Roman period. The first was the squabble between Roman Citizens and people living under Roman rule who weren't citizens. The second was between the posh and the not so posh (something which we haven't quite got over yet 2000 years later).

The scrap between the posh and the not so posh started fairly early on in the Roman Republic, but they would phrase it as patricians vs plebs. This 'Conflict of the Orders' lasted for a couple of hundred years, while the plebs tried to get equality with the patricians. The whole thing is pretty much the same as you would get through any bit of history. The patricians were a smallish group of aristocratic families. The official/semi mythical basis for being a patrician family is that they were the descendants of the first 100 men Romulus chose to be Senators. However they got the label, the initial Roman Republic was set up to give these families power. For example, some of the best jobs like Consul and Pontifex Maximus (a sort of head priest, like the Pope) were reserved for the patricians.

As early as 494 BC the plebs were kicking off. One power that they had over the patricians was going on strike. The Roman version of striking, was called seceding, and meant leaving the city altogether and heading to the Sacred Mount, which is just a hill near the city. In 494 this happened when all the plebeian soldiers walked out during a war with three other Italian tribes. Wouldn't you want to be there when the Senate got news of that. The result of this was the plebs were able to elect their own officials, called plebeian tributes. By 287 plebs had got closer to equality with the patricians, and could hold any elected position. Not that there was real equality, but in theory they had won. This doesn't exactly have a lot of bearing on Britain, but it does show these ancient people weren't some completely foreign species.

Much of the things they did, and the problems they had are roughly the same things we have today - it still seems odd having empathy for someone living more than 2000 years ago.

The State of Italy in 509 BC - Who Was Where?

Considering that when you think of the Romans, you can easily picture a group of people striding confidently across the known world surveying all the stuff they had conquered, the Roman Kingdom hadn't got all that far out of the city. They were one of the bigger cities in the local region, but they weren't even the biggest power in Italy. As you would find with a lot of the ancient world, the place wasn't really split into nice neat nations. For example, the Romans were an Italic people, which means they were of a group Italians who spoke an Indo-European language (rather than people who lean a lot). Within the Italics, the Romans were from a sub-group called Latins from Latium.

We are going to do a quick rundown of how the Romans from the city of Rome, all the way to be able to invade Britain. First, let's have a look at who the players were in Italy.

Starting in the very north of what is now Italy, around the alps, were some Celtic tribes. Below these, there were two groups, the Ligures in the west and the Veneti in the east. The Ligures had a language, which is now lost, that was heavily influenced by the Celtic tribes to the north of them. The descriptions of them make them seem a bit ltalic and a bit Celtic, which makes sense. The Romans knew them as warlike mercenaries. The Veneti, who were around the region which now has Venice in it, were similar in that they were a bit of both Italic and Celtic.

Below these Celtic style Italics were, in the north west,

the Etruscans, around what is now Tuscany and Umbria. They were the big boys in central Italy around this time. They called themselves Rasenna, and were a proper major civilisation, who peaked well before the Romans. If there was more evidence of their literature and history, we might even think of them in a similar way we do with the Romans, Ancient Greeks and Ancient Egyptians. They don't count as Italics, and are classed as their own culture.

Also in central Italy, but based on the eastern side, were the Umbrians and Picentes. The Umbrians were Italics who spoke a language in the Osco-Umbrian family, which was an Indo-European language, just different to the Latins. They were based around what is still called the region of Umbria. More on the eastern coast was the Picentes, who were another Italic/Celtic border. The south spoke an Italic language, and they were culturally similar to Umbrians. The north were a bit more multicultural, being nearer the Etruscans and the Celts.

Rome's next-door neighbours were the Sabine. They were the ones who Romulus kidnapped women from, so they were an early enemy. They really were next door, with their territory being in the modern-day Lazio region, along with Rome. Which is why Roma and Lazio are both football teams in Rome, for any football fans out there.

The Sabines weren't Latins despite being so close, and apparently spoke a similar language to the Umbrians. As with a lot of localised argy-bargy, they were close enough to Rome to be pretty similar and the population of early Rome was supplemented with Sabines (even excluding the kidnapped women).

South of the Sabines, in south central Italy, were an offshoot of them called the Samnites, although they called themselves Safineis. This lot would also be a pain in Rome's arse, or more accurately the Romans would be a big issue for the Sabines.

Below this, in the boot of Italy, were the Greeks. Which sounds a bit weird, but by the 5th century BC the Greeks had spread all around the Mediterranean. It was around this time that the Greek cities were fighting with the massive Persian Empire, who were under Xerxes (the bloke from the 300 film). It's safe to say that in Italy the Greeks were of a significant cultural and martial importance. Not that the Greeks were the only player in that part of the Mediterranean. A group of people, called Phoenicians, had spread from the Eastern Mediterranean, from around Lebanon. The big city they founded was Carthage in Tunisia, but they had also set up home in Sicily. Between the Greeks and the Carthaginians, the local tribes down there, like the Sicels, the Elymians and the Sicani from Sicily, were in serious trouble.

From City To (Known) World Domination - Italy

You probably don't need a blow by blow account of the Romans creeping control over the Italian Peninsula. The thing we think is most interesting about it is how long it took. Rome became a republic in 509 BC, but it wasn't until 338 you can say that they had control over Latium. 338 was the end of the second war against the Latin League, which had been formed by loads of other Latin groups, who were annoyed by the Romans taking over.

The Etruscans, to the north were obviously a bit of a worry, because, while that had been on the decline, they had been a pretty important group. They weren't beaten properly until the 260s BC, although there were still technically Etruscan cities, they eventually just became Roman.

The Samnites and the Sabines went the same way as the Etruscans. There were three big Roman Samnite wars between 343 BC and 290 BC. In the end they were a separate people living under Roman control, in the end they just ended up being assimilated.

Between 91 and 88 BC there was an Italian civil war, which was mostly fought because the tribes in Italy, who weren't Roman wanted to be treated equally in the Roman Republic, with voting rights and such. It makes sense, if you are going to have to be part of something, you might as well get the benefits.

While all this was going on, the Romans were having to start dealing with the Greeks in Southern Italy. The Etruscans might have been a notable civilisation at one point, but the Greeks were the biggest of big boys in the Mediterranean world, for a considerable chunk of the ancient period. You could see why the Greeks would be annoyed at the Romans starting to make moves in Italy. In that sort of scenario, it was always bound to kick off, but the match that lit that particular flame is pretty funny. The city of Tarentum (now known as Taranto) is down on the top of the inside bit of the heel of the boot. The treaty between the Greek city and Rome included the Romans not being allowed to sail about in their bit of sea. One Roman source claims that the cause of the war was from the Tarentines overreacted to seeing some Roman ships sailing around their waters taking a posh Roman on a sightseeing trip. That has to be bollocks, but it does sound funny.

The war that followed was the Pyrrhic War, named after the King of Epirus, Pyrrhus, a pretty important state in North West Greece. This war lasted from 280 BC to 275 BC, and involved the Greeks fighting in Italy, joined by some of the Italians who didn't like Rome, like the Samnites. It also involved scrapping on Sicily and in North Africa between the Greeks and the Carthaginians. The whole thing was a disaster for the Greeks. Pyrrhus started well, but he couldn't keep up with the Romans. After one battle he had won, but had lost a lot of men, he apparently said:

'If we are victorious in one more battle with the Romans,

we shall be utterly ruined.'

Which is where the phrase pyrrhic victory comes from - as in you win, but you are completely fucked after.

The war ended with Epirus going home, and the Romans taking more and more control over the Greek cities in the south.

From City To (Known) World Domination - North Africa & Spain

One of the more epic struggles the Romans had in the Mediterranean was with the Carthaginians. It started in earnest in 264 BC with wars against Carthage, who were a massive Mediterranean power based across North Africa. These wars are called the Punic Wars. 'Punic' comes from what the Romans called anything Carthaginian, which isn't handy for the modern reader. Carthaginians were a Phoenician people, meaning they came to what is now Tunisia, where their capital, Carthage, was, from around what is now Lebanon, Palestine, and Israel.

These wars were full-on ancient epics. They lasted until 146 BC, with some gaps and in those 120 off years Rome's success was far from guaranteed. The first Punic War started over Sicily which was between Rome, in Italy and Carthage, in Tunisia. The First Punic War ended in 241, and the Province of Sicily (Sicilia) was formed, although they shared the island with The Kingdom of Syracuse until 214 BC.

You might still be thinking, 'who the hell are these Carthaginians'. Well, you might not have heard much of them, but you have probably heard of their most famous generals, Hannibal. Him of elephants over the Alps fame. It was the fight with Hannibal which was one of the times that Rome could easily have lost. He surprised the Romans when he crossed the Alps, from Spain into Italy in 218 BC. Hannibal and his mates spent about 15 years marching around Italy really messing stuff up. This included the Battle of Cannae, which is usually seen as one of the Roman's worst ever defeats, as they lost the best part of a whole army of 50,000 men, dead or captured.

In the end Rome got it together and got Hannibal out of Italy by sending the General Scipio to invade North Africa. At the end of the Third Punic War, Carthage was completely destroyed, and the Romans picked up quite a few of the Carthaginian territories as provinces. They picked up the islands of Corsica and Sardinia, which makes sense, since they are next door. They also picked up provinces in Spain, Hispania Citerior and Hispania Ulterior. This means near and far Spain, respectively. Nearer Spain was the east coast of Spain and further was the southern coast of Spain. And finally, the province of Africa, which rather than being the whole continent was what is now Tunisia and a bit of Libya. This was Carthage's home turf and marked the end of them, with the close of the Third Punic War in 146 BC.

Even ignoring Sub-Saharan Africa, which is pretty big, the Romans didn't have North Africa sewn up at this point. Egypt was still its own thing and there were the Numidians in Algeria who had helped the Romans against the Carthaginians, but they would be kicking up their own fuss later on.

Spain and Portugal by 55 BC, was pretty much under Roman control, but the place was still crawling with angry Celts, so the level of control was questionable particularly in Portugal and north-western Spain.

From City To (Known) World Domination - Greece & The East

We have already met the Greeks in Italy. Getting rid of them was a winner for the Romans, but it didn't solve the problem of the Greeks in Greece.

While the Romans were still dealing with the Carthaginians, they also fought the Macedonian Wars. The Macedonians, obviously worried about Rome, had tried to negotiate supporting Hannibal. The Romans found out and just decided to fight them both. As was generally the case in the ancient world, 'Greece' was an area, which is now a few neat countries, back then had loads of smaller kingdoms, who mostly didn't get on. The First Macedonian War wasn't all that and it sort of fizzled out once Macedonia had been distracted from helping Hannibal's Carthage.

The other Macedonian Wars came from Rome now being a big player on the Mediterranean. To the east the big powers were Macedonia in Greece, Ptolemaic Egypt and the Seleucids, all three the remains of Alexander the Great's Empire, which had split up when he died.

The Seleucids had been fighting the Egyptians unsuccessfully, but in 205 BC, Ptolemy V became pharaoh of Egypt. He was 5, and the Egyptians did what a lot of states do when they have a child in charge being managed by regents. They had a civil war. The Seleucids apparently signed a nonaggression pact with Macedonia so they could have a crack at Egypt again.

The smaller Greek kingdoms saw that as ending with Macedonia taking the opportunity to take over the rest of Greece. Since the three eastern powers were busy, and were the problem in the first place, they turned to Rome. Who decided to jump in on their side. Which caused the Second Macedonian War, which lasted from 200 to 196 BC, when Rome eventually won. They then sort of tried to back out of Greek affairs rather than take over. Before That though they had a quick march around to secure their interests, including have a quick war with Sparta in 195 BC.

Now the problem wasn't the Macedonians, it was the Seleucids. The Egyptians were bollocksed and Rome had just given the Macedonians a beating, so the Seleucids saw an opportunity. The Seleucid War lasted from 192 to 188 BC They were much stronger than the Macedonians. And they had hired Hannibal as a consultant/general. It turned out the Romans could beat the Seleucids. They kicked them out of Greece and chased them into Asia.

Once again, the Romans assumed the East was fine now, since the Romans had put anyone of note down. And there was a decent gap, but when Philip of Macedonia died his son, Perseus, decided he would kick off as well in 172 BC. It sounds like the Romans struggled a bit with this one, but in 168 BC they beat the Macedonians, and decided to get properly involved in the Greek world. And by properly involved we mean, just run it by dividing it up to client kingdoms. A client kingdom was something the Romans would use quite a bit. It meant there was a king, but they did what the Romans said.

The Greeks didn't like this. So you will never guess what happened next. Yes, in 150 BC there was the fourth Macedonian War. It lasted a couple of years, although fighting also flavoured up briefly in 146 BC when the Achaean League, a group of city states, who had previously fought as Roman allies declared a crazily optimistic war against the Romans. Who absolutely hammered them.

Most of the other provinces picked up by the Romans before 55 BC are over in the east. Rome had already beat the Seleucids, so had some sort of indirect control over bits of what is now Turkey. In 133 BC the king of Pergamon dies without a direct heir and to avoid the inevitable civil war and the killing that would cause, he just gave the kingdom to the Romans, who later created the Province of Asia (it wasn't all of Asia, surprisingly)

In 98 BC a similar thing happened. The ruler of the Kingdom of Cyrenaica, which is a bit of modern Libya, died childless, and left his kingdom to Rome in his will. Later on, Cyrenaica was added to the newly conquered Crete to make a bigger province.

All of this territorial expansion east was part of a scrap with the next big baddie out East, Mithridates of the Kingdom of Pontus. Pontus was based around Eastern Turkey, and at its height spread around the Black Sea. The Romans fought three wars with them, between 88 and 63 BC and there was quite a bit of toing and froing, with the Kingdom of Armenia, led by Tigranes the Great, getting involved against the Romans. Along with the addition of Crete, the Romans also picked up the new province of Bithynia et Pontus in 63 BC, which was the core Kingdom of Pontus, around Northern Turkey. The Province of Cilicia was also established in Southern Turkey. Crete was added to this in 58 BC, but that was contested quite a bit by the Egyptians at first. Further East than Turkey, the Romans also grabbed the new province of Syria from the Armenians. A lot of the surrounding areas, which had been held by Mithridates and co, were allowed to carry on as independent client kingdoms. So, the Romans were pretty established in the middle east by the 50s BC.

From City To (Known) World Domination - Gaul

The last bit of land the Romans occupied we need to cover is Gaul, which was mostly France. in 58 BC Julius Caesar was giving the governorship of Cisalpine Gaul (Northern Italy) Illyricum (the Balkans) and Transalpine Gaul (mostly France). Transalpine Gaul had been a Roman province since 120 BC, but it wasn't particularly under control. The Celts still had the run of the place. Julius was looking to make a splash, and he wanted war with the Gauls. The opportunity came when a couple of tribes, the Helvetii and the Tigurini, migrated towards his province. Julius went big and wiped out the Helvetii and used his momentum to massacre his way up to the English Channel, usually under the guise of intervening in tribe conflicts within his province. As was often the case at the edges of Roman territory, the locals couldn't stop the Romans because they couldn't unite across tribes, so the Romans could rely on support, or at worst inaction from the enemies of the tribe they happen to be exterminating. He beat the Suebi because they were expanding across the Rhine and caused grief for the Celts in the area who were allied with the Romans. And he used a similar excuse when he waded through the Belgic tribes, like the Atrebates, who were later a bit involved in the invasion of Britain.

Not A History Of The World

It doesn't seem likely that we are going to be able to cover world history before 55 BC in this chapter. So we aren't going to try. Instead, we are going to give you a few big milestones in human history and follow that up by trying to make you feel insignificant. That's something to look forward to.

The Neolithic Revolution (First Agricultural Revolution)

In your head, you have an image of stone age people. They are in animal furs, living out of caves and moving around following the seasons and the migration of animals to get themselves food. Hunter-gatherers if you will. Well across the world, that sort of thing changed with farming.

There is evidence in Israel of people using plants and their seeds to grow food for themselves, from 23,000 years ago. However, what you would call proper farming started happening about 12,000 years ago, around Iraq and Iran. By 'proper farming' we mean people growing domesticated crops like barley. This means that 12,000 years ago, people were dabbling in modifying plants to make better crops. We aren't saying they were there in white coats with test tubes, but that still sounds impressive, considering we are talking about 12,000 years ago.

This farming revolution completely changed the way people lived. They didn't have to roam around following the food, because the food was where they planted it. It also meant they could start making use of domesticated farm animals. Goats were first, at about the same time as the plants, followed by sheep and then 10,000 years ago chickens. It makes sense it would be the domestication of plants first and then animals. Can you imagine travelling across a plain, hunting food, while dragging a goat about? It's annoying having to bring more than a couple of bags back from Tesco, so I'm not sure people could cope with that sort of inconvenience.

The spread of this revolution was slow. So slow that some regions had to come up with all on their own. Obviously, the people of the Americas caught on to the idea of farming. And it's not as if they could find out about it on their trip to Iran and taking it home to Mexico. Farming only reached Britain 4500 years ago, and we probably got it from it being passed on from those original farms in the Middle East, coming up through Turkey and the Balkans.

For perspective on how far behind the times we were, the people of Iran had already been farming for around 7000 years. That would be like us using the internet in the 90s, and Iraq only logging on in the year 8991. And we love the internet, but food is probably more important.

Cities

Farming meant people were staying on the spot. This translated, eventually into the building of cities, where people could live being supported by the food in the surrounding area. There are lots of squabbles about what the first city was, because it's not as if we have newspapers from the time reporting on the good news. However, here are some early city highlights:

- Uruk (a.k.a. Erech), was a city in Iraq, which was founded in about 4000 BC, and it grew to have as many as 80,000 people living there.

- Memphis, in Egypt, was founded in about 3000 BC. It's got a pyramid that is still standing that was built around 2600 BC.

- Aleppo, in Syria, might be the oldest continuously inhabited city, as it's been lived in since before 3000 BC. A lot of us will have laughed at an American or Canadian about how new their cities and buildings are. A Syrian could easily have the same conversation with us.

Writing

When people were starting to settle into cities, they were also getting involved with writing. It makes sense if you have people in one spot, you will need some way of organising things. Writing is useful for that. The earliest examples of 'writing' that we have are more like pictures which represent something or someone. Writing like that has been found in China dating back to 6000 BC. This developed into the Egyptian hieroglyphics style of writing, which we are sure you are familiar with. It's still using pictures to represent things, but it's more detailed.

Our favourite bit of ancient writing is in cuneiform, which was the written language from the Sumerians, who lived in Iraq. The British Museum has a tablet, written in about 1750 BC, which is a letter from a bloke named Nanni to a merchant called Ea-Nasir. The whole thing is a complaint that the copper Nanni got from Ea-Nasir was rubbish. How cool is it that we know the name of two people from more than 3500 years ago? We even know that one of them was a proper Del Boy.

Something closer to the use of an alphabet, like the one we use, came about in around 1800 BC, from the Phoenicians adapting it from Egyptian hieroglyphics. This spread to the Greeks by 800 BC, who added vowels to the constants the Phoenicians had used. The Greek version is usually seen as the first proper example of the way that we write now in Britain.

We have already complained about how we don't know much about the goings-on in Britain before the Romans. That's because we don't have anything much written down about us, and trust us, we are going to continue to whine about that even after the Romans appear. By comparison, Sun Tzu's The Art of War was written in China sometime around 500 BC. That's a book which you can go and find, even translated into English, right now.

Food, cities, and writing are just three of the most significant changes in how humans lived, that occurred ages before we have proper written evidence about anything that was going on in Britain. It's amazing how important they were and how slowly all this developed.

We will end on a fact that gets wheeled out a lot but it's particularly relevant to this book. Cleopatra VII, the Egyptian ruler (the famous one), was alive when the Romans first got to Britain. That was 2075 years ago. The Great Pyramid of Giza, a symbol of Ancient Egypt that Cleopatra ruled, was built from around 2550 BC, which is 2481 years before Cleopatra was born. That means Cleopatra was closer in time to you now, reading this, then she was the people who built the Great Pyramid of Giza.

The other one of those we wanted to include is from our earlier bit on farming. Ancient Iranians and Iraqis were planting crops 12000 years ago. Now imagine the Romans and other folks, like Jesus and his mates, at the change from BC to AD. Times the distance from them to us by six, and you make it back to those farmers. That is mental.

It makes you feel a bit less significant, and quite a lot smaller, doesn't it?

Julius Invades Twice

The Romans were not exactly strangers to the Britons in 55 BC, but Britain wasn't a part of the Roman Empire yet. There was one man who had an eye on changing that, and that man was Julius Caesar. It's quite nice that the bloke to start dragging Britain from prehistoric to historic was the most famous Roman of them all. It makes us feel wanted.

Why did Julius Want Our Rainy Island?

So, in 55 BC, Julius, as governor of Gaul, is standing at the English channel looking wistfully out at our island, and thinks to himself, 'I want me a bit of that.' But why? Why was Britain appealing to the Romans, and why was particularly Britain appealing in 55 BC?

The first potential reason for Julius wanting to invade Britain would be the fact that the people of this island have always been, and always will be, a massive pain in the arse. We are calling this the 'he came right at me' reason. Rome had been conquering Gaul for the best part of a century by this point. It started slow, but the Romans were picking up pace with Julius. But, as we will see with Britannia, conquering Gaul wasn't as easy as just beating one king and waving a celebratory flag around. The area was split up into the territories of different tribes. The Romans would beat one tribe only to have to deal with two or three other neighbouring tribes. Julius was in Gaul to finish the job, and he meant business. He was busy fighting the Belgic Celts (the people around what is now Belgium), but this was made harder by the Celts escaping to Britannia when things went against them. It must be difficult to subdue a group of Celts who, even when they are beaten, assume they will be starting to fight again as soon as their literal king across the water comes back. The traffic wasn't all one way, however, and Britons were crossing the channel to help get stuck into the Romans in Gaul. Making them all the more annoying.

Tactically, Julius might have seen the island of Britain as an obstacle to his pacifying of Gaul, and the source of a future uprising even when he had finally got control. The problem with this was that legally a governor couldn't attack tribes outside the official borders of his province. This is a surprisingly good rule. It meant that the people in Rome wouldn't get a letter from a governor at the edge of Roma territory, apologising for starting a war they weren't ready for. An invasion of Britain would be legally questionable, but the excuse of securing the stability of Gaul was a decent one. You can't be too upset at someone acting in self-defence.

The second potential reason for an invasion of Britain is linked to that idea of self-defence. We shall call it the Bush-Blair reason. Britain might be a rainy island on the edge of the known world, but it looked like it was worth having. We know that Britain had been trading with the continent, so the Romans were well aware of the potential for nice shiny things like gold, silver and tin (which was a lot more important to the Romans than you might think). There was also the potential to add decent farmland to Roman territory, as well as picking up livestock and slaves. There was literally 'gold in them thar hills.'

It's not unreasonable that a powerful leader would suggest invading a territory that contained things he would like on the pretext of self-defence. It's entirely possible that Julius felt that because of the danger from Britain's weapons of pointy destruction, which could be deployed in a matter of days, it was worth invading. Once he was there, it would be only right that Rome should take advantage of the lovely minerals to offset the costs of the invasion they made him do.

It might be we are projecting back thousands of years, but it's not inconceivable that the thought of this crossed Julius' mind. It's well documented that his time as a consul, before he was made a governor, left him with massive debts and Britain might have seemed like an excellent way for a governor to make a bit of cash. We are typically a self-deprecating bunch, but it's possible the invasion of our little island was invaded because our little island was worth having.

Our third reason is the one we like the best as the actual reason, and we are calling it the 'drink me in, for I am big Julius' reason.

In 55 BC Julius was the governor of Gaul. He was an important man, but he wasn't at his peak yet. He had already been Consul, which is the top job in the Roman Republic, and he wanted another go at it. The problem was that you needed one hell of a CV, and a lot of friends to get the job. Julius had annoyed a lot of people, and annoyed Roman politicians tended to get a bit stabby. His friends, Marcus Licinius Crassus and Gnaeus Pompeius Magnus (a.k.a. Pompey the Great) were the consuls at this point, and they had got Julius a sweet job. Actually, he had three sweet jobs as governor of Cisalpine Gaul (Northern Italy) Transalpine Gaul (Southern France) and Illyricum (miles away around Albania, Bosnia and Croatia way). He had even been given more time in the jobs than a governor usually had, which was handy because he was going to be in trouble when he went home to Rome. From those stabby politicians. Governors were immune from prosecution, but if he strolled into Rome as a private citizen, all his enemies would be straight on the prosecution bandwagon.

However, if Julius were absolutely smashing it, and he strolled back into Rome as a legend, he would be much safer. Pacifying the Gauls and securing territory into northern France was par for the course as a Roman governor. Britain, though, that was big time. It was unknown. While the Romans were familiar with the place, it was very much on the part of the map labelled 'ere be dragons. Not least because it involved an army crossing the English Channel, which in itself was no small task for people more comfortable with the pleasant warm Mediterranean. What we are saying is that Julius wanted to invade Britain so he would look hard in front of his mates.

Julius Lands in Britain - 55 BC

Julius and his friends landed in Britain in 55 BC, but he had wanted to visit in 56 BC. What had stopped him invading was some pesky Gauls. The Gauls in question were the Veneti from the Armorican peninsula, which is Brittany in France. They kicked off, and Julius had to head on over and put them in their place. This wasn't as simple as it might have been, because the Veneti were pretty good sailors and, as we mentioned, the Romans weren't particularly used to the English Channel and Atlantic. This delayed Julius by a whole year. Not because it took him a year to sort out the rebellious Gauls, but because back in the day there was a campaigning period. You couldn't do a lot of scrapping over the winter. It's too cold, and food was much harder to come by. It was very much the ancient equivalent of staying at home and eating beans because it's too cold to head out to Tesco.

Julius got over this setback, but how exactly does a general go about organising an invasion of an unknown island miles away from lovely comfortable Rome? Well, it appears badly, is how he did it.

The first way Julius messed up was trusting in the business community. He needed to know as much as possible about the Britons and what was going on in Britain. So, he gathered together his merchants, who we know had been trading across the channel. They gave it the old 'Britain you say? Nope, never heard of it.'

It may be his merchants didn't know anything useful, or maybe they spotted if Julius spent the summer ripping through Southern England, that would seriously hamper their trade. Those turkeys just didn't fancy kicking off that particular festive period.

Next up in the bad decisions was to send out a scout ship under a man names Volusenus. He was meant to have a check of the British coast and find somewhere for him to land. We will go into how this was a mistake in a bit.

The final of the trio of bad decisions was backing royalty. In particular, a chieftain called Commius. Commius was in charge of the Atrebates tribe in Belgium. He had been put in place by Julius himself following the kicking the Gauls in that region got. By the time the planning had got this far, the Britons had got wind of it, which worked in Julius' favour. A few of the Briton tribes decided to send envoys over to meet Julius and promise that they would submit to the Romans. That feels a little cowardly, but considering who they were up against it does make sense. Never mind how big the Roman Republic was, Julius himself brags about killing a million Gauls and enslaving a million more. You can see why the Britons might be keen on skipping that bit of an invasion. This is relevant to Commius because he was sent back to Britain with the envoys. His job was to visit the tribes there, probably including the branch of his Atrebates that were in Britain, and get more of them to just pre-submit. Julius was obviously keen to just turn up and immediately claim a victory without having to murder his way around the countryside. It didn't pan out like that. Puppet kings are rarely popular. Especially ones who are suggesting everyone should just give up. So the Britons just locked him up.

From all this, it seems that Julius had failed to gather any useful info and was going to face a resistant population when he landed. From there, it got worse than that for the Romans. As with the year before, with the Veneti, it was kicking off in Julius' provinces. This time the problem came from the Germanic peoples in the east. The tribes from across the Rhine were going to attack his province. The Rhine is a pretty big river, so it was a very useful natural border, with Rome on one side and heathens on the other, but rivers can be crossed. Probably sick of getting interrupted, Caesar massively overreacted to this Germanic foray over the border. He marched over and killed everyone he could find on the west (Roman) side of the Rhine. He then built a bridge to get to the east bank, taking only 10 days, which is a pretty quick bridge. The Romans had a mooch around on the side but left fairly quickly. For obvious reasons, the tribes hadn't wanted to hang around and see what was going to happen. Obviously, he had proved his point, so it was back to focusing on Britain. Unfortunately for the Romans, this delay meant it was getting late in the year, which should have meant another year's campaigning season missed. Julius wasn't going to wait another year, so he went for it, regardless of any pesky seasons.

Given it was getting late and his intelligence gathering wasn't the most effective, how did he go about with the more logistical side of getting an army together?

Well, he had himself two whole legions, which is about 10,000 soldiers, ready to go. We should pause here and mention that we don't know exactly how much this was meant to be a proper invasion. Was Julius intending to properly attack and secure a bit of Britain for a Roman rule? Was it just meant to be a quick visit to show his face, and to let the Britons know that he could take them any time he wanted? We don't know. What we do know is that 10,000 soldiers was a lot of soldiers. It's a similar number to the men historians reckon William the Conqueror took with him to England in 1066. And nobody is calling him William the Visitor are they?

While his 10,000 soldiers were all ready and raring, Julius' cavalry was getting prepared in a different port, so Julius decided to set off without them. They could catch up later. It was already the 24th of August, so it was getting late on in the year, and he had one eye on the campaign period we mentioned earlier. The bloke was in a rush. Now we get to what excellent spot had our man Volusenus, the one who had been sent out to scout, found for him? From Julius' description of the point of British coast he first got to, it's assumed where Volusenus had picked to land was at Dover. As in The White Cliffs of Dover.

For those of you wondering what's wrong with that, imagine getting off your ship to land on the beach. It sounds quite nice. I mean, who doesn't like a trip to the seaside? But now imagine that some merchants and a puppet king had told everyone that you were about to invade. So when you turn up, the cliffs above are lined with angry-looking natives. They also like a trip to the seaside and had decided to bring along their favourite heavy and pointy things along with them.

Storming a beach while having things thrown at him didn't appeal to Julius, so he decided to head down the coast a bit and find a better spot. Probably giving Volusenus a hard slap on the way. Unfortunately, they were followed by the Britons, so their next issue was landing on a beach full of Britons, who hadn't conveniently left their pointy things back in Dover. To make the situation worse, the Romans ships couldn't cope with shallow water up to the beach, so the soldiers had to jump into deeper water and fight their way from there to shallow water and then onto dry land. Thinking strategically, we believe this is known as 'having an absolute 'mare'. The whole Romans not being good sailors thing, is really starting to look important.

The story we are told about this mess comes from Roman sources. It claims that the legions were reluctant to go in the water at first. That is until a brave standard-bearer leapt into the sea, clutching the Eagle Standard. You might have seen these standards in films, they were like the Roman equivalent of medieval banners. They were symbols of each legion and was a sort of representation of the honour and pride of the men. Losing it would be unbelievably bad news for everyone involved. This brave standard-bearer jumped into the water and shouted:

'Leap, fellow soldiers, unless you wish to betray your eagle to the enemy. I, for my part, will perform my duty to the Republic and to my general.'

Isn't that a lovely story? Very Hollywood. It's more likely he screeched something along the lines of:

'I'm getting seasick on that fucking boat. Hurry up and get in the water you pack of cowardly arseholes'.

Whatever he said, it worked. The Romans got their feet wet and managed to fight their way to the beach. The Britons ran off in their speedy chariots and, since Julius' cavalry was still sailing over, he had to let them go because he didn't have anything fast enough to chase them with.

After this quick fight, the Britons had obviously decided that Julius was too hardcore for them and agreed to submit to him to avoid taking a kicking. Julius must have been looking forward to consolidating his position and just wait for the tribute to start rolling in. It was all coming up Julius. He had landed, beat the Britons and was looking all set to take charge of a good bit of South East England. Briton tribes were coming and submitting to him (again), and his cavalry was on the way over the channel.

Then disaster struck. Like a modern-day tourist from Southern Europe, he hadn't taken into account the British weather. A big storm blew up to really ruin his day. Firstly, it happened when his cavalry was sailing across the channel, forcing them to turn around and go back to Gaul. Secondly, Julius had set up a camp near where he had landed, but he hadn't pulled his ships far enough onto the beach. He wasn't used to our weather and tides, so the storm threw his ships about, and a lot of them broke. And we bet he didn't even have his brolly with him. Now the Romans had gone from a comfortable victory and a rosy immediate future to being wet, horseless and without enough ships to get home. The Britons spotted this and quickly left to start organising getting their own back.

Julius had himself two fairly big problems now. Firstly he would have to fix his ships if he wanted a route back to Gaul, and secondly, it looked like the soldiers would be forced to hang around near the beach for a bit so he would need some food for this 10,000 men. Ever the decisive general, he got one legion to set up to defend and fix his ships while the other was sent out for forage for food (foraging being a military euphemism for nicking some stuff).

Julius was hanging around, waiting for his dinner when someone spotted a massive dust cloud in the direction of his foraging legion. This either meant his soldiers were dancing for joy over how much food they had found, or they were under attack. Assuming the latter, he grabbed up men and marched over to help the foraging legion. They had indeed been attacked by a force of opportunistic Britons. It sounded pretty bad for the Romans, who were particularly freaked out by the Briton's chariots. Still, Julius and his legions managed to fight their way into a retreat to the beach.

The Britons and their chariots were a massive problem for the Romans, and Julius certainly seemed pretty impressed with them. We have been reading about all this quite a bit, and it seems unacceptable for anyone to talk about 55 BC without including this quite long quote from his book 'The Gallic Wars' So if you will excuse us, here it goes:

'In chariot fighting the Britons begin by driving all over the field hurling javelins, and generally the terror inspired by the horses and the noise of the wheels are sufficient to throw their opponents' ranks into disorder. Then, after

making their way between the squadrons of their own cavalry, they jump down from the chariot and engage on foot. In the meantime their charioteers retire a short distance from the battle and place the chariots in such a position that their masters, if hard pressed by numbers, have an easy means of retreat to their own lines. Thus they combine the mobility of cavalry with the staying power of infantry; and by daily training and practice they attain such proficiency that even on a steep incline they are able to control the horses at full gallop, and to check and turn them in a moment. They can run along the chariot pole, stand on the yoke, and get back into the chariot as quick as lightning.'

So what that is saying is that the Britons were proper ninjas on their chariots. They could ride in and get dropped off to do some fighting, and then, when it got dicey, they could call back in the chariots, jump on and ride off to safety.

Once again, the Britons decided they were probably not going to come out on top, so went and submitted to the Romans (some of them perhaps for the third time). Julius must have had enough with the whole thing. He accepted their submissions and demanded hostages to make sure they stuck to it this time. He didn't even hang around to collect the hostages and just headed back to Gaul, leaving instructions that hostages should be sent after him.

This was not a roaring success from Julius. Yes, he had technically won, but not many victories end with you racing home to get away from who you have just beaten. Most of the tribes didn't even bother to send the hostages across.

It's also worth noting that the Romans sailed back over in ten fewer ships than they sailed across in. That means it was either a cramped journey, or the Romans had lost more than 10% of their men.

That's the end of Julius' first go at Britain, but he would be back.

Julius Has A Second Go At Britain - 54 BC

Julius wasn't done with Britain, and he came back the next year, in 54 BC. We are told that this time his excuse was that the tribes hadn't sent across the hostages they had promised him. Which seems pretty straight forward as an excuse for an invasion.

The theme of the 54 BC invasion is Julius learning from his mistakes. The first example of that would be the number of men he decided to take. As we mentioned before, the 55 BC attempt may have been a bit of expedition, rather than a proper invasion. This time, it looked like he meant it. Instead of the mere two legions of 10,000 men from 55 BC, the 54 BC go involved five legions and cavalry, which was about 30,000 men. He had also learnt his lesson regarding those cool chariots the Britons used so well. We are told that he took half the Roman cavalry in Gaul with him, and historians have worked out this would be about 2,000 of them. Presumably, that would be able to neutralise those pesky charioteers as well as making it harder for the Britons to run off and regroup when the Romans were winning a battle.

We have tried getting our head around the size of this invading army. Was 30,000 soldiers loads for the ancient world? Was it loads for little ole Britain? We know that ten years later, in 44 BC there were 36 legions in the Roman army, and Julius had five of them in Britain. Clearly, the Romans could spare that many for a jaunt to Britain, but still, it was a fair chunk of the manpower of the whole Republic.

What about a bit of modern context? It's hard to know how many people lived in Britain around this time, but most estimates put it between 1 and 1.5 million. Our population is about 60 million now, so the equivalent would be an invasion of more than 1 million soldiers. Considering that Julius' initial attack would likely only see the Romans come up against the tribes of Southern England, it does start to look like overkill. Whether you think it was overkill or not, it showed an intent. This was no small expedition to have a quick look over the channel. Julius was going over there to mess some folk up.

Julius learnt a few lessons on his first trip to Britain. For a start, it was obvious that when it comes to soldiers, less is not always more. Also, horses are handy for chasing stuff. Something else he realised was that, if you are going to cross the channel, you need the right sort of ships. Not only did he build 600 new ships, but they were more suited to landing on the coast of Britain than the last year's versions. He stole the design from the Veneti, who he had beaten in 55, and mass-produced them as only a Roman could.

So he was better prepared, but you will also remember an issue he had with his current provinces kicking up a fuss and delaying him, first in Brittany, and then along the Rhine. Well, it happened again, although not as bad this time. This time the issue was in Illyricum (mostly modern Croatia) one of his three provinces he oversaw. The Germanic tribes were again gearing up for having a crack at Roman lands. Even once that was fixed, Caesar had more trouble back in Gaul. This must have been particularly frustrating as a fair chunk of the soldiers of Gaul were about to leave. In fact, this whole jaunt seemed incredibly risky.

The Gallic kerfuffle came from the Treveri Tribe, who were from around Northwest Germany. The German city of Trier is named after them. It was clear that taking soldiers out of a territory that you have just conquered was a recipe for a revolt. Julius had a plan for that, and he called a council of which the tribal leaders were meant to attend. However, the Treveri didn't fancy it, so Julius had to show them who was boss. That didn't seem too tricky, but it wasn't just the Treveri Julius had to worry about. His plan was to take the leaders of the tribes in Gaul to Britain with him as hostages, to make sure that everybody behaved themselves. One leader, Dumnorix of the Aedui, kicked up a fuss, so

Julius had to take him captive and keep a closer eye on him. Dumnorix tried to wander off while Julius was busy with his preparations, so he was chased down, and when he refused to return, they just killed him. The Aedui were from around Burgundy, which is in the middle of France. That means while it looks like it was mostly the north of Gaul which was kicking up a fuss, the problem was spread across the whole place. It was clear that Gaul would be a problem, but it was equally obvious that Julius was having none of it.

With Julius happy enough with the state of things, Julius headed off to Britain with all his ships on the 7th of July. That was months earlier than the previous year, and a far more sensible time to be dabbling in a bit of an invasion. You can't fault Julius for his ability to learn from his own stupid mistakes.

The landing was much smoother this time, without Volusenus suggesting the worst possible spot. They did get blown off course a bit, but still made it to the same landing point they eventually used in 55 BC. Now better supplied, with more men, cavalry, and some more appropriate ships, it all went to plan. The Britons had heard in advance that the Romans were coming, so they were ready to line the beach again. They were there, but seeing the hundreds of ships with the tens of thousands of soldiers, they decided not to bother and retreated, leaving the beach nice and clear for the Romans to land and disembark.

While it was no doubt a relief to any soldiers who had made the first trip, it gave Julius a new problem. You can't be invading and not fighting. That would just be a waste of time, and you would look a bit silly. Not being the most patient of men, he got his soldiers together and marched off into the night to find someone to take his anger out on.

He found the Britons hanging around the River Stour (the one in Kent). Despite having legged it at the first sniff of Roman, the Britons looked in a stronger position this time. They had taken a bit of a beating in 55 BC, but this time the tribes in the area banded together and got themselves one leader, Cassivellaunus. He was probably the chief of the Catuvellauni, a tribe from over in Hertfordshire.

Their position on the River Stour was nicely defended, and it was probably a hill fort, which was the typical sort of defended town the Britons lived in. The Roman solution to this was for one of the legions to set up in a tortoise formation. That's the one where they make a shell shape with shields above their heads and down the sides. They stormed the fort, and the Britons ran off again, but Julius, showing a bit of caution, didn't chase them, deciding not to rush off headlong across terrain he knew nothing about.

It was going well, but what happened next will sound a bit familiar. The Romans had crossed over in 800 ships; 600 of their own with the rest 'borrowed' from the tribes in Gaul. He had apparently left them at sea when they arrived, probably because he didn't want to waste men dragging that many ships onto a beach, while there were Britons to be chasing about. He couldn't have properly beached that many ships and immediately marched out to meet the Britons. Even so, less than a year earlier, he had done exactly that same thing, and it had gone horribly wrong. After the battle at the River Stour, surprisingly, Julius got the message that there had been a storm and 40 of his ships had been wrecked. Again, he had to send back to Gaul for help with making new ships. Probably to avoid looking stupid if he got done by a storm three times, Julius ordered the remaining ships onto the beach. Clearly, he hadn't completely learnt his lesson from the previous year, but he was getting there.

This delay in fixing the ships, which lasted about 10 days, definitely would have taken the edge off his quick attack on the Britons. Julius also got some personal bad news during this lull. His daughter had died in childbirth. Obviously, the death of his daughter would be devastating to anyone, but it also had a political dimension. His daughter, Julia, had been married to Pompey the Great, who was a member of

Julius alliance, the Triumvirate. Political alliances in Rome were often cemented through marriages, not dissimilar to how royalty did things until very recently. The death of his daughter meant Julius was on the edge of the world fighting crazy, almost mythical, tribesmen, while his safety net of an alliance back in Rome had taken a blow. More than ever, he needed the invasion to go well.

So Julius re-launched his attack and started by heading up towards the river where he fought the Britons 10 days earlier. Having spotted that the Romans were pretty good at fighting in an open battle, with all the classic charges and cavalry techniques, Cassivellaunus' tactic was to engage in guerrilla warfare. They would attack a group of Romans and lure them into wooded areas and give them a beating. One evening when Julius was making camp, the Britons attacked out of a wood. In his book, Julius claimed victory on that one. Still, it was obviously close enough that when he was talking about it, he mentioned how traditional Roman legion tactics were not suitable to defend against attacks like this.

Unfortunately for the Britons, they didn't get away with just popping out and having quick goes at the Romans. The next day Cassivellaunus tried it again when they came across three legions. The attack turned into a proper open battle, where the legions could do what they did best. Worse than that the Roman cavalry was able to chase down and kill Britons as the legged it off.

All this guerrilla stuff sounds a bit stalematey, but the next big event was very cinematic sounding. The tribes found themselves on the north bank of the Thames, while the Romans were on the south bank, possibly somewhere in what is now West London, around Brentford. Cassivellaunus knew they were coming and had set up defences, pointy steaks in the water and such, along the river to stop them crossing. But cross they did, with soldiers wading across the river to attack and beat the tribes.

When we were reading about all this, it felt like the whole invasion could go either way. The Romans were making good progress and heading further north, but they were on the clock, and they would want the fighting to be over by winter. At this point, our money would be on it ending in a score draw. The Britons were mostly sticking to their guerrilla tactics, including hiding away crops and livestock so the Romans couldn't get fed easily.

Despite this, and despite the natives presumably suffering under Julius' less than nice invasion tactics he tended to use, the Britons had one colossal weakness that could be exploited. Cassivellaunus was an absolute knobhead. His tribe, the Catuvellauni, had been a bit expansionist in the years before Julius pitched up. In particular, they had been warring with another sizable tribe from around Essex and Suffolk, the Trinovantes. Cassivellaunus had been getting the upper hand and had executed the Trinovantes king. There are no prizes but have a guess which group of Britons were among the first to come to the Romans and ask to deal with them. The Trinovantes wanted their own king again, and the son of the last murdered king, Mandubracius, just so happened to have fled the Catuvellauni and was with Julius on his invasion. In return, Julius was offered grain, which was handy as Cassivellaunus had been setting fire to any crops that the Romans could have got hold of.

The Trinovantes supporting the Romans seemed to start a bit of a domino effect, with the other tribes of the South East submitting to the Romans. At this point, they would have all been familiar with the Romans ability in battle, as well as their willingness to kill tribal kings if things got out of hand. These defections meant the Romans were fighting against fewer men, with the added bonus of the recently submissive tribes being free with information on Cassivellaunus' whereabouts.

The end of Cassivellaunus also sounds quite dramatic. Julius found the Britons in a fortified position in a forest. He attacked, forcing the Britons to run away. It was around this point that both Julius and Cassivellaunus got the same news. Four kings of the Cantii tribe, based down in Kent, had attacked the troops guarding all the Roman ships. How carefully the Britons were able to coordinate attacks, we don't know, but the Cantii attacks sound a bit like a roll of the dice to cause a distraction so Cassivellaunus could regroup. Cleverly coordinated or not, it failed, and the Cantii were beaten back by the Romans guarding their ships. Now Cassivellaunus was ready to come to terms with Julius, and he was going to use Commius to do his negotiating for him. Commius was the Belgic Atrebates king Julius had sent over in 55 BC to negotiate for him, so he was a suitable middleman.

The resulting treaty basically meant that the tribes of Britain, or at least the ones in the area the Romans had been in, were subject to Rome. Although, this might be overstating it. Payment of tribute was owed to Rome and hostages had to be given up. Also, the Catuvellauni were to leave the Trinovantes alone, which is a nice reward for helping Julius.

So the Romans won. Well done those Romans. But they didn't really. Julius and his men left to go back to Gaul in the autumn and never returned. They didn't even leave any sort of administration behind. Considering this was a famous military leader from the most powerful empire in the world, it didn't feel like much of a victory, except on a technicality. He had won a few battles but left about a month after he landed without having any real control over any of Britain. Not only that, but he didn't exactly cover much land when he was there, not even getting out of South East England.

The people of Rome seemed quite impressed, and the Senate granted a celebration period, called a supplicatio, which is a sort of thanksgiving. This lasted an unprecedented 20 days, so it was a big deal.

The important posh men of Rome didn't all share the population's feelings on the invasions. Cicero, a high-flier in Rome, who really didn't like Julius, wrote letters to his brother, who was with the army in Britain. In one of them, he said:

> 'On affairs in Britain I see from your letter there is nothing there for us to fear or rejoice at.'

As in there was no point in all of that, the Britons are no threat, and they don't have anything we want. Cicero was also a bit scathing on the fact that the promised riches didn't flow from the campaigns. They did get a lot of slaves, but the loot wasn't as shiny or as vast as Julius might have suggested.

What did it all mean for Britain? Julius had installed a king in a prominent tribe, the Trinovantes, and his show of strength would have dissuaded the Britons to fight Rome on the continent for fear of the return leg. There were agreements in place, and while they looked like they would be a bit short term, it put the tribes of Southern England firmly in Romans sphere of influence. They couldn't feel safe behind the English Channel anymore.

Success or not, Julius gave it the big Veni Vidi Vici and buggered off.

Except he didn't. Julius apparently did write Veni Vidi Vici (as in I came, I saw, I conquered) following a victory, but it wasn't to do with Britain. It was a few years later, after a battle in Turkey. We were sure it was about Britain, but it wasn't we're afraid. Not everything revolves around Britain, and that makes us sad.

That was it. Julius is finished with Britain. He didn't come back at all, although in his defence that was because he was very, very busy elsewhere. For a start, Gual took advantage of his little trip, and they were kicking off. Then Roman politics took over, which is the theme of our Roman history chapter coming up.

So what have we learnt? Well, the Roman's first go at Britain wasn't quite as impressive as you might think, Julius Caesar had some mistakes in him, and chariots are cool.

Civil Wars & Triumvirates

Julius Caesar's jaunt to Britain is an important part of British history. It might not have made an earth-shatteringly big difference to the life of the Britons, but it was the proper start of Roman interest in our island. It was, however, not particularly important to the rest of the world. Partly because we are just one small island on the edge of the Roman Empire, but also the Roman world was going through some mad changes. We went over the reasons Julius might have had to visit Britain, but this should give a background on what got him to that point in the first place.

Civil Wars - Roman vs Roman & Sulla vs Marius

From 91-88 BC Italy (or at least the Italian Peninsula since Italy wasn't a thing yet) had been at war with itself. The Italians, the ones who weren't Roman at least, were angry at the Romans for treating them as second class. The war was called The Social War and ended with the Romans winning, but the people on the Italian peninsula who hadn't revolted were given Roman citizenship. The Romans giving other people citizenship was nothing new, they had been doing that for a few hundred years. And it certainly wasn't weird for other Italians to be fighting the Romans. That was almost a habit by this point. What happened next was a bit more unprecedented, a Roman on Roman civil war fought for personal gain.

In Roman politics, there were two groups, the populares and the optimates. The populares were more 'for the people' and wanted more power given to the assemblies. The assemblies were the bit of Roman politics all types of normal plebs could get involved in. We say all types, but they didn't take suffrage to extreme lengths, it was only men. So by 'all' we mean at best 50%, and it was just citizens so no foreigners and no slaves, so not even that. Even so, the populares were the most open group in Roman politics, since the optimates were all about maintaining as much power as they could in the Senate, meaning real power would be held by a small number of families. These weren't political parties, so it's not precisely like Tory vs Labour, but the Romans definitely had two political 'teams.'

Between 88 and 80 BC, there were two civil wars fought between Sulla, an optimate, and Marius and his son Marius the Younger, who were team populares. The first was won by Marius, but in 83 BC Sulla was back in Rome to take control.

We mention this kerfuffle for a few reasons. Firstly, it shows that Rome was busy with fighting, with civil wars in Italy, as well as fighting the empires from the Middle East and tribes across Europe from Spain to Germany. Secondly, it shows that there was room for powerful men to jump in and start to take control of things. Lastly, it's relevant to Julius Caesar.

Julius was growing up during this, and he was related to Marius. This was good news while Marius was in charge. He was given the job of High Priest of Jupiter, who was the Roman king of the gods, and their version of Zeus. He also swung himself a marriage to Cornelia, the daughter of Lucius Cornelius Cinna, who was a bigwig working with Marius. That would have meant power and money.

The problem was this only worked for as long as the place was being run by Marius. Unfortunately, Sulla won out in the end, which meant all the good stuff given by Marius to his friends and family, like Julius, was now to be given to Sulla's mates. Sulla took Julius' priesthood off him. He then took away all his cash Julius had inherited from his dad and the dowry he had got when he married Cornelia, who he was told to divorce. He refused to do that last bit, which is nice. Probably because Julius knew the refusal wasn't sensible, and he could spot the way the wind was blowing, Julius went into hiding. He managed to survive the inevitable purge that tends to follow one faction beating another. Not just because he legged it off to hide, but because his mam's family had some influential supporters of Sulla's in it. Presumably, they called in a favour and got him taken off the shit list.

Even so, he didn't get his cash or his priest job back, so he was a bit of a loose end. Between that and probably not knowing how long he would be off the shit list for, he left Rome and joined the army.

What follows is some proper madness, but it's handy to know that it was already mad before Julius and his mates started kicking off.

The First Triumvirate - Julius Gets Some Powerful Mates

The First Triumvirate was a bizarre alliance between three important men of Rome. There was Julius Caesar who we know about, he was a prominent populares who had already had some top-end jobs, like being the Governor of Hispania Ulterior (Southern Spain). One of his teammates was Marcus Licinius Crassus, but he was an optimate. He was very much an optimate since Marius had killed his dad and his brother before Crassus made a lot of money from working with Sulla. So much money he is usually touted as being the richest man in Rome at this point. The other member of the Triumvirate was Pompey The Great. He was also an optimate and was a very popular general. He had been winning battles all over the place and was made consul for the first time when he was only 36, which is 6 years younger than was allowed at the time. Pompey shared that consulship with Crassus, but don't confuse that for them being friends. They really didn't get on, partly because Pompey had been claiming wins in wars that Crassus felt he should have got the credit for.

Even though they clearly weren't going to be a cohesive team, they joined together to get Julius the job of consul in 59 BC. They also used their power and money to effectively sideline the other consul at the time, Bibulus. Julius' big showpiece bit of legislation was the redistribution of land, helping out the poorer folk. Bibulus tried to stop it because he was an optimate, but he and his bodyguards were attacked. There were some injuries, and someone threw a bucket of shite over Bibulus. Which is, no doubt, why he legged it off and hid in his house for the rest of the year of their consulship.

Julius was understandably not popular with the posh folk in Rome. A consulship only lasted one year, and the outgoing consuls were given their next job. It was usually a governorship of a province, but Julius' enemies were keen on him getting no power, so they tried to put him in charge of woods in Italy. There probably isn't a lot of influence you can wield being a park ranger in charge of trees and squirrels, although to be fair the job was a bit more than that. Luckily, being in the Triumvirate meant he had his influential supporters. They got Julius a governorship. Actually, they overcompensated and got him three; Cisalpine Gaul (northern Italy) and Illyricum (Croatia), with Transalpine Gaul (Southern France). This was good for Julius. Not only was it nice and safe away from Rome, but it was on the edges of Roman territory, which means fighting. Fighting meant fame and lots and lots of money. It's also what allowed him to have a crack at Britain, which we know about.

All that is the background to Julius feeling the need to invade Britain. It clearly wasn't an easy time to be a Roman in, even a high-up Roman, like Julius. What happened after Julius' two trips to Britain was even spicier.

The End Of The First Triumvirate

The Triumvirate officially ended when Crassus died at the Battle of Carrhae, in 53 BC, fighting the Parthians in what is now Turkey. From 54 BC to 49 BC Julius mostly stayed in Gaul, finishing off proper Gallic resistance, and fighting a few full-on revolts. Julius had got to Northern France by 57 BC, but he was far from done as we saw in the British history chapter. Gaul had some severe problems with a revolt in central France in 52 BC, under Vercingetorix. This is not particularly significant to the end of the Roman Republic, but we didn't want to miss the opportunity to talk about the Battle of Alesia. Julius was attacking a fortified position and decided to besiege them and starve them out rather than go for a full-on attack. To do that he built temporary fortifications in a ring around the settlement, so nobody could get out. The problem for Julius was that Vercingetorix had got the other tribes involved and they were going to send reinforcements to lift the siege. So, Julius built himself another ring of fortifications around his men. That meant he had Vercingetorix in the middle of a nice safe ring of Roman soldiers and all the other angry Gauls outside. It was a Roman doughnut. It worked, and Julius kept the siege until Vercingetorix gave himself up. Not relevant, but very cool.

After all that, Gaul was much more under control by 51 BC.

Julius Takes Control

Julius' governorship was coming to an end. This was a massive problem, as he had enemies in Rome. A lot of people were worried about the power he built up for himself while he was in Gaul. The taking of the region had needed a lot of soldiers, which meant that Julius had the support of some seriously battle-hardened legions. Rome had seen what happens when a powerful man had the backing of an army, and they didn't fancy a return of the problems with Sulla. Julius was worried about giving up those legions and wandering back into Rome, having lost the immunity he enjoyed as a governor. We don't know how much this was just people trying to get to Julius, but there were claims that Julius should be put on trial for his horrible crimes in Gaul. Given the Romans weren't exactly squeamish, if what Julius did in Gaul was terrible enough to talk about trails, it must have been nudging into crimes against humanity territory.

Julius' solution to all this was to demand to be made consul. The Senate who didn't like that idea said no. Julius was now without a governorship, and any hope of advancing in Roman society lay back in Rome, where the powers that be didn't like him. Julius was in trouble, and annoyingly for him, among the people who didn't like Julius, was his old political ally Pompey the Great. He obviously felt there was only room for one great in Rome, and for Pompey, it was Pompey. There was a Roman historian, Florus, writing a bit over 100 odd years later, who wrote something very flash about the men's relationship at this point. It's been handily translated as:

> *'Caesar's power now inspired the envy of Pompey, while Pompey's eminence was offensive to Caesar; Pompey could not brook an equal or Caesar a superior.'*

With the Senate turning to Pompey for help, and Pompey wanting to get shot of Julius, Julius needed to do something. The Senate was demanding that he gave up his armies and came home to Rome. Julius didn't fancy that but offered to do it if Pompey did the same with his legions in Spain. That wasn't going to happen, so Julius took a big step. If he could get himself re-elected to an important magisterial position, he would be immune to those prosecutions and if he couldn't do that the easy way, he would do it the hard 'march into Rome' way. So, Julius crossed the Rubicon with his armies. This was important, and you might have heard 'crossed the Rubicon' used as a phrase for doing something which can't be reversed. The Rubicon was a river that separated the Province of Cisalpine Gaul and proper Roman Italian territory, so taking an army over that point was in effect an invasion.

The crossing kicked off the Great Roman Civil War, a.k.a. Caesar's' Civil War. It lasted four years and involved every prominent Roman going, but at the start, it was Julius vs Pompey. Julius ran through Italy reasonably quickly, with Pompey deciding that Rome couldn't be defended. Instead, Pompey legged it south, then carried on legging it east, where his power base was, to the province of Epirus in Greece. The war was fought all over the place, but one of the first moves was Julius attacking Spain because it was particularly pro Pompey.

He arrived back in Rome, after smashing the pro-Pompey army in Spain, and was made Dictator. The position of Dictator was an actual official title in the Roman Republic - as much as it sounds more than a little negative these days. The job was occasionally given to political leaders in times of trouble, for example, if a war was going badly, or there was a domestic revolt that was bigger than usual. The reasoning behind this thinking was that, in a nation governed by two consuls, each with the power of veto over the other, things could go badly. They could mess a war up in a 'too many cooks spoil the broth' kind of way.

It's not particularly crucial for this, but, if you want an example of why having this dictator position was a good idea, then look no further than the Battle of Cannae in 216

BC. The Romans were fighting a Carthaginian army led by world-famous elephant wrangler, Hannibal, at Cannae in Southern Italy. They were not doing well against the Carthaginians and had decided to combine their legions into one bigger army for this battle. Usually, each consul would be the general of their own army, but when the armies were combined into one, the law was that each day they took turns acting as general. The consuls at the time were Paullus and Varro. Paullus liked the cautious approach, while Varro liked a more aggressive approach. This doesn't work out in a day by day rota. For example, if the more aggressive consul ran headlong into battle on his day, and got everyone killed, there isn't a lot of room for caution the next day. According to the sources, this is what happened, and Cannae was one of the worst ever Roman defeats. Sometimes two heads aren't better than one, and too many cooks can indeed spoil the death count.

Anyway, Julius was made a dictator, and he took the job for 11 whole days. During which he made sure he was re-elected as consul, giving a beautiful legitimising sheen over his civil war, and making sure he couldn't be prosecuted. Although who is going to try and prosecute the bloke whose army was ripping through Italy and beyond? This use of the dictatorship did somewhat go against the spirit of the dictator rule, but it got the job done.

All this happened in less than a year. The next four years saw fighting all over the place, including Greece, Albania and Tunisia. It didn't all go Julius' way, and he lost the odd battle, but it was clear who was winning. In 48 BC, Pompey escaped to Egypt, where they were enjoying their own civil war, with King Ptolemy XIII fighting his sister Cleopatra (yep, that one). In a bold move, Ptolemy had Pompey assassinated in an attempt to make a friend of Julius. Which, sort of made sense, as the Romans were obviously going to have a say in who ran Egypt sooner or later. The problem was that Julius didn't like an Egyptian killing a Roman general. So either for his own political benefit or because he really was angry at Ptolemy killing his friend-turned-enemy, Julius dived in on Cleopatra's side. He laid siege to Alexander, beating Pompey's old army in the process. The fighting continued for another 3 years, until 45 BC, with Julius winning his last victory at the Battle of Munda, in Spain.

Civil wars generally aren't very nice, and this one was no exception. Which made Julius' celebration of the win a bit controversial and got him into a bit of trouble. When a big war was won, or some other significant military event had taken place, the people in charge of them were celebrated in a triumph. This involved a big parade through Rome with everyone waving a cheering. In 46 BC, Julius had one of these, and he paraded with things to celebrate his wins. Like the tribal leader from Gaul, Vercingetorix, who he had beaten, and Cleopatra's half-sister, who had joined the wrong side in the Egyptian fight that had been going on. That's pretty standard, but he also paraded things to celebrate his successes against other Romans, including paintings of the deaths of prominent supporters of Pompey. That was a bit much for a lot of Romans.

However, it was less his tone-deaf celebration of beating his fellow Romans that got him in trouble and more his political actions. We mentioned that Julius was made a dictator in 49 BC, but he got the title again in 48, and then again in 46, for ten years this time. The Romans quite liked being a republic, and they had got to be that by kicking out tyrannical kings. They were a bit like the Americans, and the Romans being a republic became 'the thing' that they were. So, Julius giving himself all this power didn't go down too well. At one point, Marc Antony, who you might have heard of and will be getting some airtime in a bit, offered Julius a crown during a religious ceremony. Julius turned it down, and historians generally assume this was a bit of propaganda to show that Julius didn't really want to be king. Maybe, though, it was testing the waters. If the crowd had gone wild and had a good ole' cheer about the idea of King Julius, maybe he would have swapped his famous laurel wreath for a shiny new crown.

Julius reformed a load of stuff, including setting up the Julian calendar, which is what Europeans used until the 16th century. He also took advantage of a lot of senators being dead, what with a civil war going on, and in 47 BC he just appointed loads of new senators, he even increased the total number of them from somewhere between 500 and 600 to 900. Surprisingly, these new senators were fairly agreeable in terms of letting Julius do what he wanted.

The move to Julius being all-powerful, with the rest of the republic being side-lined, wasn't well-received by a lot of people. Julius was very popular amongst the Roman people, but you really can only take that so far. In 44 BC, on the Ides of March, Julius was assassinated. For anyone interested, 'Ides' just means the middle of a month. His assassins were a group of about 20 Roman Senators. They didn't hire an assassin or gang to do the killing, they surrounded Julius themselves on his way to a session of the Senate and stabbed him to death. The most famous of these 20 men was Julius' friend (clearly not a friend), Brutus. He is most memorable because of the phrase 'Et Tu Brute?', as in 'You Too, Brutus?' Which you might know from Shakespeare.

And that was the end of Julius, but not quite the end of the Roman Republic yet.

The Second Triumvirate, More Civil War & An Empire

Basically, what happened was another Civil War. A lot of people were still very pro-Julius at his death, and as a populares, he had done a lot to benefit those Romans not lucky enough to be of the senatorial class. One bloke who looked like he could take over Julius' support was Marc Antony. He had been one of Julius' right-hand men and had been with him in Gaul, although he was very important in his own right. Marc Antony looked to take advantage of Julius' death and whipped up Julius' supporters into a frenzy, hoping to ride the wave to the top. The frenzy bit of that worked, with those men involved in the assassination having their houses attacked. Unfortunately for Marc Antony, Julius had made his grandnephew Gaius Octavian his sole heir, effectively announcing him as the head of things, not to mention making him phenomenally wealthy.

The start of all this post-Julius fighting isn't quite what you would expect. Marc Antony was in a solid position, he was recognised as Julius' right-hand man, he was in Rome, and the army knew him. His problem was that a chunk of the Senate had just got together to assassinate Julius, so they weren't too happy with Marc Antony running about the place. There is an enjoyable quote from Cicero on the matter. Cicero is famous for his letters, a lot of which we still have, and he is a pretty funny man. Although we imagine he grated a bit on people at the time. On the decision to assassinate Julius, but leave Marc Antony, he later said:

'I could wish that you had invited me to the banquet of the Ides of March: there would have been nothing left over! As it is, your leavings give me much trouble.'

Luckily for Cicero and the other member of the Senate who wanted this done with, Octavian was travelling back from the East. He was angry at Marc Antony for not giving up what Julius had left Octavian. Here is Cicero again, showing what their plan was for Octavian.

'He is a young man to be praised, honoured and removed"

Octavian might have been young, being 18 in the year Julius was killed, but he was no mug. Roman politics was all over the place. Octavian used his leverage as a potential counter to Marc Antony to get himself some extra power, to go along with the army he controlled. He then had to go fight Marc Antony, which is what the Senate really wanted. In the end, it couldn't have gone worse for the Senate. Brutus and Cassius were sent to the eastern provinces, basically in exile. Octavian and Marc Antony didn't fight to the death, instead teamed up and even added in a third bloke to create the Second Triumvirate (you can't Triumvirate with two). The third member of this tribute band was a bloke named Marcus Aemilius Lepidus, who had been Julius' Master of the Horse. The Master of the Horse wasn't, as the name suggests, the man in charge of the stables. It was in effect Lieutenant of the Dictator, so a significant role. This agreement was formed in November 43 BC, which is 20 months after Julius was assassinated. Things were moving pretty slowly, although for fans of excitement this was just the preamble.

All this was accompanied by the sort of murder spree you would expect from big swings of control, and this was a big swing. The Second Triumvirate split control of the republic between the three men, with the agreement set to last five years. They basically all had all the power in the Roman Republic, so they took their pick of provinces and controlled all elections. This was a full-on coup, although since they had armies, we suppose it was more of a junta. For fans of snark, you will be sad to hear that Cicero was a victim of these murder spree, with him being killed, having his head and hand chopped off, brought into Rome and pinned up in the Forum. Not a pleasant way to go.

The other bigwigs of the 'Liberators' as they called themselves, Brutus and Cassius didn't go down as easily. They lasted until October 42 BC when the armies of the Triumvirate beat the Liberators armies at Phillipi in Greece, with both generals committing suicide after being defeated.

We made it clear that the First Triumvirate didn't get on at all. However, their relationship made the Lannister family look like the Waltons compared to the Second Triumvirate. The Liberators were gone, but there was a second scuffle shortly after in 41 BC. When Octavian had returned to Italy, he set about a big reform programme, which involved confiscating lands and giving them to the soldiers he had brought back from his war in the east. This was controversial and caused a bit of a fight, called the Perusian War.

As we said, the Roman territory had been split with Marc Antony being out in the East, Octavian controlling the west, with Lepidus down in North Africa. That didn't exactly solve the problems, as while the 41 BC squabble was fought in Italy, miles away from Marc Antony in the East you can't help but feel he was a touch involved. Mostly because the two leaders of the army which fought Octavian were Fulvia and Lucius Antonius, also known as Marc Antony's wife and brother. Octavian beat these rebels, but we are sure you see where this is going.

Lepidus is a bit of a footnote in all this, and he was removed from power in 36 BC. He had been fighting a usurper, called Sextus Pompey, in Sicily. He won, but then got bullied by Octavian when they argued over who would control the island. Octavian accused Lepidus of trying to do a bit of usurpation himself (which is a bit rich) and the legions sided with Octavian. So Lepidus retired and moved back to Rome. That can't be the way a man as rich and important as he was would want to be remembered.

Incidentally, anybody looking to open a strip club in Portsmouth - Sextus Pompey would be a phenomenal business name.

Lepidus was always a sideshow; the real battle of the ages was Octavian vs Marc Antony. Marc Antony was out in the East, with Cleopatra, the Egyptian Queen, and their three children. As another indicator about how messed up this all was, Marc Antony was, by this point, married to Octavian's sister, after his last wife Fulvia had fought a war against Octavian. So, him living with Cleopatra and their family was probably a bit of a kick in the teeth.

A few years after Lepidus' retirement, in 33 BC, the Second Triumvirate deal expired, and a proper civil war kicked off not long after. Octavian was on a big propaganda kick, using

Cleopatra as a weapon against Marc Antony. To be fair Marc Antony had made it easy with his Donations of Alexandria in 34 BC, where he gave titles to his children by Cleopatra, making them kings and queens in the Middle East and North Africa. By 31 BC, this cold war turned hot, with Octavian fighting Marc Antony for control over the whole republic. Although that's not how Octavian phrased it. In fact, he didn't declare war on Marc Antony, he declared war on Cleopatra. Romans didn't like civil wars but slapping down an uppity Egyptian was very much in their wheelhouse. Despite the official line on it, the war was very much a civil war. The republic was split and hundreds of thousands of men fighting land and sea battles.

This was the end of both Marc Antony and Cleopatra, who both committed suicide after losing decisive battles in 30 BC. That was the end of the Second Triumvirate and was near enough the end of the Roman Republic.

Octavian was ruling alone as the most important man in what was still technically the Roman Republic. By 30 BC he was pretty much in control over everything, and almost as a technicality, he was the consul. You can easily call this year the end of the republic and the start of the empire. Saying all that, Octavian was made consul for the 7th time in 27 BC, so he was still technically elected. After what happened to Julius, Octavian was very keen on not looking like he was trying to make himself into a king, which can't have been easy considering he pretty much was. In 27 BC he was given the title of Princeps Senatus, which is a sort of 'first among equals' sort of title. It's a bit like 'Prime Minister,' as in saying they are the 'top' minister among all their ministerial colleagues, even though they are clearly in charge. It's a bit of a silly title.

By 23 BC, Octavian gave up even pretending, and he was given the title of Augustus, which is the name we know him by. Now Augustus was an emperor, meaning the Romans were now an empire and not a republic. Although it had been a few years since the Senate had proper control of the place, with the likes of Sulla, Marius, Julius, Pompey, and Marc Antony marching about the place.

And that is the end of the Roman Republic. And more importantly, for us anyway, that is why Julius didn't follow up with his invasion of Britain. It's safe to say he was busy.

The Nabataean Kingdom

The Nabataeans were a group from Arabia, who were from the corner of the Arabian Peninsula between the Red Sea and the Mediterranean. We don't know a massive amount about them, but the Nabataeans were relatively significant. For a start, they were nicely placed to earn from the trade going from the rest of Arabia out to the coast to be shipped elsewhere.

In fact, their position on the peninsula suggests they were no mugs, being nestled between Egypt and the Seleucids. In fact, they were able to take advantage of the Seleucids suffering a bit in the 2nd century BC, and they started nicking more land up the coast of the Mediterranean, including Damascus.

This was under their king, Aretas III. Unfortunately, one of the reasons we know more about Aretas than some of the other Nabatean kings was because of those pesky Romans. In 63 BC Pompey the Great was running riot in the region and he gave the Nabataean a bit of a beating. From then on, they were a Roman client, which meant they could carry on being their own thing, but only as long as everything they did met Roman approval. Luckily though they were still able to cash in on their position in trade, so they did a lot better than some of the other client kingdoms. Which is probably why they lasted all the way up to 106 AD before the Romans properly annexed them and turned the area into the province of Arabia.

Part of the reason we wanted to mention the Nabataeans was that they were attacked by Pompey in the short time we are talking about. However, the main reason they are getting a mention is we wanted to talk about their architecture. The Nabataeans were big on a style of rock-cut building. This is pretty much what it sounds like; you take a solid bit of rock, like a cliff, and you carve something out of it. To see what we mean, find your nearest search engine and search 'Ad Deir-Petra'. This is called The Monastery in English, and it was repurposed into a church much later. Basically, it is a big chamber carved into the side of a massive rock, but the front has been carved to look like the front of a temple. It must have taken ages. That's our favourite one, but apparently the more popular building of this type is the nearby Al-Khazneh (The Treasury).

The Nabataeans had a second city (as in the second most important, they had more than two) in what is now Saudi Arabia. There is another example of the rock-cutting, called Hegra, and that one is a UNESCO World Heritage site. Go and have a look at that lot as well, we will wait here.

While we are on the Arabian Peninsula let's give a mention to the southern part of the peninsula. You may have heard the name Queen of Sheba, usually used as a phrase for someone who thinks they are class and deserves all the finer things in life. The Queen of Sheba story is used in a lot of cultures and is mentioned in the bible. She turned up at the court of King Solomon the Israelite King, offering all sorts of fancy gifts of gold and spices. Well, historians tend to believe this Sheba kingdom was, what we know as the Kingdom of Saba, in what is now Yemen. The Sabaeans had been about, possibly, as early as 1200 BC, but they were a decent sized kingdom by the 800s BC and lasted until the 400s AD. How cool is that? In 21st Century Britain we can just casually throw around a name that originated in ancient Yemen.

Britain After Julius Caesar

Julius Caesar's invasions of Britain in 55 and 54 BC, were pretty significant events in British history and were probably more than a bit significant for the tribes in the South East of England at the time. For those of you who were paying attention in our last Roman history chapter, you will remember that Roman politics was in a bit of a state. That meant that Julius, or anyone else, was too busy to bring an army back to Britain until 43 BC. It turns out the emperors of the newly minted Roman empire would be too busy for Britain for a while, although they certainly hadn't forgotten about us. In this chapter, we will have a look at the times they did remember Britain and what difference having the Romans as next-door neighbours had on the Britons.

In this chapter, we ask ourselves, what's wrong with Britain, and why does no one want us? What else is money useful for? And has anyone ever made cash from selling seashells?

Augustus Gearing Up For Britain

Our next Roman history chapter covers the period between Julius taking over the whole Republic and the three Roman Emperors between him and 43 BC. It won't be too much of a spoiler for you to know that two of the three thought about invading Britain but didn't. We are told that Augustus planned invasions of Britain three times: in 34, 27 and 26 BC, so he must have really fancied it.

It's all a bit vague as to why in particular Augustus did fancy attacking Britain so much. You certainly can't discount the fact that Britain was an island on the edge of his territory, and Romans liked nothing more than taking control of new places. It was a case of 'when in Rome' if you will. Augustus was also pretty keen on associated himself with Julius. He was born with the name, Gaius Octavius, but when he was adopted by Julius, his name became Gaius Julius Caesar Octavianus, which is some unsubtle linking to his new dad there. While Augustus couldn't re-conquer Gaul, because it had mostly stayed conquered, he could re-invade Britain. That would have been a nice reminder to people that he was just as cool as his dad. We get told about the first planned invasion by Cassius Dio, an ancient Roman historian who was writing about 200 years later. He also says why it didn't happen:

'In emulation of his father he had set out to lead an expedition into Britain also, and had already advanced into Gaul after the winter in which Antony (for the second time) and Lucius Libo became consuls, when some of the newly-conquered people and Dalmatians along with them rose in revolt.'

So it looks like a tribe in Croatia kicking off was all there was between the Romans and another invasion of Britain.

Dio also says that Augustus got as far as Gaul in 27 BC, to invade Britain. This time the problem was with Gaul itself distracting the emperor from crossing the English Channel. The next year, in 26 BC, Augustus was winding up for another go, because apparently, the Britons 'would not come to terms.' That means Augustus wanted them to do something, but the Britons were refusing. Luckily the

Roman emperor had no attention span, and Augustus was called off to solve revolts in Northern Italy, from the Salassi, and in Spain from the Cantabrians and Asturians. You can see why Augustus didn't get around to Britain, between Roman civil wars and angry Celtic folk across Southern Europe.

Annoyingly, none of that tells us what 'terms' the Britons were meant to come to terms over in 26/27 BC. There are a few reasons why Augustus might have for demanding things from the Britons. Technically a lot of the tribes in Britain, certainly a lot of them in the South East of England had submitted to Julius in 54 BC. That meant the Romans could make demands of them; demands which include money or other goods. They weren't part of the empire, so they weren't paying taxes, but there is a word for taxes you have to pay even if you aren't under the control of a government, and that is tribute. Perhaps the Britons weren't paying their protection money, and Augustus wanted it. Civil wars are expensive, and he had a lot of soldiers who needed paying, so maybe Augustus didn't take kindly to not getting his money.

A less economic reason for Augustus to get involved in Britain would be that, as he technically oversaw the tribes there, he would be the ultimate judge in inter-tribal arguments. And you can believe there were plenty of them. We know that one of the terms in the treaty that Julius put in place was that the Catuvellauni tribe were meant to leave the Trinovantes. It does look like some shenanigans were going on there, with the Catuvellauni minting coins from the Trinovantes capital of Colchester (Camulodunum). Unless they were sharing a mint, it looks like the Catuvellauni had decided to take over again.

We are also told by know that at least two rulers from Britain ran to Rome when things got dicey at home. You have to assume that these Britons wanted to be somewhere safe, but also that they were angling after Augustus to head over to Britain and put them on the thrones they believed were theirs.

Caligula Has A Breakdown On The Coast

After Augustus, we have to skip an emperor and go straight to Gaius Caesar. You could be forgiven for not having heard of this particular emperor, who was obviously named after Julius, but you will probably recognise him from his nickname, Caligula. The nickname incidentally came from 'little boot' because of him wearing soldiers' boots when his dad was on campaign in Germany.

His attempt on Britain is beyond bizarre, and nobody really trusts what the sources say happened. We are told that the son of a Briton king, Adminius, ran to Caligula when he argued with his dad. Adminius persuaded Caligula that it would be dead easy to roll into Britain and take proper control, presumably giving Adminius a crown in the process. The campaign was set in motion and Caligula marched through Gaul to the English Channel, but it all went wrong when the soldiers he took with him showed signs of being close to mutiny. That meant it would be a bad idea to take them across the channel into a relatively unknown area full of potentially angry natives. His solution to this worrying problem was mad. We have two versions of the story from Roman historians, both writing quite a bit after the period.

The first story comes from Suetonius. We are told that Caligula didn't cross the English Channel, so there was no invasion. Despite that, because Adminius, who was king of nowhere, was on his side, Caligula claimed a victory and:

'sent a pompous letter to Rome and ordered the couriers to drive their vehicles right into the Forum and up to the Senate House and not to hand it over to the consuls except in the Temple of Mars and before a full meeting of the Senate.'

That's an odd way of celebrating a victory you didn't have.

It wasn't even trying to talk up your achievements in a war which nobody really won, or even trying to cover up a loss. There was no fight to claim victory from. That isn't even the weird bit. When he was on the coast of Northern France, looking at Britain, he:

'drew up his battleline on the shore if the Ocean and moved his ballistas and other artillery into position. Then, with no one knowing or able to guess what he was about, he suddenly ordered them to gather shells and fill their helmets and the fold of their tunics with them, calling the spoils from Ocean owed to the Capitol and Palatine.'

So, he got ready for a fight by lining up his men, on the wrong side of a sea, and got them to collect seashells so he could pretend he had returned from a battle with some sweet, sweet loot.

Dio tells a remarkably similar story, but in his version, Caligula sails out to sea on a boat a bit, before ordering soldiers to collect seashells, as if he was claiming that he had tamed the sea. He also says the seashells were to take back to show off in Rome, which would have been seriously awkward for everyone watching that procession.

Caligula was not a popular emperor, so it's worth saying that the Romans would have something to gain for hamming up any embarrassing episode for Caligula, so it probably didn't go down quite like that. If you really want to give him the benefit of the doubt, there is a possibility he was trying to embarrass soldiers who were refusing to get involved in an invasion of Britain. That's possible, especially since we would imagine the soldiers involved would not have enjoyed being ordered to walk about the beach with the ancient equivalent of a bucket and spade. Either way, there was no invasion of Britain under the three emperors following the rule of Julius.

What Was Going On In Britain?

How did the Romans more significant influence on Britain impact the people of Britain? We have some clues about that, but we don't exactly know what was going on. We don't have any written records, and since the Romans weren't exactly over there, we don't have much from them either.

We do know that despite the occasional threat of invasion, the Romans seemed relatively happy with the arrangements with the Britons. For example, Strabo says:

'they submit so readily to heavy duties both on the exports from there to Gaul and on the imports from Gaul – these consist of ivory chains, necklaces, amber, glassware and other such trinkets – that there is no need to garrison the island.'

Meaning the Britons were doing as they were told and paying the taxes due for being involved in trade with the Roman Empire. So there was no need for a proper occupation, as long as the Romans were earning, they were fine.

He also makes a guess that:

'For at the very least one legion and some cavalry would be needed to exact tribute from them, and the expense of the army would equal the money brought in.'

We hate to spoil the story, but Strabo was not wrong, although phrasing as 'at the very least one legion' suggests he didn't really predict how mad Britain would be for the Romans.

The general view from people like Strabo and the statesman/philosopher Cicero was that the Britons were no threat. While there might be some benefit to having control, we weren't worth the effort to take over properly.

Despite saying we don't know much, we do have some clues on the goings-on in the south of England. Specifically, we know bits about the Atrebates, from south of the Thames, the Catuvellauni, from north of London and Trinovantes, from over in Suffolk.

The reason we know about the Atrebates is because of a character we have already met, Commius. He was one of the leaders of the Gallic Atrebates and had been sent to Britain in advance of Julius' invasion in 55 BC. He wasn't always a big fan of the Romans. In 53 BC, when there was a significant uprising against the Romans in Gaul, Commius ended up being one of the leaders of the resistance, which must have annoyed Julius a bit. That annoyance would explain why Julius sent one of his generals, Volusenus to kill him. This is the same Volusensus who managed to find Julius a less than ideal spot to land during the 55 BC invasion. So it's not surprising that, during the assassination attempt on Commius, Volusensus only managed to wound him. Commius managed to get away with annoying the Romans, and he struck a deal with them. Commius promised to stay in one spot and do what he was told, under the condition that he wouldn't have to deal with any Romans. That place he ended up living was with the Atrebates tribe in Britain.

We also have a half-decent idea of what happened with the Atrebates after Commius, mostly thanks to coins. We will be banging on about coins a lot. They are pretty useful for figuring out what was going on in the Roman world for a few reasons. Firstly, they are metal, so they have lasted. Secondly, they can be dated, but probably most importantly, they put images and text on their money, just like we do. For example, historians are fairly sure that Commius was succeeded as an Atrebates king by a bloke named Tincomarus, who was his son. We know this because we have coins with his name on.

The Britons had coins before the Romans appeared, with the first ones being minted in Kent in around 100 BC. What's interesting about Tincomarus coins is that they used

Roman images and Latin phrases. It's not important, but it's cool that from the 1st century BC, Britain had coins that are weirdly like the ones we still use. Round, with two sides decorated with 'nationally' significant images and names. If I handed you one from ancient Britain and asked you what it was, you would know.

It's not surprising that the Britons started acting a bit more Roman after Julius' visit. The Romans had a strategy of taking hostages from the families of leaders they have recently beaten. It was something they had done all over their new territories. Commius was a client king of sorts. In the Roman world, a client kingdom was somewhere the Romans had control of, but as long as everyone behaved and paid up, the natives could keep their leaders and their laws. This would probably have involved Coummius giving close family members to the Romans to take to Rome as hostages. Including his son. So, by the time, Tincomarus was king he had lived in Rome, would have Roman friends, would speak Latin and would have seen how Rome works. Considering the status of Rome vs the Atrebates tribe, you could see why he would want to introduce a few of the trappings of 'civilisation' to Southern England.

From these coins, we know about Commius, his successor, Tincomarus and the next king, Eppillus. We also get the name of Verica, who would be next up for the job. We will meet Verica in the next Roman Britain chapter, but it's safe to say Verica was a very silly boy.

The other two Briton tribes we have an idea of what was going on were the Catuvellauni and Trinovantes. This is for much the same reason as with the Atrebates. The Romans had installed 'their man' as the leader of the Trinovantes, Mandubracius. He had been the member of the Trinovantes tribe who had sided with Julius and told the Romans where the leader of the resistance, Cassivellaunus, was. To be fair to Mandubracius, he was the son of the old Trinovates king, who had been overthrown and killed by Cassivellaunus and his Catuvellauni friends. You can see why Mandubracian had sold them out. At the end of all that, the treaty Julius made with the Britons involved Mandubracian being given control of the Trinovantes, and the Catuvellauni were told to leave them alone.

It doesn't look like that panned out like he might have hoped. By around 9 AD, the Catuvellauni had a new king called Cunobelin, and he was a pretty big deal. We know that from his coins, which were just as handily made as the Atrebates versions were. We also know that he minted these coins in St Albans, which was the main settlement of the Catuvellauni, and Colchester, which was the main settlement of the Trinovantes. Which means the Catuvellauni were up to their old tricks and were spreading their influence. To be fair, the Romans seemed to be OK with this. The Roman historian, Suetonius, calls Cunobelin' rex Britannorum', which is King of the Britons. That suggests that he controlled a pretty significant area, although don't be fooled by the grand title, we are still talking about South East England rather than Britain. It wasn't just the Trinovantes who had to watch out for the Catuvellauni. Epaticcus, who was probably Cunobelin's brother, started minting coins from within Atrebate territory, suggesting Cunobelin and his family were spreading south as well as east.

Cunobelin was king for a pretty long time, and he was obviously there with the Romans blessing. The use of rex is interesting. The Celtic word for a king that the Britons used was rigon. The fact that kings of both the Catuvellauni and the Atrebates started using the Latin version of rex shows how they were both leaning into Roman ways.

A major part of being a client kingdom of the Romans was the management of succession. Romans were very keen on making sure the right leaders (as in pro-Roman) leaders were running their client kingdoms. The second-best way the Romans could guarantee the right man got the job was to threaten them with the legions. The best way was to actually use the legion to give the client kingdom in question a kicking. This became a big problem for Britain after the

Catuvellauni king, Cunobelin, died in 40 AD. It ended up being a red rag to a massive bull.

So what have we learnt? Well, Britain was desirable, but not enough to actually do anything about it. If you are rich enough, you can just claim to have won things, and everyone has to nod along. And coins are cool.

Clever, Apathetic Yet Brutal, and Mad

We know that the first three emperors, Augustus, Tiberius, and Caligula didn't invade Britain. However, that doesn't mean they weren't busy doing things elsewhere. We should probably fill in those gaps.

Augustus: 27 BC - 14 AD

We left Augustus in 23 BC when he was finally a proper Roman emperor with all the power and not much pretence that he was going to share. He lasted another 37 years before he died at the age of 75. Which, considering he had fought half to the Roman world at one point or another, is fairly good going. We are going to see a lot of emperors who would last nowhere near that long while being much less controversial.

Considering the action-packed life of young Octavian, and the newly minted Augustus, old man Octavian/Augustus was pretty calm. His reign was the start of something called Pax Romana (Roman Peace), which is 200ish years of relative peace in the Roman world. The fact that these 200 years includes some very unpeaceful things means two things. Firstly, it's a load of all PR bollocks and secondly, the rest of the Roman period was absolutely mental.

Something which Augustus did, which really did solve a lot of the argy-bargy in the Roman Empire, was to make the army professional. With Sulla, Marius, Julius, Pompey, Mark Antony, and Augustus himself, the Romans had had quite a few people raising armies over the last century. So, Augustus made the army into a proper professional standing army. That meant there was a bit less chance of someone else raising an army to fight him with. By the end of the fight with Marc Antony, the armies involved added up to half a million soldiers. Augustus decided to trim that down to about 25 legions, with each legion being made up of about 5000 men. With nearly twice as many again in the auxiliaries and the navy. Estimates put the total number of men at around a much more manageable, 290,000 men. He also gave himself direct control of the provinces where these armies were posted, with the other provinces given to the Senate to control. You are going to see throughout this whole story, just what a clever move that was. The best way of staying emperor was to have the control and backing of as many of these legions as you can. The last thing he wanted was someone else having control over his armies, he, more than most, knew what could happen with that.

Since Augustus was founding a new dynasty for a new empire, his successor would be an important pick. Augustus had a daughter, Julia the Elder, but he didn't have sons, and the Romans weren't up for an Empress. That makes the succession of an emperorship a bit awkward. Luckily for the Romans, this didn't matter all that much, and he could just adopt whoever he liked as a successor. Julius had adopted Augustus as his son and successor, even though he was his great-nephew. Augustus did seem keen to keep it in the family as well, and luckily, he had three grandsons. Lucius, Gaius, and Agrippa were all adopted by Augustus. Unfortunately, Agrippa turned out to be an arsehole, and he was exiled from Rome. Lucius died in 2 AD while travelling through Gaul, and Gaius died in 4 AD after being wounded by the leader of a revolt in Armenia.

This was a bit of a nightmare for the Romans, but they had a bloke waiting in the wings, Tiberius. He was Augustus' son-in-law, but not the dad of Lucius and Gaius. Roman families were complicated, and it seems rare to find an influential Roman having only one spouse - Augustus had three wives himself, having divorced two of them. Either way, Tiberius was apparently the obvious choice after the death of Augustus' non-twatty grandsons/adopted sons. That's true even though Tiberius had retired from politics in 6 BC, by running off to Rhodes and refusing to get involved. Augusts lived for another decade after the death of Gaius, so Tiberius had ages to get up to speed again, and that's how we had a 55-year-old Tiberius as the second Roman emperor.

Tiberius: 14 - 37

Tiberius' reign lasted 22 years, which means he got to the age of 77, which is a ripe old age for an emperor. He was an odd emperor, and the Roman historians of the time didn't like him all that much. According to Suetonius, who was around the end of the century/beginning of the next, Augustus said about Tiberius:

'Alas for the Roman people, to be ground by jaws that crunch so slowly!'

Which makes it sound like Tiberius was going to be rubbish, yet boring. Suetonius also says that it probably crossed Augustus' mind that having a less than stellar successor would make Augustus look even better by comparison. Anyone who has been involved in interviewing for their replacement will sympathise with that.

We know that Tiberius had already retired and had to come back, but it sounds like he really didn't want the job. He didn't use the fancy titles he was allowed, like 'Imperator,' which roughly means commander. He also wasn't big on birthday celebrations, and he didn't allow too many statues of him put up. Which is weirder than it sounds. Roman emperors love statues. What's the point in being the most powerful man in an empire, in fact, the most powerful man within thousands of miles, if you can't throw up a statue or two.

Tiberius had been a successful general in his time, but when Augustus died, he had to deal with some significant mutinies from some of the 25 legions he had inherited. Three legions stationed on the Danube mutinied, complaining about their conditions. The Danube is the river that flows from Germany through Austria and Hungary out towards the black sea, and it was a crucial Roman border, with mad Germanic tribes usually being kept on the other side of it. It's also blue.

The revolt was fixed by Tiberius' son, Drusus Julius, and a bloke named Sejanus, who we will meet in a minute. It also kicked off on the Rhine where four of the eight legions there also mutinied. This was solved by Tiberius' adopted son Germanicus. You might think Germanicus knocking about in Germany is some sort of nominative determinism (doing the thing you name is - like a John Baker becoming a baker), but he got the name from his dad who had won impressive victories in Germany, and it means something like' victorious in Germany.' Drusus, Sejanus, and Germanicus were three of the most significant men in Tiberius' emperorship.

Having a long reign meant that Tiberius had a similar problem to Augustus in terms of succession. The obvious candidates were his sons, Drusus Julius and Germanicus. Unfortunately, like with Augustus, neither outlived their dad. Germanicus died while out in Syria, and there is a chance that he was poisoned by one of his enemies, Piso. There is also a claim that it was done on Tiberius' orders because Germanicus was getting too big for his boots. Piso was ordered back to Rome for a trial but conveniently committed suicide before it happened. Now that is dark.

Drusus Julius died a few years later, but much less suspiciously. This was a bugger for Tiberius because they were not only successors, but they had been doing a lot of leg work for him. Drusus Julius died in 23 AD, and by 26 AD Tiberius had basically given up and had buggered off to the island of Capri, which is just off the coast of Naples. If you are going to hide from your responsibilities, there are worse looking places to do it. Leaving to go sunbathing meant Tiberius had left the running of the empire to his Prefect of the Praetorian Guard, Sejanus. A Prefect of the Praetorian Guard is the title for someone who was in charge of the Praetorian Guard. This was an elite military unit, which Augustus had turned into the emperor's bodyguard, and the Praetorian Prefect became a significant figure in the government of the empire. You will see this lot pop up consistently. They are always bad news, and Sejanus was no different. He was a proper wrong'un.

Sejanus was back in Rome running things, getting rid of all his opponents, and being emperor in all but name. He did something in 31 AD, that tipped it over the edge, and Tiberius had him executed. We exactly aren't sure what the particular straw that broke the Tiberian camel was, but whatever it was it ended badly for Sejanus, his family and pretty much everyone he knew.

Sejanus was not a good regent, and apparently, things had all gone wrong while he was in charge, with governor positions not being filled and enemies of the empire nibbling away its edges in the East. However, Tiberius being back in action was not good news for a lot of people. He went on a spate of treason trials against prominent people of Rome. We have said that he wasn't a popular man, so it's hard to know exactly what's true, and what is claimed just to stick the boot into a bloke they didn't like. A lot of what we are told is the sort stuff that we don't really want to write, but as a taste of what he got up to, here is a quote from Suetonius:

'Those of the Jews who were of military age he assigned to provinces of less healthy climate, ostensibly to serve in

the army; the others of that same race or of similar beliefs he banished from the city, on pain of slavery for life if they did not obey.'

So he sent a few thousand Jewish men to die in a nasty place and kicked the rest he kicked of out Rome by threatening to enslave them. The nasty place was Sardinia, which we hear is very nice these days, but back then had issues with malaria.

Tiberius' lacklustre approach to ruling extended to him not putting a lot of effort into finding a successor after the death of his sons. In the end, the most obvious successor was Germanicus' son. This new emperor was called Gaius Caesar, but you definitely know him as Caligula.

Caligula: 37 - 41

Let's start off by saying that Gaius Caesar being called Caligula seems a bit left field. Romans tended to have long drawn out names, but Caligula wasn't even one of his. In fact, it meant something like 'little soldier's boot', or bootikins, which he had picked up as a nickname from soldiers when he, as a little kid, accompanied his dad, Germanicus on a campaign in Germania. Apparently, he used to dress up as a soldier, including little boots, hence bootikins.

Caligula also wasn't a popular emperor. The rumour was that Caligula had killed Tiberius to get hold of the top job. Bear in mind Tiberius was 77 when he died, it might not be true, but even the rumour shows what the Romans thought of the pair of them. That means we have the same problem with Caligula as we do with Tiberius, it's hard to know how much of the mad stuff you hear is true.

Saying all that, it looks like Caligula got a bit of a popularity bump early on, just by not being Tiberius. He brought back people that Tiberius had exiled and stopped the treason trials. He was also apparently generous with money to the poorer people of Rome. Something which is always going to go down well.

Soon though, he was executing potential enemies with gay abandon and spending Rome's money like it was going out of fashion. Which will have gone down less well. Suetonius was not a fan. Although, he does list the good stuff that Caligula did at the start of his reign, like finishing up the public works that Tiberius had started, which was a temple and a theatre, as well as beginning some other useful projects, like aqueducts. Then he says:

'So much for Caligula as emperor; we must now tell of his career as a monster.'

After that is a list of some horrible stuff, like putting treason trials back on the menu, removing the heads from statues of gods, to be replaced with his own and holding sham gladiatorial fights, with old gladiators. He apparently also had a massive gold statue of himself made and each day it was dressed like him. That kind of thing and setting himself up as a living god was a bit much for the people of Rome. Emperors were usually made into gods after they were dead, so jumping the gun like that wasn't the done thing. The list is full of horrible things, which you don't like to see, but they are also exactly the way you want your mad emperors from history to act. Historians generally think that Caligula became ill shortly after he got the job, and it seemed to tip him over the edge. It's hard to say, and it might just be that he really was a horrible human being. Or maybe it's all a load of bollocks.

Not everything we know about Caligula is all rumour and madness, he did do some proper emperoring during his three and a bit years in charge. He brought the client kingdom of Mauretania, which is modern Algeria and Morocco, closer into Roman control. Although he did that in a fairly Caligulan way. He invited the ruler of Mauritania, Ptolemy, to Rome. Ptolemy is interesting because, while he was a

Berber, which was an ethnic group in North Africa, he was also the son of Cleopatra's and Marc Anthony's daughter. Making him of Macedonian (through Cleopatra) and Roman descent. It also meant he was Caligula's second cousin. Which goes to show that, even in the ancient world, the leaders of all of these Mediterranean kingdoms were all dealing with each other enough to be related. And that was just a polite way of saying there was a lot of shagging in Roman diplomacy.

Anyway, back in Mauritania, Ptolemy was invited to Rome to be confirmed as King of Mauritania and given all the honours you would expect for a friendly king. Then, Caligula had him assassinated. We don't really know why, but it probably had something to do with how rich Mauritania was. A client kingdom would owe dues to the Romans, but a full-on Roman province, full of cash, meant lots of money for Caligula to play with. Caligula was big on extravagance, and he had frittered away all the funds Tiberius had built up for the running of the empire. Predictably, Ptolemy being bumped off started a revolt, but Mauritania was soon a well-controlled Roman Province.

We would be lacking if the story of Caligula that you would have been most likely to have heard didn't get a mention. Which is that Caligula was planning to make his favourite horse, Incitatus, consul. It looks like that stupid story was just made up and repeated by later Roman historians, like Suetonius and Dio Cassius. It was probably just the ancient version of clickbait. I don't know about you, but I'm having a read of that if it's advertised with horse consuls as a headline.

It's safe to say that, with all this, Caligula fell out with all the important people in Rome. He had been exerting the piss with the senators, making their life an absolute hell, and in some cases quite short. Caligula apparently enjoyed the quote:

'Let them hate me, so they but fear me'

His reign lasted less than 4 years, and we will go over its end, and his successor, in the next British history chapter. For now, let's just say Caligula's emperorship didn't end with him tragically dying in his sleep. Something which had massive consequences for Britain.

Ancient Egypt

The history of Egypt is one of the better documented of the ancient world, and it's absolutely mind-boggling. The First Dynasty started in about 3100 BC, when a man named Narmer united Upper and Lower Egypt, to create a unified kingdom. The fact that we know about an Egyptian ruler from 5000 years ago is mad. For a sense of scale on how long the history of Egypt was before the Romans got involved; probably the most famous pharaoh of them all, Tutankhamun lived in the 1330s BC. Which means there were more than a thousand years between Narmer and Tutankhamun and another millennium or so between Tutankhamun and Cleopatra VII, the one who was knocking about with Julius Caesar and Marc Antony.

The Romans finally took over Egypt as a province in 30 BC, but they had been interfering for a while. Augustus, who turned it into a province, knew how important it was. Egypt was a huge source of food for the Roman Empire. The floodplain around the Nile was very fertile and covered a significant amount of space. Any Roman emperor who lost control of that would be in trouble. Hungry armies are bad news, and a hungry Rome means someone is getting lynched.

For those sorts of reasons, Augustus set up Egypt as a very special province. No senators could enter the province, which meant the governor of the province couldn't be chosen from the usual suspects. The governors were always of the equestrian class, which were the slightly lower class 'knights' of the Roman Empire, and they were chosen directly by the emperor. It was a clever neat process to make sure that the person in charge of the 'breadbasket' of the empire, and it's two or three legions, was loyal to the emperor.

The ancient Egyptians being around for as long as they were, means it shouldn't be surprising that it wasn't always the Egyptians who were in charge of Egypt. In fact, when the Romans took over, they nicked it from the Ptolemaic Dynasty, who weren't originally Egyptian. The dynasty was named after Ptolemy, who was its first pharaoh. He had been one of the top blokes under Alexander the Great when he had gone conquering from Macedonia out southwards and eastward. When he died in 323 BC, his top men ended up splitting the empire between them: Cassander got Macedonia, Lysimachus got what is mostly Turkey, Seleucus got the Middle East, setting up the Seleucid Empire and Ptolemy got Egypt. By 305 BC, Alexander's empire had completely broken apart, and Ptolemy declared himself a pharaoh.

That all means that, 250 odd years later, Cleopatra was descended from Macedonians. It does go to show how the ancient world from Italy to North Africa to Persia was surprisingly connected. As further proof of that, Alexander the Great wasn't the first time Egypt had been ruled from afar. From 525 to 404 BC, there was a dynasty which was ruled by the Achaemenid Empire, a Persian Empire whose capital was Babylon, in Iraq.

See, Egyptian history isn't all pyramids, sarcophagi and women being rolled about in carpets (that's a thing, we aren't being weird).

Claudius Invades

So far, in our history of Britain, our relationship with the Roman world has been a bit tentative. We've had a couple of invasions, three serious-sounding threats of invasion and a threat that was mostly a trip to the seaside. The Romans have been thinking about taking over the British Isles for nearly 100 years. We've had Julius Caesar turning up in Britain, as a proper token effort, to make people think he was doing important stuff. We've had Augustus putting us on a to-do list, with the best of intentions, but ultimately being distracted by something shiny. Then we have had Caligula looking like he was going to achieve something, but really being too shit. Anyone who has ever had an office job will completely understand this process.

In this chapter, we ask ourselves; what would tip an emperor over into an actual invasion? What's the most glory a boss has ever stolen from someone? And what's the worst possible way to deal with bullies?

Who's In Charge Here?

Now we are finally getting to the bit where the Romans properly invade Britain. In 43 AD, there was a new emperor in town, and he kicked off the invasion that started the Roman occupation of Britain. So, who was this heroic, imperial figure who upped the stakes against the mighty

Julius Caesar? Which man-mountain finally dragged the British Isles towards a place in written history? It was Claudius, the half-deaf uncle of the mad Emperor Caligula, who walked with a limp. We are being flippant about his disabilities, but it strikes us as impressive he got to where he did. The modern diagnosis of Claudius' disabilities has mostly settled on cerebral palsy. Being an emperor was in effect an administrative job, but the whole Roman world does come across as a bit more hyper-masculine than you would like. They were very into the military, and Claudius had no military background to speak of. Maybe the Romans were more 'woke' than we have given them credit for. In fact, it may have been because of his disabilities that he got the top job in the first place. For anyone with visions of an early version of positive discrimination, hang on a minute before you get too impressed.

The predecessor to Claudius was Caligula, and we have previously mentioned that he wasn't the most popular of blokes, and we hinted he may have come to a sticky end. To be honest, it's not 100% clear exactly how erratically Caligula did act. It's also not 100% agreed upon whether he had some serious mental illness, or if he was just a horrible bloke given too much power. It's not too dissimilar to people asking whether Donald Trump has dementia or if he is just a terrible human being. Either way, what happened to Caligula should make Trump take a closer look at his bodyguards. Can you imagine having to spend all day in a room listening to that?

By January 41 AD, Caligula had pissed off everyone far too much. There were apparently plenty of conspiracies to get rid of him, but in the end, the one that worked was a nice and straightforward route-one approach. Members of his Praetorian Guard stabbed him. So, he died. Easy. What happened after was a bit messy. The Praetorian Guard were the main guards of the emperor and his household. However, there were another set of guards, called the Germanic Guard, who were closer personal bodyguards. The point of these soldiers is that they would be recruited from Roman controlled regions of Germany, and surrounding areas, meaning they had no loyalty to anyone else in Rome. The point was that they would be less likely to get involved in Roman politics than the locals, and were more likely to be unquestioningly pro-emperor. In the event these Germanic Guards didn't like the killing of Caligula, so the pro-emperor thing clearly worked. They kicked off and went on a revenge spree. Killing and wounding anyone who looked even vaguely guilty. The members of the Praetorian Guard went on their own counter spree, killing Caligula's family. Which should have included his uncle, Claudius.

The story goes that Claudius went off and hid, but some pro-Caligula, or at least pro-emperor Praetorians, found him hiding behind a curtain. Instead of chopping him up, they made him emperor. Right, let's just stop there a sec. You don't have to spend too long with the Romans and the way they worked to smell a bit of a rat, and even if that turn of events seemed reasonable, which they do, who doesn't love an imperial conspiracy? The tale of an unassuming, unthreatening Claudius being made a reluctant Emperor to replace the mad Caligula is quite a nice story if you skip over the bits with the duelling massacres. However, it has been suggested that maybe Claudius knew this was going to happen. We will probably never know if Claudius was behind it. Still, I would bet my last fiver on any Roman emperor being given the job in suspicious circumstances being as guilty as sin. Romans make a Tory leadership contest look like friendly chat in a nunnery. It would be wrong to assume that Claudius would make a bad emperor, just because of his disabilities. In the same vein, we should give the disabled community the credit they deserve and acknowledge that they have it in them to be just as shifty and conniving as anyone.

However he came to be offered the job, any Praetorians hoping to have themselves a weak Emperor limping about the place shouting 'you what?' made a mistake. Claudius really was a rather good Emperor, especially after the Caligula debacle. All this is very much Rome's problem, but it is still crucial for our Roman Britain story, as you will see.

Why, Claudius?

For all our saying it was a bit of a fluke Claudius had become emperor, on paper Claudius wasn't completely unlikely to get the job. He was the nephew to a previous emperor and the uncle of another, so it's not like it's a butcher or farmer getting the job. However, Rome was all about the military. You could be forgiven for thinking that the Roman Empire was an army supported by the state, rather than the other way around. You don't very often come across many important men of Roman history who had not at the very least served in the army, and more typically they would have been involved in some great achievement. Which makes it sound odd that Claudius' emperorship was backed by the military, but the Senate didn't like him. This was an error from the political class. Claudius went on an execution bender, that was impressive even for the time. It does cast extra doubt on the whole innocently hiding before being thrust into the limelight emperor origin story Claudius went with.

This is directly linked to when, two years into his reign, Claudius was going to turn up in Britain with a fair few legionaries. But why did he fancy a crack at Britain when the Romans before him couldn't find the time? Like with Julius Caesar's run in Britain, we have a few reasons why Claudius might have gone for it, and they are all army related.

It probably boils down to how Claudius was backed by the army, yet he had no great military experience of his own. You are as likely to find a Roman emperor with no military experience, as finding a taxi driver without a range of robust views on the state of the nation. A century before Claudius was on the scene, Julius invaded Britain to look hard in front of his friends. Claudius, a half-deaf emperor with a limp and no military experience, really needed to look hard. That sort of thing would be literally life and death. He couldn't just do a Caligula, standing on the French coast screaming 'What the fuck are you looking at mate' at Dover, wasn't an option. No one was going to take him seriously, so Claudius went big. During his reign, he did some solid work on expanding the empire. He added in parts of modern Greece, Bulgaria, Slovenia Austria, Turkey, Palestine, Algeria, and Morocco. However, a lot of these regions were already under Roman influence, or at least had already taken a kicking. If we do say ourselves, it was the invasion of Britain which was the most impressive of the expansions; it was the thing that made him look the hardest.

The second reason for invading Britain is more of a standard problem that leaders of armies have. Back in Back in the day, when Julius and Augustus were looking into Britain, they ended up being distracted from Britain by the Celts in Gaul and the Germanic tribes, or maybe the odd massive civil war. Claudius didn't have that problem, Gaul was well settled, and the Germanic tribes were relatively quiet. A fair few of them were even fighting in the Roman army. This was handy for an emperor who wanted to focus on doing a bit of invading. The problem with everyone being calmer than usual is that Claudius didn't have anyone for his armies to fight. Having spare legions waiting around, not invading anywhere was a bad idea. Soldiers like a fight, and they certainly liked the profit that can be made from those fights. Claudius, having just benefited from a soldier sponsored massacre of his family in Rome, probably didn't want to spend too much time thinking about how those bored soldiers might try and entertain themselves. Throughout history, soldiers have made it very clear they are there to mess things up. If you don't point them at someone else to mess with, they will likely look themselves at you.

Now have seen the actual reasons that historians give for an invasion, do you want to hear the official reason for the attack? The weapons of mass destruction of the Roman world? Claudius was invited over by a Briton.

In our last Roman Britain chapter, we covered some of the intertribal shenanigans in South East England. When Julius had left Britain, he had taken the dominant tribe, the Catervaulaunni, down a peg or two. A hundred years later, they were back on top and back to ruining other tribes' day. They had taken over the Trinovantes main settlement of Colchester (Camulodunum). The Catuvellauni also had a go at the Atrebates and started taking their territory as well. Apparently, they did so well that they managed to kick out the Atrebates king, Verica. The solution Verica's came up with was to ask Claudius to get him his old job back. Obviously, despite the Romans not running the place, they must have been viewed as some sort of arbitrator in those situations, which is a classic part of the client kingdom arrangement. All in all, Verica running to Rome to ask for help was a perfect opportunity for Claudius to expand Roman influence and look like an absolute boss as he did it.

If you allow us a pause; when you study a little bit of history, you become amazed by how often different people around the world do what Verica did. You are being bullied by some bigger boys, so you appeal to an even bigger bully to sort them out. In your desperate, deluded state you believe they will sort out the original bully and then leave. What really happens is that you then have a new, scarier bully stealing your lunch money. People are amazing. We just won't learn. We are not saying that the Romans wouldn't have taken control of Britain anyway, it has a feeling of inevitability about it when you know how the Romans go about stuff. However, Verica should be applauded for being so annoyed by the Catuvellauni that he was willing to usher in four centuries of Roman rule for most of the island, just to get back at them. You, sir, are a petty man and we salute you.

Finally, An Actual Invasion

So now we have had our real 'oil' reasons and our official

'weapon of mass destruction' reason, but how did the actual invasion go down?

Claudius' invasion of Britain was a pretty big affair, using four legions which adds up to about 20,000 legionaries. The force also included auxiliaries, meaning the total number could have been about 40,000 men. Auxiliaries were not legionaries, and only Roman citizens could be legionaries. That means that auxiliaries were soldiers from around the Roman Empire, like those from Gaul or Germania. The size of this army was similar to Julius's second attempt, the one when he had a bit more luck. They sailed from either Boulogne or the Rhine, or maybe some from each. They landed in Kent, or perhaps somewhere near Southampton. It's a bit unclear.

Get used to this vagueness. A lot of our information for this comes from Cassius Dio. He wasn't even born until more than 100 years after these events, so it's not exactly fully reliable. The Romans wrote a lot down, but not necessarily all the stuff we would like to know now. Also, to be fair to the Romans, consider all the things you have written down and then lost: phone numbers, shopping lists, Memento style lists of people you can and can't trust. So keeping documents safe over a couple of millenniums seems like a big ask, and we have lost a lot.

Something strange about this Claudian invasion of Britain is that Claudius wasn't there. He wasn't in Kent or around Southampton. He wasn't even knocking about on the Rhine or in Boulogne. He was back at home in Rome. Even so, the cast of the Roman invasion was pretty good. The overall command of a bloke called Aulus Plautius, who had been an interim consul and a governor of Pannonia (a bit of Hungary and Austria) One other person involved worth mentioning was Vespasian, because we will see him again when he becomes an emperor. It just goes to show their politicians and rulers really had to put a shift in. There was no sitting on the board of a bank, or spending a few years working in PR for them.

Mind you, our all-star cast didn't start that well, and the launch of the invasion was a bit of a shambles like it always was with the Romans and Britain. There must have been something about the English Channel that upset the Italians and their friends from across the empire. Plautius had his legions ready to embark for Britain, and they all just agreed that 'no thanks, we quite like it here.' We are told by Dio that the soldiers were:

'were indignant at the prospect of campaigning outside the known world'.

Rome, as an institution, knew more about the island that they did under Julius, but we doubt the average legionary had flicked through a copy of Strabo's Geography. It was still the end of the world to a lot of Romans, and far away from home across a ropey bit of sea. Even so, at least Julius had got to the other side of the Channel before the legions decided it was all a bit much. Plautius didn't even have a handy sweary standard-bearer to get things moving.

Plautius, being stuck on the wrong side of the Channel, decided to roll the dice, and made a crazy gamble. He sent off to Emperor Claudius for help. It's usually a good idea to ask your supervisor for assistance when you come across a problem. However, when your supervisor is a Roman emperor, it's a bit questionable. Emperors don't tend to be above being a bit free with the executions, and it was particularly risky in this instance. Claudius had been bumping off senators like it was going out of fashion, so the emperor probably wouldn't have lost much sleep over having Pluatius executed. Asking that man for help with your job was the definition of a high-risk strategy. Luckily for Plautius, instead of sending an executioner with a big axe, Claudius sent a freed slave. That does sound like it was meant to be sarcastic, as in:

'This is so easy, even this bloke, who used to be a slave, is going to be able to get them across the sea.'

Admittedly the ex-slave in question, Narcissus, was an important man on Claudius' staff, so maybe it wasn't meant to be that much of a burn. If the story of what happened is to be believed, Narcissus made Plautius look a bit of a knob. He arrived and went to speak to the stubborn soldiers, but they started shouting 'Io Saturnalia'. Saturnalia was a Roman festival held for the god Saturn. A fun sounding part of the festival was that masters and slaves would partake in a bit of role reversal, and the slaves would be served dinner by their master. Obviously, the joke was that the slave was in charge now, and the Plautius would have to do what he was told. Absolute banter. Whatever the intent behind sending Narcissus, it worked, and the legions set sail. That could be because the legions were shamed into action. Or maybe it was the realisation that an emperor taking the mickey was the best possible outcome in a list of otherwise very, very bad outcomes.

Once Plautius reached the British side of the English Channel it started going pretty well for the Romans. Roman historian, Cassius Dio, claims that Plautius arrived in Britain in three waves, although we don't know if that meant in three different places, or if three groups hit the same beach at three different times. It doesn't matter much, because, however they did it, there weren't any Britons there to meet them.

The Catuvellauni were up first and were handily beaten with both leaders, Caratacus and Togodumnus, separately losing out to the Romans. Since the Catuvellauni were a big player, it looks like the smaller tribes under their control started submitting to the Romans. Obviously, there was no point in taking a kicking when the tribe that controlled you had already been done over. It's worth pointing out that Claudius' invasion seemed to focus on the kingdoms that were already 'clients' of Rome. It was the Catevaullini that appeared to be taking the brunt of the attack.

After the initial Roman wins, the next battle sounds very cinematic. We know Dio might not be the most reliable source since he got all this second hand, but what he lacks in useful detailed descriptions he makes up for in dramatic flair. The Britons had set themselves up on a riverbank opposite the Romans, which made them hard to attack. Plautius' solution to this was to send some of his auxiliary troops further along the river to swim across. Once across they came back along the river and attacked the camp of the overconfident Britons. Crucially they targeted their horses, meaning the Britons couldn't use their chariots to attack the Romans or to escape them if it all went wrong. Despite giving it a good go, it did indeed go wrong for the Britons. The fighting lasted until the next day, but the Britons were defeated and ran away to set up again on a different river, this time the Thames, possibly near where London is today.

According to Dio, the Britons on the Thames were undone by the same' crossing the river somewhere else and attacking a camp which otherwise thought itself safe' rouse. Amateur stuff from the Britons there. It was looking bad for them by this point. The Catuvellauni had been thoroughly beaten by now; Togodumnus was dead, and their other leader, Caratacus had run away west, although there is more on him later.

With the Britons having an absolute nightmare, Plautius set his sights on the important city of Camulodunum (Colchester) With his Roman's bearing down on this doomed stronghold, the impressive general made a decisive military manoeuvre. He stopped.

It was time for a phenomenal bit of PR activity. Apparently, Plautius had been told to send for Claudius if he was having any trouble. However, since he seemed to be doing quite well, it's not likely that this was why he stopped. His problem was the conquering of Britain wasn't to be Plautius' success but Claudius'. Which would be a hard sell for an emperor who was in Rome at the time. Plautus either sent word he was about to finish off the Catuvellauni, or Claudius was already on his way after hearing Palutius had landed in Britain safely. Whichever way it happened, Claudius had hopped a couple of ships and arrived in Britain. He headed straight to where Plautius and his men had been waiting, presumably for weeks now, and 'took control' of the attack on Camulodunum.

And so Britain was conquered by Claudius, with eleven kings of Briton tribes submitting to him.

Right. Obviously, we have a few problems with this.

Firstly, no, he didn't. He was barely there at all. Earlier we covered all the reasons that Claudius might have invaded, but really, we think it was all about Claudius, and he didn't much care about any other benefits. For further evidence of this, please consider the following three points.

Secondly, Claudius claimed the title Britannicus, which was a title that was given to Claudius, and any following emperor, who it was felt had conquered Britain. It meant 'Victorious in Britain'. Not only did Claudius have the fact that he conquered Britain in his title, but he also named his son Britannicus. Creating a living, breathing reminder to show everyone. 'Sorry, what do you mean you disagree with me? Have you met my son Britannicus, by the way?' Subtle as a brick. It would be like a player coming off the bench in the last 30 seconds of a cup final and calling his firstborn 'FA Cup.'

Thirdly, Claudius took elephants with him to Britain. It wasn't the first time elephants had been used in battle. They were handy for scaring the enemy half to death, before trampling them fully to death. However, Britain is far away from anywhere with easy access to elephants. Plautius didn't take any elephants with him for all of the proper battles he won. So why did Claudius need them for a sure thing? Because they sound epic and to be fair to Claudius if you battle using elephants, it's going to get a mention, and everyone who reads about it is going to think; 'Nice! That Claudius was a pretty cool emperor.'

Lastly, he spent a total of 16 days in Britain. That is a token effort at best. People go on longer holidays than that.

Anyone who has ever had a boss that claimed the credit for your work should think that Claudius was an absolute bellend.

We will accept that all the above points are maybe a bit petty. If you want a good reason for why we think Claudius was full of shit for claiming he had conquered Britain, how about the fact that he just plain hadn't. Not even Plautius, who put a shift in, had conquered Britain. We know that eleven kings submitted to Claudius, but unhelpfully, we don't really know who they were. The Catuvellauni were definitely one. The Iceni, from around Norfolk, are assumed to be one, as are a tribe from Northern England, called the Brigantes. We specifically mention these two tribes as we are soon going find out precisely what that submission was worth (spoiler: varying degrees of fuck all) These tribes probably covered a fair bit of what is now England, but the Romans themselves hadn't really strayed too far out of the South East. As for Wales and Scotland, the Romans hadn't touched them. It's a bit rich claiming to have conquered a place you haven't even seen most of. You should bear in mind that, at this point, the Romans weren't 100% sure that Britain was an island, and they certainly had no clue what was going on at the top of it. Either way, Britain wasn't exactly a Roman province yet. The bits the Romans had control over were mostly run by client kings, so technically the rulers of the tribes became middle managers under their new Roman boss. However much control the Romans directly had over South East England, it's more than a bit of a stretch to say Claudius had conquered Britain.

As a side note, Verica, who had gone asking for the invasion, isn't mentioned anywhere again. Presumably, karma caught up with him. His assumed successor, Togidubnus, seemed to have been made a major client king, probably putting him in charge of the tribes who caused the Romans the most problems. There is no way this went to plan for

Verica. He wasn't a king, and now there were Romans all over the place.

Despite all our cynical misgivings, the conquering of Britain was well received back in Rome. Claudius had a triumph thrown for him. A triumph was a massive party where you get to parade in front of the people of Rome showing off how mighty you are. He even had two triumphal arches built and minted some commemorative coins. It's Plautius we feel sorry for. I bet his party was a lot more low key.

So what have we learnt? Well, bosses have been claiming the work of their employees for millennia. If you put off doing that big project at work, you do risk your eventual replacement coming along and finishing it really quickly, making you look a bit rubbish. And, finally, if you overclaim your achievements loudly and often, people just believe what you did was better than it was. That's a relevant life lesson. The sort of lesson you can only read in a book which has won its author a Nobel Prize in History Writing, like this one.

Claudius - A Very Mixed Bag

We have already heard how Claudius came to power and why that was important for Britain. However, the specifics of how he got from hiding behind a curtain to actually being emperor are quite telling. Specifically telling us that the Roman Empire was a bit badly set up from the off.

The Praetorian Guard picked Claudius, and he was supported by the Urban Prefect (praefectus urbi), who was basically a sort of mayor of Rome, and his accompanying soldiers. That left the Senate not a lot of choice in acknowledging him as emperor. The Senate was still a major feature of the Roman Empire, but by now it wasn't looking all that important. Augustus had been careful to pander to them, to make them feel important, even though he was busy transferring all their powers to himself. Tiberius went big on treason trials featuring senators, and Caligula carried that on and added in humiliating individual senators at the same time. The Praetorian Guard, and the army as a whole, are going to pop up a lot when it comes to new emperors. They basically picked who it was going to be, or at least the army had to be happy with whoever got the job. To modern ears, that is a terrifying way to do things, and you will see throughout this whole story that your modern ears are mostly right.

We quite liked Claudius when we read about him, but the Senate wasn't too big on him. Or at least they weren't a fan of how he got the job. Generally posh, self-important people don't like being side-lined, and the relationship never warmed up. In fact, Claudius made one move in particular which would never have gone well with the senators. He added new senators from the provinces, specifically from Gaul. They weren't even from the nice near bit of Gaul, but the full-on 'long-hair' Gaul. Claudius was born in Lyon (Lugdunum), which was in Gaul Narbonensis, a more civilized bit of Gaul in South West France, so he was familiar with the region.

The speech that Claudius made to the Senate about these new senators, or at least something like the speech he might have made, has been found printed on a bronze tablet. It's surprisingly progressive and is about inclusion and diversity of the empire and the republic before that. That must have done down really badly in the room. The original basis of who could and couldn't be a senator was that they were the descendants of the men who Romulus had picked for the first Senate in the Roman Kingdom. These were not people who were going to be big on diversity and social mobility.

It seems like an error for the Senate to be going toe to toe with an emperor, considering the damage that Tiberius and Caligula did to them with the treason trials. And it went exactly the way you would expect. Claudius didn't stick to just mugging them off with Gallic senators. He executed about as many important people as any other emperor of the time had and would. The figures have it as being somewhere around 35 senators and between 200 and 300 equestrians, who were the social rung below the senators - so important people themselves.

Scrapping with the Senate aside, Claudius did some pretty sensible stuff. Claudius started using freedmen (as in ex-slaves) in the administration of the empire, probably because he couldn't trust the senators who would usually hold positions of responsibility. Which we assume meant people got jobs based on ability rather than who their dad was, which is a novel idea.

Claudius also got involved in a bit of empire improvement and according to Suetonius:

'The public works which he completed were great and essential rather than numerous.'

Which suggests he made useful stuff rather than loads of flashy buildings. It included things like aqueducts, and an impressive-sounding lighthouse at a harbour he had built in Rome.

He also righted a few wrongs that Caligula had been involved in. Caligula had been particularly unpleasant to Jews, and Claudius let them practice their religion with a bit more freedom. He did, however, come down against them in a ruling about Alexandria, in Egypt. The locals there were annoyed about the level of Jewish immigration, so Claudius' response was to ban further mass immigration of Jews to Egypt. That doesn't seem particularly nice.

On the other hand, Claudius did come down on the Jewish population's side in the Province of Judea, which was a region around modern Israel and Palestine. Judea had been a Roman Province since 6 AD, but like with Mauritania, Caligula messed it up. The place was run by a procurator, a Roman in charge of admin. Caligula, being a twat, decided it would be a brilliant idea to turn the Temple in Jerusalem into an imperial shrine, with a whacking great big gold statue of himself in it. The Jews didn't fancy that. Can't think why. So, even after Caligula's death, there was a lot of tension in the area, which is probably why Claudius decided to downgrade the Roman rule a bit there in 41. The Romans were clearly still in charge, but Judea made a move towards more of a client kingdom situation than a Roman province when he put Herod Agrippa in place as King of Judea. Incidentally, Herod Agrippa was the grandson of Herod The Great. As in Herod' kill all the boys under two' the Great of

New Testament fame. Herod died in 44, and Judea reverted back to being a proper Roman province.

What we are saying was that Claudius mostly seems like a pretty sensible ruler, which is a bit refreshing after boring, but somehow also brutal, Tiberius and probably insane Caligula. Where Claudius loses points would be his personal life. Considering his family, you can't blame him for being a bit dysfunctional, but it's safe to say he didn't do well with wives.

He was engaged twice before he was emperor. The first wedding didn't happen for political reasons (not his fault) the second didn't go ahead because the bride to be, Livia Medullina, died on the day of the wedding (you have to hope that's not his fault because that would be dark).

His first actual marriage was to a woman called Plautia Urgulanilla, but they were divorced due to adultery and accusations of murder (her, not him). They had two children, Drusus and Claudia. Drusus died when 'he was strangled by a pear which he had thrown into the air in play and caught in his open mouth.' That's horrible. Claudius was a magnet for tragedy.

His next wife was Aelia Paetina, who he later divorced so he could marry another woman who was 30 odd years younger than him. Now that was a dick move, but at least it didn't involve a body count.

The younger woman was Valeria Messalina. This is still all before Claudius was emperor, by the way. It's worth mentioning here that it's hard when talking about the female family members of famous men from history. They often end up with a bad reputation as slappers or manipulative shrews, particularly if the husband isn't much liked. A lot of them probably deserved it, but often it seems a bit forced. That means that wife number three, Messalina, may not have been as bad as she sounds. And she sounds terrible. We are told that she had an influential position, especially when they had a son, who later became called Britannicus. She clearly liked her power, and she cemented her position by bumping off rivals, including Claudius' sister.

Ignoring all the general slurs, in 48 AD, when Claudius had been emperor for a few years, he went away from Rome on general emperor business. When he came back, he found that Messalina had gone and married some other bloke. A senator nonetheless, which will not have helped that happy go lucky feel about the place. Both the senator, Gaius Silius, and Messalina ended up dead as a result of that. They can't have thought that was going to end any other way.

His fourth wife, Agrippina the Younger, has a similarly bad reputation, if not quite a bit worse. She certainly seemed to have put a fair bit of effort into making sure her children, particularly her son from an earlier marriage, Nero, inherited the empire. But that is relatively standard stuff.

A bit less standard is that Agrippina was generally accused of killing Claudius. The reason given for it is that she and Claudius hadn't been getting on towards the end and Claudius was looking at changing his mind and making his other son, Britannicus, his heir. However, if Claudius died before Britannicus was an adult, then this would be less of an issue, and Agrippina was really, really keen on having her son, and Claudius' adopted son, Nero, take charge. Again, this might just be folk blaming an ambitious woman. Claudius was 63 at the time, so particularly in the ancient world, him dying could easily have been natural. Saying that, I would wait until you have read our Roman history chapter on Nero before you pass judgement on Agrippina. It takes a turn.

We just want to finish up by showing how mad the marriages at the top of the Roman Empire really were. Agrippina was Claudius' fourth marriage. It was Agrippina's third. She was also the daughter of Germanicus, meaning she was Caligula's sister and, disturbingly, that makes Claudius her uncle. And husband. No wonder they were all crazy. However, you should be a bit careful about applying modern standards to historical figures, often they are doing things which seem massively wrong, but it was generally seen as alright at the time. Maybe sometimes the benefit of the doubt is fine. After all that, I don't think I like Claudius anymore. And that's before we found out that an uncle-niece marriage wasn't acceptable to Romans either.

So that is the man who dragged Britain into the Roman Empire. Considering the goings-on during this whole period, you can't help but think we might have been better off staying on the outside.

Nam Viet

43 was a big year for British history, but it is also a significant date in Vietnamese history. Vietnam, as we know it now, has only been around since 1976, when north and south was reunified, but the Vietnamese trace their history back to the 2800s BC.

In the 1st century, what is now Northern Vietnam was under the control of the Chinese Han Dynasty. The region was known as Nam Viet, which had been the name of the kingdom before the Han took over the place in 111 BC. Nam Viet, wasn't precisely what is now Northern Vietnam, because the ancient peoples didn't have a lot of respect for modern borders. It was actually Northern Vietnam and some of the Chinese provinces of Guangdong and Guangxi.

We are aware that you will have paid no attention to that last bit of geography chat because you will have spotted that Vietnam is clearly named after an ancient kingdom which had the reverse name. Nam Viet to Vietnam. The old name was resurrected, and swapped around, by a 19th-century Vietnamese emperor, Gia Long, when he unified the country after beating another dynasty. It's weird stuff like that which makes us love reading history. We are sure it made absolute sense in the time and place, but why just pick an old name and then tweak it a bit?

The name Nam Viet comes from 'southern Viet', with the Viet being an ethnic group in the region. That means that Nam Viet was where the southernmost of those people lived. Which is nice and simple. It also won't have escaped your notice that this means that Vietnam, which is probably best known to you for its war between north and south, is named after the southern Viet, who lived in Northern Vietnam. It's a topsy-turvy kind of country.

Anyway, as you can imagine the native people of Nam Viet, were not always keen on being run by the Chinese Han. 43 was the year that a rebellion against the Han ended, with the deaths of the Trung Sisters, Trung Trac and Trung Nhi. For those of you who weren't aware, the Vietnamese naming convention is to put the family name first, so the Trung Sisters weren't just two women with the same first name. Trung Trac's husband had been killed when he was found out to be plotting a revolt against the Chinese. Unfortunately for the Chinese, the Trung sisters, along with other important Vietnamese people, didn't fancy giving up and declared themselves independent in 39.

The newly independent state, with the Trung sisters as queens, was pretty big, going from the bottom of China, down to the city of Hue, which is about halfway up modern-day Vietnam. They lasted for four years before the Chinese could send a general to beat them. That is a decent amount of time, considering that the Han were no mugs themselves. The final battles were around Hanoi, which is the capital of modern Vietnam, up in the north. In the end, the sisters knew they were well beaten, and we are told they both committed suicide by drowning in a river.

As we know, that wasn't the end of the Vietnamese, but the Chinese would be in control, on and off, until the 15th-century. However, it seems the Vietnamese still celebrate the Trung Sisters. There is even a whole district in central Hanoi named after them, which is quite cool.

Scapula, Suetonius & The Brigantes

In our last visit to Roman Britain, we finally got around to the Romans establishing themselves on our little island in 43 AD. However, as we made painfully clear, Claudius not only didn't have proper control over all that much of the island, but he also contributed very little to getting the control over the bits the Romans did have. He claimed the invasion as a win for himself, but really it was his general Plautius who did all the work. Claudius was in Britain for a grand total of 16 days, after that he buggered off and left Plautius to get on with things. 'Things' being the subjugation of more Britons.

In this chapter, we ask ourselves; Who could replace undervalued Plautius? And who gives a shit about Anglesey? And begging for your life is undignified, but can it work?

I'm Starting To Think We Aren't Welcome Here

Plautius' attempts at conquering Britain, beyond that first foray, aren't, as ever, all that clear. But luckily for us, he and the governors coming after him did it all in stages, so we can piece bits of it together.

The first stage was keeping control over what he already had. We know that, even before Claudius left, some of the Britons had their weapons confiscated. Although not all the tribes in the area were disarmed. That becomes significant later on. Exactly who had to do what, we don't know. Still, it's safe to assume that at the very least the Catuvellauni were disarmed, presumably along with any other tribe who gave Plautius undue grief during the initial invasion.

As with a lot of these things we really aren't sure how far the Roman control might have gone, or how much control they had over the bits they were technically the boss in. There is, however, a handy line we can draw along the country, with the theory being that everything below it was, to a certain extent, Roman territory. This line was a road called the Fosse Way. Romans are famous for their straight road building, and this is an excellent example, which ran from Devon, in South West England, towards the Humber through the East Midlands. This road took them through the settlements of Exeter (Isca), Leicester (Ratae) and Lincoln (Lindum). It became a major pathway for the rest of the Roman Britain period and was used long after that. In fact, you can still drive along a fair bit of its route; some of it is now the A46 around Leicester, which is a little bit depressing, but quite cool at the same time. Historians don't typically seem happy with the idea that this road was a border the Romans used, and there is no way it was that simple. However, it's too convenient to ignore, and without a better idea of what and when Roman movements were happening, it will do as a rough guide.

The clearest picture we get from this early Roman consolidation is the activity of one of the celebrities of the invasion, the future Emperor Vespasian. The sources say he fought 30 battles and took 20 settlements, beating two major tribes. Maybe he did, but given he was later an emperor, you should take that with whatever sized pinch of salt you fancy. Especially considering the source was a bit vague on where exactly these battles and settlements were. It does mention the Isle of Wight (Vectis, as the Romans called it) as one of the places he fought, and his legion ended up in Exeter, in Devon. That would mean he came up against a couple of tribes we haven't really seen much of yet, the Durotriges and Dumnonii tribes, who were from the part of the South West around Devon and Cornwall. We also know less famous Romans also headed north, along the Fosse Way, since they established forts in Leicestershire and Lincoln. This would have put the Romans in the territory of the Brigantes and the Corieltauvi. The Brigantes had a massive territory around Yorkshire, Lancashire and spreading into North East England. The Corieltauvi were a sizable tribe who were based around the settlement at Leicester.

Plautius was in charge until 47 AD, so he had three years in Britain, and he seemed to do a half-decent job of controlling a big chunk of England before he was recalled to Rome. He was replaced as governor by a bloke called Ostorius Scapula. We only have a few sources for these governors and how they ran things, so we are at the mercy of the opinion of a few men, and what they chose to write down. The impression we get from them is that Plautius was competent and got stuff done. He had successfully invaded after all and spent three years in hostile territory without any major mishaps. Or at least any disasters embarrassing enough that they were bothered to be recorded. Scapula, on the other hand, was probably an arsehole.

It looks like Scapula's job was to expand Roman control further across the island, and he gave it a good go, but he had two problems. Firstly, there was the Britons in front of him and, secondly, there was the Britons behind him. We are told, by Roman historian Tacitus, that when Scapula arrived, the situation wasn't the best. The tribes had decided that because the new governor was new to the island, and because it was winter, they could chance their arm and cause some trouble. That means Scapula's early activity was defending the territory of the Britons allied to Roman. It looks like this was the lands of the Dobunni, who were from Gloucestershire, and were under attack from the Silures. The Silures were a tribe from South East Wales, and they were a massive pain in the arse for the Romans. Scapula sent men to protect Roman-controlled territories from the Silures, which would have involved a more prominent presence of Roman soldiers in the region, in the lands of tribes like the Dobunni. It must have been hard to pretend you are the boss when a load of foreign soldiers are marching about the place. We imagine the more Romans around the less in control these client kings looked.

In a more aggressive move towards the Britons who lived in Roman-controlled territory, Scapula decided to disarm some of the more suspicious tribes. We are told the new policy was in place between the Trent (a river that flows through Nottingham) and the Severn (a river on the Welsh border), which would cover the whole of Southern England. This included the Iceni tribe, who were based over East Anglia way. They didn't like that because the Iceni were one of the tribes who had submitted to the Romans without fighting them, so they thought they had earned a certain level of treatment for them.

Do you know when you are watching the news from America, and they are talking about potential gun control laws? You get angry folk screaming about conspiracies and how they need those guns to fight corrupt governments and red coats. Well, that. Except instead of drunk, angry men sitting at home going mad on Twitter, you had loads of hard-as-nails ancient Celts. In 47, the Iceni response was to hole up in a defensible position and give the Romans the finger. They inevitably lost to the Romans, who now had a better excuse than ever to disarm them, although they were allowed to keep their client kingdom status. That was a decision the Romans would regret in a few years.

Scapula might have softened enough to let them have a bit of self-rule, but he couldn't just trust everyone in that part of the world to start behaving themselves. Luckily, the Romans had themselves a big fort in Colchester (Camulodunum) in the area where the Catuvellauni had been in control before the Romans arrived. As a Roman settlement, Colchester was handily placed to keep control, but Scapula needed soldiers elsewhere if he was going to spread control west into Wales. His solution was to scrap the fort in 49 and build up a town which could be settled by retired legionaries. Part of the deal for serving in the Roman army was that you got some land when you finished your service. Assuming some angry Briton hadn't chopped you in half first. For Scapula, this was a neat little solution. He had found land for his veterans, and he had a town of ex-soldiers he could rely on to look after that part of the island while he was off elsewhere.

With Scapula feeling a bit more confident about what was behind him, he could have a proper look at what was going on beyond the Fosse Way. He started with the Deceangli, who were in North Wales. It sounds like Scapula was fairly successful there, with the Tacitus quote on it sounding quite painful:

'Their territory was devastated, and booty seized far and wide, while the enemy dared not risk an open engagement and, if they attempted to harass the Roman column by stealth, their treachery was punished.'

Which sounds like the Deceangli knew they couldn't beat the Romans in a toe to toe fight, which meant Scapula felt the need to punish them for 'shifty' tactics. We will be quoting Tacitus quite a bit, and you will realise quite quickly, Tacitus loves that blook and thunder stuff.

Scapula didn't get much further than the Deceangali before he had to do a bit of fire fighting in a supposedly calmer region, once again. It wasn't exactly behind him in the core Roman lands, but instead, it was further north with the client kingdom of the Brigantes. That tribes were under the rule of Queen Cartimandua, who was pro-Roman. Or at least pro-give-the-Romans-want-they-want-so-they-will-leave-the-Brigantes-alone. This wasn't a view shared by everyone she ruled. The Brigantes lands were massive and covered a lot of Northern England, split by the Pennines, so realistically the Brigantes must have been a tribe made up of smaller groups who had banded together. And it's not surprising that not everyone in the Brigantes was on the same page. A civil war kicked off, on a scale which must have been reasonably significant because Scapula stopped what he was doing and headed in the direction of Wales to dive into the scrap to make sure Cartimandua stayed in charge up there. Which she did.

Now, finally, Scapula could get on with having a crack at Wales, starting with the Silures in South Wales, and we have the return of a Briton from the previous chapter; Caractacus. Caractacus had got himself in with the Silures tribe, who seemed to be the main cause of problems for the Romans in Wales. It's hard to figure out how Caractacus managed to go from leading the Catuvellauni, pre-43 invasion, to heading up the inter-tribal resistance against Plautius and Claudius, to being a big wig in opposition to Scapula from Wales. It wasn't just the Silures who were causing grief, it looks like Caratacus was involved with folk from other tribes as well. Unfortunately, for the Romans, causing a rebellion, like with the Iceni, which they had to violently put down, then getting involved in a Briton civil dispute, again violently, did wonders for Caractacus' recruitment drive. It's a lesson the human race just will not learn. One group goes about maiming and killing people and then wondering why they are being shouted at and attacked by everyone. Rinse and repeat until you have a shiny glossy arms industry.

In a nod to modern conflicts, the Welsh Briton's tactics involved fighting in the mountains and hills, making them hard to catch. Which is something the Taliban in Afghanistan has had a bit of luck within recent decades. Guerilla warfare, Welsh-style, was especially a problem for the Romans. In terms of their armies, the Romans had fully specced into dominating battles in open spaces. The scrap with the Silures was difficult and would have needed manpower, so a fort was established near Glouster which is on the border of what is now England and Wales. This possibly housed the legion which had been back east, at Colchester, and was no doubt handy as a base to work from. It sounded like a pain, but, as is often inevitable with the Romans, they did manage to beat the Silures, and Caractacus was forced to leg it again. This time he went further north to base himself with the Ordovices, who were a tribe in Central Wales.

After the Silures, the field of battle had moved north with Caractcus, and it was the Ordovices' turn. The Britons had holed themselves up in a defensible position, which was assaulted by the Romans. It sounded like it was hard-fought but, eventually, the Romans won, again. Even this wasn't the end of Caractacus because he managed to escape, again. The man has more lives than Lazarus. It must have been a close-cut escape though since he left his wife and kid behind. Either that or he didn't like his family. We have covered this Welsh adventure in a few hundred words, but it's worth pointing out that this happened in 51 AD. That's eight years after Plautius and Claudius popped over from Rome, and four years after Scapula was given the job as governor. This was no nice jog through South East England and into the Welsh Valleys. This was a slog.

What Happened To Everyone?

This win over Caractacus was nowhere near the end of this part of the story. For a start, the Welsh Britons weren't done for. Even the Silures who had taken a proper beating weren't done. The Romans had moved north following Caractacus, but they were a touch overconfident about how willing the Silures were to properly submit. The Welsh tribe got together again and gave the Romans a couple of embarrassingly big beatings and reverted back to their guerrilla tactics. For a bit of a clue just how annoying they were to the Romans, we have Scapula's reaction to them. Apparently, the constant attacks by the tribe got up Scapula's nose so much that he ordered the annihilation of the whole tribe. As in full-on genocidal extermination. Maybe there was a point to that, but it seems to us that if a group is facing annihilation, they might as well fight as hard as they can. The only way up is up from genocide. Now there's an inspirational quote to put on a poster. For anyone worried, the

Silures weren't wiped out and the Welsh Britons, in general, would carry on being a pain in the arse for years to come, even if they couldn't chalk this one up as a win.

As for Scapula, this was pretty much the end of him in this story, since he died in 52, after five years in charge of a fledgeling Roman Britain. According to Tacitus, he had been 'worn out with care.' We can't say we warmed to the bloke. It was probably the attempted genocide that did it; call us over-sensitive, but it puts you off a bloke. It's not clear if he left the place in better condition than when he found it, and he seemed a touch too aggressive, but as for 'worn with care', to be fair it did sound pretty stressful.

Handily for us, the story of the other big player in all this ends quite neatly after all this. As we know, after the loss in North Wales, Caractacus legged it, yet again. This time he legged to Northern England to the Brigantes and their Queen Cartimandua. It was quite the national tour he went on. Caractacus showing up gave Cartimandua an extremely easy decision to make. Should she support, or at least hide, the most wanted man in Britain? Scapula had just intervened in a civil war in her favour, and the last thing she needed was the poster boy for the resistance skulking around her territory, riling up the already tetchy locals. Even if she had been tempted to help him, Caractacus' track record wasn't particularly impressive. He had lost in South East England followed by losses in both South and North Wales. Add to that the fact that the Romans had just hammered the Iceni and half of her own Brigantes, and she probably handed the man back to Scapula with a little bow on.

It would be reasonable to assume that being handed over to the Romans would mean bad times for Caractacus. And you would assume wrong. We were expecting the next line in that story to be somewhere between 'he was never heard of again' and 'he was brutally executed.' What really happened was that he got very, very lucky. How exactly did Caractacus avoid being the guest of honour at his own execution? The story goes that he was allowed to speak in front of the Senate, and he gave this speech:

'If the degree of my nobility and fortune had been matched by moderation in success, I would have come to this City as a friend rather than a captive, nor would you have disdained to receive with a treaty of peace one sprung from brilliant ancestors and commanding a great many nations. But my present lot, disfiguring as it is for me, is magnificent for you. I had horses, men, arms, and wealth: what wonder if I was unwilling to lose them? If you wish to command everyone, does it really follow that everyone should accept your slavery? If I were now being handed over as one who had surrendered immediately, neither my fortune nor your glory would have achieved brilliance. It is also true that in my case any reprisal will be followed by oblivion. On the other hand, if you preserve me safe and sound, I shall be an eternal example of your clemency.'

We think what he is saying there is:

'Obviously, I was going to fight back. I had loads of good shit, and you were going to nick it. Now you've won I can't do anything about it, you've already got all my good shit. So letting me live makes no difference to you, and you would look proper sound.'

The Senate bought that hook, line and sinker, and Caractacus was allowed to live in Rome instead of being strung up.

That is how it went down as recorded by Tacitus. As ever,

we are overly cynical, but this seems a convenient story to make the Romans seem cool. Especially when you add in another quote attributed to Caractacus after he saw Rome:

'And can you, then, who have got such possessions and so many of them, covet our poor tents?'

As in:

'I thought I had loads of good shit, but you have loads better stuff then I had. Why did you even bother coming and taking what we had?'

Who knows, maybe it did happen like that, and the Romans really were that cool. Or perhaps the Romans just really like tents, even if they are rubbish.

Calm Down Everyone

Caractacus was no longer a problem, but there was some important admin to be getting on with. With Scapula dead, Claudius needed to find a new governor. His choice suggested that he wanted everyone in Britain to calm down a bit, which they did. Sort of. The new governor was a bloke called Aulus Didius Gallus. He got the job in 52, and his thing was consolidation rather than swinging big at conquering new territory. Not that consolidating the Roman position in Britain would be easy after Scapula spent so long pissing everyone off. They didn't calm down just because he was dead. It will be a bit of a running theme for new governors, but when Didius got to Britain, he found the place in a bit of disarray. The Silures were continuing to cause them grief, and the defeat of Caractacus hadn't slowed them down at all. In fact, we are told that a Roman legion took a proper beating from the Silures before Didius got there.

If Didius was hoping for a quiet life, he would have been a

bit disappointed. The Britons in Wales were still raging, but there were also problems from further north. In a previous chapter, we mentioned that Cartimandua, the ruler of the Brigantes tribe, and her trouble with a faction of the tribe who weren't up for Roman rule. Back when Scapula had been governor, there had been a bit of Brigantes on Brigantes fighting up there, so he had sent soldiers up there to help Cartimandua beat the anti-Roman faction. Nine odd years later, with Didius on the scene, it happened again. In an embarrassing Jeremy Kyle style twist, it was Cartimandua's husband, Venutius, who was causing the trouble. He wanted to take on the role of head-rebel after Caractacus had conformably retired to Rome. Roman historian, Tacitus, reckoned Venutius was the best military leader the Britons had to offer, so he might have been the real deal. Cartimandua certainly didn't take kindly to all this, and when the fighting started, she managed to defeat and imprison members of Venutius' family. What we are saying is that any divorce court would have had two sides to hear.

As we know, England and Wales were now full of tribes under varying levels of control by the Romans. The Brigantes were probably allowed a fair bit of freedom as one of the client kingdoms. It must have been very handy for Didius' that his northern border had friendly-ish folk on it. If only to be a buffer between the Romans and other Britons further north. If Venutius got his way, that border of lunatic Britons would be a lot closer to home. Not to mention, the idea of a Caractacus Mk II running about the place would not have been a pleasing thought.

For a bit of added spice to an already dodgy situation, at some point, Cartimandua remarried. Which isn't too surprising, what with the civil war and imprisonment of in-laws it would be odd if the Brigantian power couple had stayed in wedded bliss. However, in a move which must have really annoyed Venutius, Cartimandua married a bloke called Vellocatus, who had been Venutius' shield-bearer. We assume that was the ancient equivalent to the stereotype of leaving a husband for a tennis coach. That must have got to Venutius. Luckily for everyone, considering the pace this was escalating at, Didius sent a force up there to make sure Cartimandua came out on top. The Romans chased Ventius and his mates out of Brigantian territory but decided not to follow up and beat him for good. Long-term, this wasn't a good plan, and it wasn't the end of this squabble between husband and wife. The Romans should really be learning that just subduing a group doesn't mean that's the problem solved. However, for now, Didius and his Romans felt a bit better about their northern border.

Romans Get Back To It

Didius, as governor, wasn't very well received by some Romans, such as Tacitus. He is a bloke whose opinion gets given lots of weight because he is one of the relatively few authors whose writings have survived this long, and Tacitus had no time for Didius. We've heard Britain was in a bit of a state when Didus turned up. However, Tacitus claimed that when Didius arrived, he found that those stories of the dire situation had been a bit of an exaggeration. Instead of just getting on with the job, and being pleased everything was going smoothly, Didus doubled down on the exaggeration and 'magnified' how bad things were to make his wins look more impressive. Or maybe as a helpful safety net of an excuse if it all went against him. We've all done it at work. It's the imperial governor equivalent of telling your boss something is going to take two weeks to do, so you look like a genius when you do it in one.

Tacitus, like a lot of Romans, liked a particular type of governor. For them, unless you are wading through lakes of blood to expand the empire, then you might as well have stayed at home. Didius didn't fit that mould, he was more about consolidation than expansion. To be fair to Didius, he was probably just following instructions. Claudius was a bit more cautious after the initial invasion, and his successor, Nero started off much the same. When Didius was recalled in 57, he left the place calmer than when he turned up, and he probably can't be blamed for a marital dispute playing out in Yorkshire.

Didius' replacement was a man called Quintus Veranius. He took a different approach and dove straight into scrapping with the Silures. There are suggestions that Nero had been considering abandoning Britain altogether around this time. It makes sense, as it was taking up some serious manpower just to keep hold of what they had on the island. Instead, he went from the cautious approach and moved into all guns blazing. The aim was to get everything properly pacified. Saying that, Tacitus doesn't give Veranius a lot of credit as governor either. He refers to his scrap with the Silures as 'plundering raids.'

Veranius only lasted a year or so before he died on the job, so there's not much to say about him. In his defence, the Siluires don't make as much of an impact after this, even according to Tacitus. That suggests he had done a decent job with the pacification. We would say this would count as a bit of a win for Veranius; the Silures had been a royal pain in the arse since the Romans had arrived on the island. If Veranius finally got them to calm down enough not to cause any more disasters for the Romans, we reckon that's decent going.

For some insight into how Veranius annoyed Tacitus, we have a quote from him about the governor:

'he claimed that if he had lived another two years, he would have laid the (whole) province at his feet.'

Hindsight is 20/20, but considering what happened after this, for Veranius to claim he would have the whole of Britain wrapped up in two years is a Trumpian level of over self-confidence. That might have rubbed Tacitus up the wrong way.

Even if Veranius wasn't hardcore enough for Tacitus,

his replacement, Suetonius Paulinus, will have been more to his liking. He followed up on the work of Veranius and dove straight into Wales, fighting the Ordovices. Handily, he had relevant work experience that would have come in useful battling the Britons in Wales. He was a veteran of the fighting in Mauritania, around the Atlas Mountains in North Africa. So he was used to folk hiding in the hills and occasionally appearing to really wreck your day.

Suetonius conquered the Ordovices territory in two years. Obviously, Veranius would have been soaking in the delights of John o' Groats by then, but for mere mortals, it was a pretty impressive achievement. However, the most significant bit of Suetonius' Welsh jaunt was the Romans taking the Isle of Anglesey, which they called Mona, an island just off the northwestern coast of Wales. This was important for two reasons. The first was that it was a step towards the Romans properly wrapping up Wales. Secondly, we are told that it was a handy place for people running from the Romans to lay low and regroup. If the Romans had left them there, they would have been worried about someone whipping up the tribes into an anti-Roman fervour again.

The other important reason for the Romans taking control of Anglesey was the druids. These days if someone invaded Anglesey, it would take a couple of weeks for the rest of us to notice. Back then it was a major religious centre for Druidism, which was the religion of the Celts. This wasn't just a big deal for Britons, it was a significant site for Celts on the continent as well. Important Gauls sent their children over to learn from the Druids there, so taking that was a big deal.

The issue was that the Romans disliked druids, so Anglesey was an obvious target for them, even if it wasn't receiving refugees fleeing from the Romans tearing up Wales. Traditionally the Romans took a relaxed view of other people's religions. They were usually fine with them, to the point of adopting their gods, generally after renaming them to something more Roman sounding. Sometimes though, they were having none of it. As we will see later with Christianity and have already seen with Judaism, the line the Romans draw with other people's religions is when they impact the running of things. They certainly didn't seem to like prothletising (as in trying to get people to convert to their religion) However, what they really didn't like was when the people in charge of a religion decided to tell people that Roman rule was a bad thing. We are told one of the reasons the Romans didn't like Druidism, in particular, was that the druids worked against Roman occupation, getting the locals all het up about armed resistance.

As with a lot of stuff, anything to do with the druids is, to some extent, guesswork. We weren't joking when we said the Romans didn't like them, and they were wiped out by the end of the 2nd century, so we don't have too much written about them, let along by them. We saw at least one historian call them 'enigmatic.' Strangely, one of our main sources on the Druids is Julius Caesar. He wrote about them, referring to them as priests, judges, and teachers. He also said they practised human sacrifice, including the building of massive wicker men, which was filled with people and set on fire. One thing we do know is that the folk who dance around Stonehenge these days aren't druids in the ancient sense (although good luck to them, it looks like a laugh).

It's a safe bet that the druids would be involved in the anti-Roman movements. It's not too much of a stretch that the people high up in the druidic scene would come from the same families as the tribal leaders. That's what would happen centuries later with Christianity in Europe. Being part of the leaders of the Britons means druids had plenty to lose from a Roman invasion, and they wouldn't have wanted to stand aside while their brothers etc. took a beating.

Whatever the reason, Anglesey, as a centre of British Druidism, with all the accompanying shrines and holy places, was presumably a bit of an epicentre of the anti-Roman feeling. It was also important to the natives, a bit like a Mecca or a Jerusalem. But rainier. So what happens next was always going to be unpopular.

Apparently, when the Romans arrived on the Welsh shore opposite Anglesey, the Britons were waiting on their side. The Menai Strait between the island and mainland is pretty small, with the narrowest bit only being 400 meters. These days there is a bridge across, and it's about a four-minute walk. As the strait was so narrow, the Romans easily sailed across in flat bottomed boats, or swam and waded across to get to the Britons. Tacitus has quite a dramatic telling of the battle, and here is a pretty lengthy translation of what Tacitus said happened:

'On the beach stood the adverse array, a serried mass of arms and men, with women flitting between the ranks. In the style of Furies, in robes of deathly black and with dishevelled hair, they brandished their torches; while a circle of Druids, lifting their hands to heaven and showering imprecations, struck the troops with such an awe at the extraordinary spectacle that, as though their limbs were paralysed, they exposed their bodies to wounds without an attempt at movement. Then, reassured by their general, and inciting each other never to flinch before a band of females and fanatics, they charged behind the standards, cut down all who met them, and enveloped the enemy in his own flames. The next step was to install a garrison among the conquered population, and to demolish the groves consecrated to their savage cults: for they considered it a duty to consult their deities by means of human entrails.'

Basically, the Romans got there and all the Britons, men and women, were waiting for them. The druids were there as well, doing mad druid things which scared the shit out of the Romans. But the legionaries got over it, killed all the Britons and messed up their sacred groves. A grove is a fancy word for a group of trees. The excuse for knocking down the trees was that the clearings they surrounded were used for ceremonies of human sacrifice, which was a bit of a no-no for Romans by this time. Although they had dabbled in it themselves in the past, and it is a little strange for the Romans to be fussy on this point, considering everything else they got up to.

Tacitus' telling of the attack is a bit dramatic, and he certainly wasn't there, given he was only born around about this time. He did, however, have a link to the attack. His father-in-law, Agricola, was there, so he probably had it second hand from him. We will be hearing from Agricola again in a later chapter. He was an important bloke in Roman Britain.

So, Suetonius and his Romans had knackered Anglesey and dealt a big blow to the Welsh Briton tribes. It looked like he was about to put the Welsh tribes down and add them to the apparently relatively calm Roman-controlled territories. However, it didn't work out like that. Just as he was finishing pulling up trees, he got some news that messed up his plans. And what was this news? One word for you. Boudicca. She kicked up quite the fuss, do we will be giving her a whole other chapter.

So what have we learnt? Don't divorce your husband, he might gather support for himself and invade your house. Having mad priests chanting round you before a battle doesn't make you a dead cert for the win. And don't fuck with mountain folk. Whether it's Afghanistan or Wales, they are a bugger to beat, and it's never worth it.

Nero

In our last Roman Britain chapter, we transitioned from the Roman Empire being ruled by Emperor Claudius to Emperor Nero. Since he is an emperor everyone has heard of, if only for his excellent coffee franchises, we thought he should get his own chapter.

Dead Relations

Nero was born in 37 AD into quite the posh family. He descended from Augustus and, Agrippina, his mother, was Caligula's sister. Which means he was the great-nephew of Claudius. Then Claudius, who married Agrippina, adopted him as a son, which is how he got the job as emperor. Although as we say in the Claudius chapter, it was a bit more intriguing than that (as in palace intrigue rather than just interesting). Agrippina was possibly involved in the death of Claudius, to stop Claudius' son from a previous marriage, Britannicus, getting the job.

Lots of people have messed up parents, so you can't really be held accountable for their madness and Nero was only 16 when he became emperor in 54 AD. The fact that you have heard of Nero before suggests he was a bit mental. You just don't hear about the ones who were big into admin and fair ruling. We should spend a bit of time with Nero, and his family, because it shows how important family, and the relationships between the emperor and the posher subjects, were.

Nero's early reign was dominated by his mam, which makes sense as she had put so much effort into getting him there in the first place. That sort of thing does set off some alarms, but to be fair, pretty much every 16-year-old boy is a dickhead, never mind a 16-year-old ruler of the biggest empire ever known. So a bit of maternal guidance could have been a good thing. Or maybe a terrible thing, depending on the mam in question.

It wasn't just his mam who was involved. Nero had a couple of advisers, Burrus and Seneca. Apparently, they were very sensible and managed the place in a decent fashion, although we will see Seneca in a British chapter later being very not sensible. The general view from the sources is that in the first few years of Emperor Nero, Burrus and Seneca tried to manage things to a background of Nero and Agrippina squabbling.

A big downside to Nero's reign, which is attributed at least a bit to Agrippina, was the higher than average number of posh people getting murdered. This wasn't new, and Claudius had been bumping off Senators at quite a rate, but the Nero era killing was a bit more Jeremy Kyle in tone. For a start, to get the job in the first place, his adopted dad apparently got poisoned. It might be a bit harsh to blame Nero for this, but his mam carried on getting stuck in it even after Claudius was dead and buried. She seemed to be keen on making sure she was the one that Nero trusted to help run things. This meant killing a range of people who might loosen her grip on power. One of Augustus' grandsons got offed, but that's a fairly standard removal of an obvious rival. She also did for one of Nero's aunties, Domitia Lepida. This one is particularly harsh because she had helped Nero when he was growing up. Back when Nero was a kid, Agrippina fell out with her brother, Emperor Caligula. The falling out was because she was involved in a plot to kill Caligula and replace him with the widower of her dead sister. When

Caligula found out about the plot, the brother-in-law was executed, and Agrippina, along with another sister was exiled. Nero got sent to live with his aunt, Domitia. Which obviously meant she might have more influence over Nero than Agrippina would like. So, she needed to go.

It didn't end there either. Agrippina got involved again and is accused of organising the execution of a man we have already met, Narcissus. He was the freedman who Claudius sent to help Plautius get his soldiers across the channel. He had to go, presumably because he had become powerful under Claudius and maybe Nero trusted him since Narcissus had been pretty good to his adopted dad Claudius.

This spree isn't exactly Nero's fault, teenagers, even emperor teenagers, don't exactly have a lot of control over their mams. However, we do get to a couple of deaths which Nero gets the blame for. After a while, Nero started to act a bit more independently from his mum. She was forced to move out of the palace and was generally side-lined. You can imagine how she took that considering she had 'rightfully' murdered her way to that influence. Her response to that was to start to side with Britannicus, Claudius' eldest son, as a possible replacement for her son Nero. Britannicus was a particularly good pick, he had about as much claim to being emperor as Nero, and for ages had been the heir apparent anyway. He also had a cooler name. All that meant people might have got behind him if he challenged Nero so, what with the apple not falling too far from the tree, Nero had him killed.

The next killing is a bit more extreme, but in the circumstances, we imagine you can see where we are going. Nero had his mam killed. The Romans were off it, but you don't hear of matricide too often in these things. It takes a special kind of dickhead for that, but the Agrippina was a special kind of mam we suppose.

The killing itself was quite inventive, if it hadn't been nearly 2000 years ago, we would say that Nero had been watching too much CSI. He invited his mam to visit him at his house in Naples. When she was sailing back home, a shipwreck was organised, using a system of weights to put a hole in the bottom of the ship. But Agrippina didn't drown and got to shore, where he sent a message to Nero saying she was fine. His reply was to send some men to kill her and claim to everyone that she committed suicide. We have two questions about this. Firstly, presumably, there were other people on this ship, was it 100% necessary to organise an accident with such a big body count? Secondly, who would have believed the suicide thing? Who nearly drowns on a sinking ship, survives by swimming to shore and then just decides to top themselves? That's an optimistic lie. This happened in 59, so about five years after Nero became emperor. Five years is quite a long time, so this family-sponsored murder rampage was a bit slower pace than we made it seem, but it does show just how dangerous and insane it was at the top of Roman politics and society. Which is why his advisors Burrus and Seneca got off lightly when they just got less important over time after Agrippina's death. Apparently, the five years where Burrus, Seneca and, we suppose, Agrippina had a bit of control was pretty good, and is occasionally referred to a 'golden era.'

So far we have put a lot of blame on Agrippina for things. We wouldn't want to go around excusing the murders committed by an emperor just because he had parent issues. Hence, it's important to acknowledge a few more killings which were not really Agrippina's fault. Nero went through a few political rivals of his own from the Senate. Including the grandson of Emperor Tiberius, the son-in-law of Claudius, and a few other relatives of other past emperors. Which incidentally meant they were part of Nero's family. Aggressive? Yes. Fairly standard Roman emperor behaviour? It's a bit beyond normal, but not unheard of. However, if you want something a bit spicier, he did have his wife, Octavia, executed in 62. That's five years after Agrippina died. The same year he married again to a woman called Poppaea Sabin. She and Nero had a child who didn't survive infancy, and while she was pregnant with their second, we are told that Nero kicked her to death. That's a bit edgier (or horrendous and evil, but you know what we mean), but considering he had his mum killed, it's not too surprising. It sounds like the killing of a couple of wives, if not all those other people, was not a popular move with the people of Rome. Not being popular with the general public is a risky move for an emperor who is going toe to toe with the Senate.

If you read enough history, you do start to get a bit suspicious of modern writers applying psychology to historical figures. It can sound a bit weird sometimes. However, as we have said about quite a few things so far, if Nero's family issues were half as bad as we are led to believe, then if he was living now there would 100% be a Netflix documentary series being made. The Roman historians tended to talk about a change in his behaviour around the time Agrippina was killed. He started behaving erratically and doing exactly what he wanted. One of the odd things he did after this period was, at a festival celebration, in 64, he married a freedman named Pythagoras. We have seen these ex-slaves pop up as important men doing important work, what we didn't expect to see was one of them being the husband to the emperor. We are told that, in this wedding, Nero played the role of the bride, because presumably the ceremony wasn't set up for same-sex marriages. We doubt this went down well with the political class of the time. They certainly wouldn't have liked the emperor marrying someone who wasn't posh. In terms of the same-sex marriage, that also will have been held in a dim light. The Romans were surprisingly open-minded about homosexuality, but they were also all about masculinity. That means Nero being the bride wouldn't have impressed many folk. All in all, it doesn't sound like the behaviour of a normal emperor.

The same year he married Pythagoras; the thing Nero is most famous for happened. Rome got a bit burned down, when a fire started in the posh bit of town, just around the Circus Maximus. It began on the 18th of July and apparently lasted for a week, which is crazy sounding. We just can't imagine a fire in a city lasting that long. That is one shit fire brigade. So we had a check at a few other famous fires, and it going for that long isn't all that weird. The Great Fire of London lasted about five days. Either way, Rome's fire certainly wiped out a fair bit of the city.

Now, we are all familiar with political leaders being blamed for bad stuff which happens on their watch, but it does seem a bit much to blame a leader for a fire. However, not only does Nero get blamed for the fire, he gets blamed for actually starting it. The reason given for Nero being keen on there being a fire in Rome was that he wanted to build himself a new palace, and there were loads of buildings and people in the way. Whether he planned it or not, Nero did build himself a nice new palace in the space created by the fire. It was called the Domus Aurea, or Golden House, so you can imagine it was a little, subtle building. It was, in fact, a not so little, subtle building with a statue of himself put in it. A statue that was over 30 feet tall. Absolutely mental. And absolutely suspicious.

The famous thing about Nero and the fire is that he fiddled while Rome burnt. That was pretty much bollocks and made up later on. For a start, if Nero was fiddling, it wasn't like you are imagining. If he was putting on a show, his instrument of choice was a kithara, which is a plucky string type thing, like a lyre. Nero fancied himself as an artist, and he enjoyed singing, poetry and art. He was particularly a big fan of Greek culture. Unfortunately, he was rubbish at it. But when you are an emperor who was killing off people at an impressive rate, nobody is going to tell you. It would be a bit like Putin entering Russia's Got Talent. Those judges are going to be on their feet clapping before he opens his mouth.

All in all, we think it's fairly safe to say that Nero was a messed-up bloke, who went on to do some messed up things as emperor. It also goes to show just how powerful the emperor was at this point. Past emperors had been putting important people on trial and executing them for ages, so much so it was pretty standard stuff. Clearly, they had the control to do that, but the fact that a man like Nero, a bit like Caligula, could do that while being obviously unstable shows how untouchable they were. Until they really weren't.

Foreign Relations

All that family strife and poor fire management gives an insight into the man, and quite a lot into what it was like to live at the top end of Rome society. However, Rome is nothing if not an empire. So, what was going on in the wider Roman world? It doesn't look like Nero managed anything too impressive in terms of expansions, but after Claudius did his bit, you can't really hold that against him.

There were some significant and still famous troubles in Britain, which gets its own chapter in a bit. However, as a self-important Englishman, we hate to say it, but Britain was just a bit of a sideshow during this period. The main event was, as it had been for a while, in the east. Nero spent quite a few years squaring up to the big threat to Roman dominance over there, the Parthians. The Romans and the Parthians had been scrapping for a century before this, so this wasn't exactly Nero's fault. The problem Nero had was to do with the Kingdom of Armenia. The Armenians were in the unfortunate position of being in the middle of the Romans and the Parthians, acting as a buffer state. They kept the big boys separate to avoid any off-the-cuff agro.

The Armenians had been handily in the pocket of the Romans since Augustus, making this buffer state more pro-Roman than pro-Parthian. Although how pro-Roman did depend on the circumstances. The Armenians had been very successful at playing off east vs west, and Tacitus refers to them as 'ambiguous people.' which is a semi-polite way of saying 'shifty buggers.' It had all been kicking off in Armenia for a few years before Nero got the top job, in 54 AD. In 51 AD, there had been a bit of a kerfuffle. A bloke called Rhadamistus had killed his uncle, Mithridates, who happened to be the king of Armenia. The ancient world really did have no respect for family. The Romans in charge of the region went in swinging but managed to proclaim Rhadamistus as the rightful king, even though he had done the killing. There was some arguing, and the Parthian king decided to invade and install a bloke called Tiridates as the Armenian king instead. Tiridates just happened to be the Parthian king's brother.

By the time Nero became emperor, it was all getting a bit tetchy, and in 58 he decided he was having none of it, so he launched Rome into a war with Parthia. It went ok for the Romans at the start, and they gave the Parthians a bit of a beating, to the point where they could install their own king in Armenia, Tigranes IV. The Parthians came back into the scrap and started doing quite well themselves. In the end, there was a peace made in 63, with the Treaty of Rhandeia (which is in Turkey). The terms of the treaty suggest that maybe the Romans had come off worse, or at least nobody had really won. It did mean that the king of Armenia was to be crowned by the Roman emperor, meaning he technically got to pick who it was, which would make Armenia a Roman client kingdom. However, Rome got to choose who was the Armenian king as long as who they chose was a Parthian Prince. Which means the king of Armenia would come from the same family as the king of Parthia. So, we doubt he was particularly neutral. All in all, it wasn't a win.

Another couple of groups in the east that Nero came into conflict with was the Jews and the Christians. Rome had been in control of bits of the Middle East for a while by this point, which is where most Jews lived. Relations had been tetchy for a while, as we saw with Tiberius kicking them out of Rome, Caligula riling them up and Claudius making some harsh rules about Jews in Egypt. This culminated in The Great Jewish Revolt, a.k.a. The First Roman Jewish War, starting in 66. The revolt lasted until 73, after the end of Nero's reign, and was the first of three big Roman-Jewish wars. It may have been coming, but the starting pistol came from anti-taxation riots threatening Roman citizens, followed by a heavy-handed response from the governor, including the plundering of Jewish temples and execution of thousands. That sort of thing isn't going to calm anyone down. The attempts to gain control over Jerusalem didn't work, and Nero sent an army of 30,000 men to get the job done. That went just as badly, not only could they not take the city, but when the army retreated, they got caught, and 6000 roman soldiers were killed. In the end, it worked out for the Romans, as it usually did, but not while Nero was around to enjoy it.

It wasn't just the Jewish who didn't get on with Nero, the Christians also have a bit of a dim view of the man. Nero was emperor between 54 and 68, so he oversaw the epicentre of the religion in its formative years. Let's say Jesus was born in 1 AD, although the historical date is usually put a bit after that, and that he was executed at 33. That would mean Nero became emperor about 20 years after Jesus was doing his thing, making it prime bible times. Nero wasn't named in the Bible, but he was there. According to Christian tradition, Nero ordered the execution of Saint Peter in Rome. Saint Peter was the first Pope and a good mate of Jesus. Who knows if Nero did order that particular execution, but what does seem clear is that Nero didn't like Christians and he definitely had a go at them.

Christians, by all accounts, were not very popular at the time. In the sources from the period, it seems like the view of the Romans was very similar to the opinion people had of Jews for a long time after - and still now if you wander into the wrong corner of social media. We are talking secret societies, dodgy dealing and evil rituals involving cannibalism. Although to be fair, when it comes to Christians, that could be a literal interpretation of the eucharist, with the whole' body of Christ' thing. These rumours and the general suspicions presumably made them very convenient scapegoats for the Great Fire in Rome. So when Nero started executing Christians for their 'crimes' the population generally thought justice was being done. Or, if we are being cynical, given the temperament of a lot of emperors the population were generally pleased justice wasn't being done to them.

However, in the end, it looked like it backfired. Nero started executing Christians in cruel and unusual ways, like being eaten by wild animals or turned into human torches. The Tacitus quote is:

> 'In spite of a guilt which had earned the most exemplary punishment, there arose a sentiment of pity, due to the impression that they were being sacrificed not for the welfare of the state but the ferocity of a single man.'

As in 'even though folk thought they were guilty, the way they were killed looked like it was more for the benefit of a bloodthirsty maniac emperor than law and order.' It must have looked extra ropey considering Nero was also rumoured to have started the fire. A far too obvious bit of misdirection maybe?

Life in the ancient world was probably less brutal than you have pictured in your head, but it was still unbelievably cruel. Considering the empire was built on conquering everyone within marching distance of Italy, these people will have seen some things. Which gives us two thoughts. The first is, how far must he have gone to disturb that crowd. The second is, to modern ears, it's a bit of a weird place to draw the line. It reminds me of an episode in the American TV programme, The West Wing, when they point out that they don't execute people on Sundays. Such an odd attempt to inject some civility into killing someone.

Before we have a look at the end of Nero's reign, is there anything nice to say about the man? Well, first, it's worth pointing out what we have sort of been saying all the way through this. Maybe the stories about Nero are exaggerated. Nero didn't get on with the Senate for quite a lot of his reign, what with the executions and whatnot. He was also the last of his family to be emperor. This means when he was gone, anyone writing about him had no reason to suck up to him or his descendants. So writers were free to be honest about him, but equally, maybe the writers were sucking up to the new emperors and the senatorial class who hadn't liked

Nero. Perhaps this started a competition to slag him off, and his bad reputation snowballed from there.

Saying all that, it would be easier to give the man the benefit of the doubt if he and his family didn't have a history of murdering their way to power. Also, it's fun to believe all the bad shit you read about evil emperors. All this means any good stuff from Nero's reign is hard to find. It's possible he was quite popular with some people. In the same way that Caligula was occasionally popular with the common folk because he would do populist things like throw money around. Nero was big into entertaining stuff like chariot racing and music. That means it is likely chariot fans got to see loads of cool racing, which they will have enjoyed. Nero might have got the blame for the fire that burnt down Rome, but according to Tacitus, he did pay a lot to help rebuild the place, which probably won him some friends. Although the benevolent nature of that will have had the shine taken off it by the 30-foot statue of himself he had built at the same time. It wouldn't have screamed philanthropy. The Bill and Melinda Gates Foundation is investing a lot of money in getting rid of polio, but you would be less impressed with him if they celebrated that by putting a 30-foot gold statue of themselves up outside a children's ward. God knows they could afford to.

The End Is Nigh

So now, the end of Nero. It's worth covering, because

a) the end of an emperor would always be significant for the Roman Empire.

b) The odds are good that the end of a maniac emperor is going to be worth a read.

c) it kicks off an unbelievable year on Roman history which is going to get its own chapter in a bit.

The end wasn't pretty. Nero, being unpopular with the Senate, did have the odd conspiracy against him throughout his reign. For example, in 65, some politicians and some of the Praetorian Guard were planning to kill him. They got found out, and everyone was executed, but it does go to show Nero had a few enemies. Crucially, throughout this period of history, a good indicator of bad times ahead is when the Praetorian Guard takes a disliking to someone.

It all came to a head in March 68. A governor in Gaul (France), called Vindex, went into open rebellion against Nero. Incidentally, Vindex was from a Senatorial family from Gaul, who had been given the rank when Claudius started making people from Gaul Senators. Which throws up the possibility that this wasn't a Roman being Roman, and gunning for promotion through warfare. Maybe it was a group of Gauls upset by the Romans in Italy ruling over them. Either way, the emperor's solution to this rebellion was to get Virginius, the governor in Germania (Germany), to sort him out. Usually, that would be job done, but spurred on by Vindex getting involved, the governor of Hispania Tarraconensis (Spain), Galba, also decided to have a go at Nero and make himself the emperor. The Senate declared Galba an enemy of the state, or an enemy to the public, as the Romans put it. The only problem was that the public wasn't all that sure Galba was an enemy. People stopped supporting Nero, including his head of the Praetorian Guard. Which we know means curtains.

It escalated until Nero felt the need to leg it from Rome. The Senate in the meantime was a bit stuck. The emperor and his family were deities, so it's not that easy to square away getting rid of one. You can't just swap out your support for a god on a whim. They are like football teams. In the end, it didn't matter what the Senate wanted to do. Someone found Nero hiding in the villa of a freedman, not far from Rome, and they told him that the Senate had ordered him to be executed, even though they hadn't. So Nero committed suicide. This left the Senate to posthumously declare Nero an enemy of the state to avoid upsetting Galba, who was about to turn up with a massive army and make himself emperor.

Potentially a fitting end to what was, probably, a crazy example of a megalomaniac Roman emperor. As with most of what we are writing about, we don't really know how much of it is true. Did Nero kill himself? Maybe. Whatever happened he was dead, and as a final kick in the teeth to the emperor, his last words are generally given as some variation of 'Dead. And so great an artist!' Like a cringy emo. Surely, he didn't say that.

Nero was only emperor for 13 years, but it's safe to say he made quite the impression. His immediate legacy involved leaving Rome in a right old state. We are going to go over the year or so that followed his death later, so stay tuned because it's full of proper Game of Thrones stuff (except with a more interesting ending).

Nubia

When it comes to the ancient world, there is only one game in town in Africa: the Egyptians. They get all the coverage. To be fair, it helps that the Egyptians were on the Mediterranean and were heavily involved in the Roman, Greek, and Persian empires. However, one of ancient Egypt's neighbours barely gets a mention and probably deserves it. Nubia was a region between the Egyptian city of Aswan all the way down south towards Khartoum, the capital of Sudan. Like with Egypt, this area was discussed by the Nile. In fact, the top of this region was at a place called the First Cataract. A cataract was an area of the Nile where it became shallow and rocky, so you couldn't easily sail up it. The southern border of the region was at the Sixth Cataract.

The Ancient Nubians had a history that was as long as the Ancient Egyptians. From 3800 BC to 3100 BC there was a group who lived there known as the A-Group culture. To prove they are just as ancient, they were wiped out by the 1st Egyptian Dynasty. This is a poor start, and we do want to say that the Nubian people were far more interesting than the name 'A-Group culture' suggests. Even worse than that the people who archaeologists called B-Group, turned out to just be a skint part of A-Group, so they skip straight to C-Group.

The C-Groups were in Lower Nubia, but the part was up in Upper Nubia, where, between 2500 BC and 1400 BC the Nubian Kingdom of Kerma popped up in Northern Sudan.

They controlled things from the Fourth Cataract (in Sudan) and the First Cataract (in Egypt). In the end, Kerma got taken over by the Egyptians, but things swung in a Nubian direction in 754 BC, when a Kushite leader, called Piye, invaded Egypt. The Kushites, from Kush, were the group who had established themselves in Nubia in the 11th-century BC. When Piye invaded and beat the Egyptians he established the 25th Dynasty, meaning that Egypt was part of a Kushite Empire, and were controlled from their capital of Napata, in Sudan.

Later on, the Egyptians tried to erase the records of the Kushite Dynasty, by taking their statues down and the like, so clearly, they weren't fans. But by the time we get to the period we are looking at with the Romans, the Kushite Kingdom, Meroe, was kicking off, also in Sudan. This period lasted from 200 BC up until the 300s AD, and were still doing alright from themselves, making decent money from trade. The Nubian region was handily placed to be involved in trade between their own region, Egypt, and Arabia, with the Red Sea being a useful alternative where the Nile wasn't navigable.

In the end, the Kushite Kingdom had the same problem as the Egyptians; the Romans wrecked thinks. The Kushites had a habit of raiding into Egypt, which had become a Roman province, and the Romans responded to that like they always did. With soldiers. This weakened the Kushites, having lost to the Romans in both the fighting and in trading. Eventually, the capital of Meroe was abandoned in the middle of the 4th-century.

The history of the Nubians has them very closely linked with the Egyptians, which makes sense, as they are next door, and as we have seen, they conquered each other a few times. That means they shared a lot of their cultures. So, what is the first thing you think of when you think of ancient Egyptians? Correct. Pyramids. This link between the two cultures means that the Nubians also had pyramids. In fact, they had more pyramids than the Egyptians did, and they built them over a longer period. Although they started 500 years after the Egyptians, meaning that they were an Egyptian import. The archaeological sites around Meroe are UNESCO heritage sites, and the pictures are very cool. We are big fans of the Nubians, it turns out.

Boudicca Loses It

Some bits of Britain had been under Roman control from when Claudius and Plautius turned up in 43 AD. However, even in those regions, some Britons weren't on board with the whole Roman Britain thing. One of the most famous of them was Boudicca, and she gave the Romans a proper black eye in a sizable revolt.

Now before we go into who she was and what happened, let's address the whole name thing. We are old enough to have been told in school that the name was Boadicea. She has been called all sorts of names over the centuries, but apparently, Boadicea was a mediaeval typo. So really it should be Boudicca, although that could be bollocks as well. Part of the problem is that when it comes to important Celtic figures like Commius, Caractacus and Boudicca, all the sources are written by Romans and not Britons, or any other type of Celts for that matter. And much like the British Empire, the Roman Empire didn't always have a lot of time for regional languages. They had a habit of hearing a name, trying it, deciding it was silly and making up their own version. As far as we are concerned, we don't usually like change, and would be tempted to stick with Boadicea as we learnt at school, but we think Boudicca sounds cooler. So we are going with that.

In this chapter, we ask, how far can you annoy people before they kick-off? How nice does a place have to be for you to stay in it even though it's on fire? And what's with Britain and celebrating glorious failure.

Where Did It All Go Wrong?

In our last British History chapter, we left in 60 AD, with Suetonius having just given the Welsh Britons on Anglesey (Mona) a kicking. He was all set to wrap up there and head back out into Wales proper, to finish the job on the annoyingly resilient Welsh tribes. Then he got a message saying it was all going off again in the bit of Britain which was meant to be safe. Boudicca had got herself together with an army, and her Iceni tribe along with the Trinovantes, were looking menacingly at Colchester (Camulodunum). That was a massive problem for Suetonius because that was the Roman-built colony city, which had been specifically made to be full of Roman veteran ex-soldiers, who were meant to be keeping an eye on the place while Suetonius was elsewhere.

But before we go into all that, we should rewind a bit and have a look at who the hell Boudicca was, why she and her mates were so angry, and how she found herself in the ruins of ancient Colchester.

As ever we are relying on Roman sources for this, mostly Tacitus and Dio. They firmly point the finger of blame at the Romans for this one, although they point the finger at individuals rather than 'Romans'. As you will see, you can see it both ways. Some individuals were acting like arseholes and were asking for a kicking. However, the arsehole acts were very much set up to be the way it worked in the places the Romans governed, like Britain. It was just Romans being Romans if you will. Tactius' main reason for the revolt is particular to the Iceni, but you can see a version of it happening all over the empire. The Iceni were a fair-sized group living in the East of England, around Norfolk and a bit of Cambridgeshire. Back when the Romans were invading the Iceni had been one of the ones to submit to the Romans early doors, and so they kept more control over themselves. We saw a bit of a revolt from them when Scapula tried to take their weapons away from them in 47. It's generally thought that when Scapula put down that bit of unpleasantness, he made Boudicca's husband, Prasutagus, king of the Iceni. That means that Prasutagus was a Pro-Roman client king. So, what went wrong? Well, Prasutagus wasn't going to live forever.

If you read enough history books, you start to see that even in the event of a clear succession to the throne, when a monarch dies, there is a fair chance it's some other bugger who grabs themselves a crown. That's even without the Romans looming over everything, making sure they approve of who gets the job. The real issue this time was a pretty standard Roman approach to the death of a local leader in a territory they want to take full control of. When a friendly ruler died, and if the timing was right, the Romans had a habit of folding their kingdom into their own lands and blaming the locals for it. Prasatagus looked like he knew it would happen, and in a sad attempt to butter up the Romans to prove how on-side the Iceni were, he named Emperor Nero as co-heir to his kingdom along with his two daughters. Tacitus had this down as an act of deference, as in 'look we think you are class Mr Nero, don't hurt us.' It does make sense. In reality, Nero could do what he wanted with the Iceni anyway, so a little nod to the Roman emperor probably couldn't hurt. It didn't work though, and the Romans decided to take the Iceni lands and add them to the province being directly administered by Roman officials.

This sort of thing is likely to kick up a fuss at the best of times. However, the way they did it this time was straight out of 'My First Big Book of Causing Revolts.' We are told by Tacitus that the kingdom was 'plundered.' Lands were taken from the posh Iceni, Boudicca, their queen, was flogged, and her daughters, the named new rulers of the Iceni, were raped. How was that not going to end badly?

Dio adds an, almost comfortingly familiar, financial element to the revolt, one that went well beyond just the Iceni. When the Romans turned up, Claudius had thrown money around the Briton elites. This was to get the locals on board with the Romans. It's hard to work up the effort for armed resistance when you are comfortable at home surrounded by the finer things in life. Seventeen years later, the procurator of the region, Catus Decianus, decided that this money hadn't been a gift, but that it was a loan that had to be paid in full. Immediately. A procurator was a Roman official, who typically was in charge of a province's finances. The Trinovantes, who joined the Iceni in the revolt, were also a victim of this imperial loan sharking. In their case, there is evidence of an even more appalling approach. Claudius and his mates turned up and took lands and money from the Trinovantian aristocracy. At the same time, they were required to contribute to building up Colchester into a proper Roman town, including the funding of a temple dedicated to Claudius himself. So now the Trinovantes were made to loan money to pay Romans for things, to be able to build a temple dedicated to their oppressor, in their own city. There are mafia bosses who would call that going too far.

It wasn't just these imperial 'loans' which were causing problems. It looks like there was a full-on racket going on. Dio points the finger at Seneca, who was a big wig in the early days of Nero's emperorship. He had loaned Britons an unbelievable massive amount. It's put at 40 million sestertii. Sestertii was the Roman currency, and at the time 40 million equates to a multi-million-pound loan in modern terms. Seneca decided it was time to get paid and asked for all of what was owed. To be paid immediately.

It has to be said that these things clearly would contribute to some seriously bad feelings between the Britons and the Romans, but we imagine this was more the lighting of the touch paper of a massive, ready-made, bonfire. Seventeen years of invasion, conflicts and rule would have included some things that would have stuck in the memory of the average Briton. Just look at the Trinovantes. Even without the money aspect, they had every reason to kick off. To lay it out again; Colchester, which was now a Roman town, filled with Roman ex-soldiers, had been their capital. Now, their city was filled with foreigners and a massive temple dedicated to the god-emperor who had conquered them. Then you have the fact that Romans were targeting the druids, who were the leaders of their religion. People being a bit sensitive about religion isn't new, and you would struggle to label someone as being 'sensitive' about someone trying to eradicate their faith. We doubt anyone needed much of an excuse to dust off their swords.

Whatever the cause, it was all going off in the East of England. Hindsight is 20-20 and all that, but we would say that assaulting the royal family of a tribe in East Anglia, while your governor is on Anglesey, is high up on our list of 'really daft things historical folk have done.' Colchester was to be the revolt's first target. It wasn't in Iceni territory, but it's the right sort of region, and they had been joined by the Trinovantes, who would have wanted to punish the people living in their city.

For context on how screwed the Romans around Colchester were, let's say you were in Colchester now, and you were about to get beaten up by a local you had pissed off. You might ring your mate to come and help you fight off the said local. The only problem is he's on a family holiday on Anglesey. That's getting on for a 6-hour drive, depending on traffic. You are going to get beaten up. Unfortunately for the Romans of Colchester, Suetonius couldn't just jump in his car, so he and his army would have to march the 270 odd miles over, what is almost, the widest west to east trip in Britain.

The Remodelling Of South East England

So, what exactly happened? This time we know a fair bit

about the events. It feels like the Romans really got involved in the story of this. It was a significant event, but even so, you get the same sort of details we last saw when talking about Plautius and Claudius invading our little island.

We know the first major action was the Britons heading to Colchester. They got the jump on the town, and they proper knacked the place. Even so, the locals in Colchester had time to call for reinforcements. We laughed about Suetonius being miles away, but he wasn't the only Roman force who could help. Colchester called for help, but only got 200 men sent to help them. Considering a legion was about 5000 men, 200 seems like a mickey take. Particularly, as it looks like they were sent there from London by a man named Catus. That's the bloke who had riled up the Iceni in the first place. If that is true, and then he only sent 200 men, who, according to Tacitus, were not even correctly armed, he really wasn't making any friends.

The Britons tore through Colchester, and the locals holed up in the temple where the Britons had them under siege. The temple was presumably, strategically, and structurally, the best place to hide out from the Britons. Symbolically it was a bit of an own goal. This was the temple had been built by the Romans as part of the Imperial Cult, where the Roman emperors are gods. It was constructed to worship Claudius, the bloke who took the credit for conquering the Britons in the first place. A group of oppressors, hiding in a symbol of oppression, from the oppressed. That's not going to calm anyone down. The siege lasted 2 days before the Britons got to them. That must have been a rough two days, but not as bad as the third. We are told that the Britons weren't taking prisoners, so that was death all round.

Colchester was the largest settlement in Britain, which means that the Britons killed as many as 10,000 people there. The numbers around these sorts of events are hard to know. The Roman sources usually give us some, but they are hard to trust, as they always inflate them. Bigger numbers of Roman dead make the Britons look like the villains, and vast numbers of Briton warriors make eventual Roman wins look even better. The only people we have seen have as much trouble with counting crowd numbers are the Metropolitan Police, Donald Trump and whoever announces the crowd size at Arsenal home games.

As we said, there were Roman legions closer to Colchester than Suetonius. It's hard to know exactly where they were, the Romans had a habit of splitting legions in half to have them in two places or having detachments of one legion added to another. Which causes historians all sorts of headaches. However, the best guess is that when Boudicca was charging about, there were two legions in Wales with Suetonius. Half of one legion was in the East Midlands, presumably to keep an eye on the Brigantes in the north. Another legion was based in Exeter, but some of them were probably near Gloucester at the time. Finally, the other half of the East Midlands legion appeared to have been a bit closer to Colchester, at Longthorpe near Peterborough. The commander of this half legion, Petillius Cerialis, ran down to stop the Britons moving away from Colchester. He did not do well, and the end result was him escaping, with about 120 cavalrymen, leaving about 2000 dead Roman infantrymen behind him.

With the destruction of Colchester and the beating of half a Roman legion under their belts, Boudicca and her mates headed to London (Londinium) This wasn't exactly the major global city it is today, but, it had been founded by the Romans. It had made a decent start as a trade centre. Suetonius knew that was where they were heading, and the race was on. The Britons didn't have as far to go as Suetonius and his legions, but they moved much slower. They weren't exactly trained for forced marching and were slowed down by their families. The problem with raising up and attacking Roman settlements was, if you left your family at home, the Romans might sneak around the back and kill them all. In warfare, getting everyone killed is generally seen as an own goal.

When Suetonius arrived at London, he realised he was outnumbered, which Cerialis had proved was a bad thing. So Suetonius decided to leave London to it. He was pretty sure that he wouldn't win, so the decision was made to sacrifice the whole settlement so he could find a better place for a battle. That's probably a decent strategic decision, but there is a line in the translation of Tacitus' account of it which nicely shows how harsh that was.

'he determined to save the country as a whole at the cost of one town. The laments and tears of the inhabitants, as they implored his protection, found him inflexible: he gave the signal for departure, and embodied in the column those capable of accompanying the march: all who had been detained by the disabilities of sex, by the lassitude of age, or by local attachment, fell into the hands of the enemy.'

So that's women, the old and people who just like the neighbourhood, all completely fucked. Harsh.

Unsurprisingly, it ended up with London going the same way as Colchester. Archaeologists have found evidence of destruction and burning around London from this time. She was there for a few days, and it looks like they completely totalled the settlement and anyone left in it. Incidentally, there is a statue of Boudicca in both Colchester and London, which is a weird tribute to a woman who wrecked both places.

The next stop on the revenge express was St Albans (Verulamium), although if anyone was still hanging around in these towns not sure what was about to happen, clearly they hadn't been watching the news. Predictably, St Albans went the way of London and Colchester. We had a look, but as far as we can tell there isn't a Boudicca statue there, which suggests the people of St Albans know how to hold a grudge.

By now Suetonius had been joined by more soldiers. There was even one spare legion down towards Exeter, who had been asked to join in. Only they didn't fancy it, so stayed at home. Historians reckon Suetonius managed to get together an army of around 10,000 men. We aren't sure how many the Britons had, later Roman sources had it down at 200,000+, but, as we mentioned before, it's likely that they were massively overstating it to make themselves look extra hard. Regardless of the poor reporting, when they met, it was a big event.

We aren't sure where the two sides finally met in battle. Generally, it's thought to be somewhere around the West Midlands, and probably along Watling Street. Watling Street was a route used by the Britons and then the Romans, to get from down in Kent up into Wales. It was the route that Suetonius would have gone down to get from Wales to London.

By all accounts, the setup of the battle was in the Romans favour even though they were outnumbered. The Romans had found a spot in a confined space, where they could only be attacked by so many Britons at a time, as they were funnelled in towards them. The Britons might have had the numbers and the belief, but the monied, well-trained Romans had the edge. It was very much like an early round of the FA Cup. The lower league team can often start well and make it difficult for you, but, ultimately, it's not often an inferior team can last the full ninety before they collapse. Once that collapse started, the Britons broke and began to run from the Romans. Unfortunately, they had brought their families, who were arrayed at the back of the battlefield, right in the path of the fleeing Briton soldiers. Cue an absolute massacre. Tacitus has the score as 400 dead Romans and 80,000 dead Britons. Which is probably miles off, but even so it will have been a proper beating. And that was the end of that attempt to give the Romans a kicking. To be fair, it seems to be a decent effort, although it was probably not a good idea. What was surprising about all this was how nobody comes out of it with any proper credit.

Finger Pointing

We aren't sure what happened with Boudicca. Tacitus has her down as poisoning herself, while Dio says she got sick and died. Although, we suppose she might have got ill from poisoning herself? Who knows? Either way, she was gone and doesn't come up again in our story. She is celebrated as a heroic figure, hence the statues, but she did kick off a rebellion which ended badly, and with the deaths of what must have been tens of thousands of Britons. So, statues aside, she wasn't exactly a glowing success. We do tend to enjoy a glorious defeat in Britain, which says a lot about us. It's also worth mentioning that the Romans see this whole thing as very embarrassing. We are told that the Britons killed 80,000 people in all this, which sounds like a lot. That sort of thing would be embarrassing anyway, but they didn't seem to enjoy being beaten by a woman. The Britons didn't seem to mind women being in charge. We have already met Cartimandua as the queen of the Brigantes, and now we have not only war leader Boudica, but her two daughters, who Prasutagus, made his heirs to the top job in the Iceni. You can find them easily enough if you look, but in the grand scheme of things there are relatively few examples of that sort of thing in European history, so it's odd to see a few of them all at once.

On the Roman side, they won, so surely some of them came out of it looking good? Not so much. We have already mentioned Seneca, who gets a shoeing in the historical record by Tacitus, Dio and the like. Catus gets a similar rough time of it, but even worse than that, we didn't mention just how shitty he had been. When he sent those 200 men to defend Colchester, he obviously did know how hairy it was getting, because he snuck off to hide in Gaul, all nice and safe. What a dick. He was replaced by a new procurator, Julius Classicianus.

Even the leaders of legions didn't do overly well out of it. We mentioned the legion in Exeter who didn't fancy joining Suetonius. Well, the general of that legion, Postumus, obviously regretted that. Hearing that Suetonius had won, and realising he was in quite a bit of trouble, Postumus topped himself.

What about Suetonius? He turned up and won the day, surely he got some plaudits? No such luck. We suppose that's to be expected. He oversaw the place when this whole mess kicked off, and while he put down the rebellion, the fact it happened at all wasn't ideal. Suetonius did stay as governor for at least a year after the final battle against Boudicca. He had plenty to do, for a start getting new men from Germany to replenish his legions. He then went about putting down any other bits of resistance and generally reminding folk who was in charge.

In the end, he got replaced as governor because the Romans were worried this aggressive approach might kick off another rebellion. The new procurator, Julius Classicianus, was a Roman citizen, but he was from Gaul, so he probably was a bit more sensitive to how annoyed the Britons would still be. Classicianus fell out with Suetonius in the aftermath of the revolt. By all accounts, Suetonius decided the best way of putting down any remaining desire for the rebellion was to kill people, and not just the people involved. The Britons who didn't pick up a sword but weren't 1000% vocal in their support for the Romans, got some as well. At the same time, there was a famine which caused even more death and suffering. This wasn't all Suetonius' fault, as the Britons had been too busy for proper farming. Revolt is a full-time job. However, any requisitioning of food by the Romans wouldn't have helped things. This repressive approach was definitely bold, considering the initial revolt was caused by ill feelings coming from oppressive measures by Romans. You can see why Classicianus, as procurator, would have disagreed with how this was going. It would be hard to get a province up and running financially after a fight this big at the best of times. Even more, dead people means less production, less trade and less tax. That's just basic strategy video game stuff.

Classicianus petitioned to get Suetinius replaced, which happened under the excuse that after the revolt Suetonius lost a few ships. That was apparently enough for him to get the elbow. It all sounds oddly bureaucratic, but it was a good way of everyone getting what they needed and everybody saving face.

So there you go. A massive uprising, huge battles, cities destroyed, and nothing achieved. The Romans were embarrassed, but they were still in charge of big chunks of England and Wales. What a waste of everyone's time. On that note, that's the end of Boudicca and her revolt tour, but we do have something a bit less exciting to talk about. It's about this point in the history of Roman Britain, it gets a bit confusing as to who was who. What exactly is a Roman? A lot of the people who will have been killed in the sacking of Colchester, London and St Albans won't have been 'Roman,' they will have been traders and hangers-on from across the empire, including next door from Gaul.

Not only that, but the dead would also have included Britons who had moved into those towns. They would have been people who were getting on with living their lives working with the Romans. You don't have to use too much imagination to see a world where these Britons would have been called traitors by Boudicca and her mates. The rampaging Britons wouldn't have seen them as proper Britons, they would have been traitor Roman-British. That's before you get to the point that Britons didn't necessarily care about other Britons. Would an Iceni give a shit about a Catenvaulaii? Not particularly, if the history of the region before Claudius arrived is anything to go by.

Then we have the Romans themselves. Does a Roman need to be from Italy, or even Rome? No. A lot of the 'Romans' in Britain this time will have been members of the Roman army posted on the island. These soldiers weren't all Roman. Even the Roman citizens won't have all been from Rome, or even Italy. Then you had the auxiliaries, like the 200 men sent to reinforce Colchester, a lot of them would have been Celts from around the French or German regions, fighting for the Roman Empire. It seems a bit odd calling everything Briton vs Roman.

We hate to ruin the whole story for you, but the Romans were in Britain for a very long time. This means as the centuries rolled on, Britain became more and more Roman. There is no reasonable way that we can be consistent on who exactly we are talking about when we say 'Roman.' So we are going to carry on simplifying it as if it was easy. If only to avoid our brain dribbling out of our nose, but it's an interesting point.

So what have we learnt? Well, people don't like it when you attack them. Armed rebellion against a much better army isn't always a good long-term plan. And bankers have always been causing people problems.

The Roman Army

Our chapter on Boudicca and the revolt in Britain, while action-packed only covered a short time over 60-61. That leaves us in a bit of a bind for our companion Roman history chapter. A blow by blow of everything that happened in Rome over the course of a year might stray into the boring. So instead we are going to throw in a bit about something crucial to the Romans: the army.

The Legions

Rome was all about the military. We have already seen how the backing of armies meant that important men like Julius, Pompey and Augustus could try to take complete control over the whole thing. We have already mentioned that Augustus standardised the army a bit more and tried to stop them from being near enough mercenary armies for these sort of men. But how was the Roman army organised?

It changed a lot over the whole Roman period, obviously, because that would be a long time with no change. During the period of the first few Roman emperors, the set up was what most people would see as the 'classic' Roman army. It's the army you see in the films, so if it's good enough for Hollywood it's good enough for us.

The legions were the backbone of the whole thing. In the

past, the Roman army had been made up of men conscripted when someone needed an army, and then they were sent home when they didn't need that army anymore. Assuming they weren't all dead in the meantime. That had changed when Gaius Marius implemented the Marian Reforms in 107 BC. Marius was the bloke who was fighting Sulla when Julius was a young' un. Part of these reforms was making standing armies, meaning armies full of soldiers only had one job: being soldiers. They didn't go home at the end of a war, which is sad, but it also meant they were more practised at soldiering than average. It was a bit like we do it now.

By the time Augustus was in power, he had decided that it was important to limit the number of legions. A limited number of legions meant it would be harder for a group of men to all raise massive armies themselves and have a big civil war. They would all be fighting for the support of only 25 legions, which limits the options. Since Augustus had managed to amass far more men than that, he didn't want to allow anyone else to copy him. While during this period, there were about 25 legions in the empire. Later, more would be added, so it did go up to more than 30 legions at points.

So, what was a legion? A legion was between 5000 and 6000 soldiers. It was commanded by a legionary legate, who was basically a general, and they were appointed by the emperor. Which makes sense, if you are going to have 6000 soldiers running around, you want them to be commanded by someone you can trust.

6000 men would be a lot for one bloke to manage, so he had help. Under him were six military tribunes. The highest rank tribune was a 'broad-stripe' tribune, named after the stripe on his uniform. This was usually a posh bloke in his 20s, from the senatorial class, near the beginning of his career.

Under the broad stripe tribune, and above the other five,

was the third in command; the camp perfect, who was a sort of quartermaster. He oversaw the camp and things like equipment. Unlike the man above him, the camp prefect would be experienced and would have worked his way up.

The next rung down was five 'thin stripe' tribunes, and you can guess where the name comes from. These were from the lower equestrian class, or 'knights.' So, still posh, but not silver spoon posh. They would have also usually have had previous military experience.

Below these top-end officers were centurions. This lot were usually plebeians, so were normal people, who had been promoted from the rank and file of the legionaries. The most important centurion got the job of the senior centurion (primus pilus), and he ranked below the thin stripes. A centurion was in charge of a century, which against all logic was made up of 80 legionaries. Six of the centuries made up a cohort, and a legion had ten of these cohorts.

At this point in history, to be a legionary, you had to be a Roman citizen. As we have said, the legions were standing armies, so being a legionary was their job. And it was their job for a term of 25 years, with one prominent, undesirable, get-out clause. This meant that the legions were an elite force, and they didn't just take anyone on as a soldier - it wasn't just a place for the dregs of Roman society. You can see why they had the edge over people like the tribes in Britain. No matter how fundamental fighting and martial skills were the tribesmen in Boudicca's army, we doubt they could compete with men whose sole job it was to be in the army. For as long as 25 years.

Auxiliaries

The legions were the backbone of the Roman army, but they were only about half of it. The other half were auxiliaries. These were units of men, who weren't Roman citizens but served in the army, and they were recruited from all the different groups of people from the empire. They often formed up units that played a specific role that would support the regions. There were archers from Crete, for example, and the Numidians had light cavalry. There was even a unit of camel cavalry that came out of Syria. We are sure that was entirely sensible, and it's probably not too different from your horse-based cavalry, but the image of loads of blokes legging it about on camels is funny to us. The camels were usually part of a Roman force in the East, with only a few of them in a unit, but later, Emperor Trajan would raise a unit of 1000 of them. Imagine 1000 camels with soldiers on their backs running about. That's good stuff.

We have seen the auxiliaries in action already. It was a group of them that Plautius' sent to swim across the river to head round the back of a camp of Britons. That's a handy example of a task that would be given to the auxiliaries, rather than the legionaries. Auxiliaries didn't have the prestige of the legions, but it's safe to say that they did plenty of work and that they were no slouches themselves.

Something that must be really annoying for historians is trying to keep tabs on these auxiliary units, particularly, who was in them and where they were. For an example of the problems they would have, an auxiliary unit might have been raised from the Batavian tribe in Germany, and it would be named after them. They then might be posted somewhere like Britain, where due to the hazards of the business, vacancies might come up in the unit. These vacancies would be filled by whoever, and not just Batavians. Eventually, the Batavian unit might have hardly any Batavians in it, but they would keep its name. The Romans were practical like that, but it's not handy 2000 years later.

Being the practical people that they were, the auxiliary units were also standardised under Augustus. Infantry units had a similar structure to the legions, with 6 centuries of 80 men making a cohort. The centuries were commanded by a centurion as well. However, these cohorts weren't added together to make a unit the size of a legion, so in the early Roman Empire, auxiliaries were originally 480 men. The cavalry units were a bit bigger, being 512 men in 16 groups of 32. There were also mixed units of both cavalry and infantry, to add in a bit of the best of both worlds. The command of these auxiliaries could be commanded by a local chief/king, but most of the time they were placed under the control of a military tribune

Auxiliaries didn't have the prestige of the legions, so why did people join the auxiliaries? For the non-citizen auxiliaries, the eventual benefit was citizenship for them and their children. At the end of their 25 years, the heathens would be given a diploma that granted citizenship, making them into a civilised member of the Roman empire. That was a carrot that was dangled, but we imagine that the fact that they got paid and fed was a good recruitment tool.

This all had sod all to do with the year 60 AD Britain, although to be fair soldiers were involved. It just seemed to us that 90% of what we talk about is army based, so it's handy to make sure everyone is on the same page for what we are banging on about.

Han China

The Roman Empire was big, but it didn't get to be big enough to come up against the Chinese, who had their own thing going on in the Far East. In 221 BC several warring regions were unified by a bloke called Emperor Qin, who kicked off the short-lived Qin Dynasty. This ended the Warring States period, and counts as a unification of China, although those states only cover less than a third of current China.

The Qin lasted from 221 to 206 BC, but they were involved in some stuff you will definitely have heard of. For a start, the second Qin emperor, Qin Shi Huang, built the Terracotta Army, to protect him in the afterlife. If you haven't heard of the Terracotta Army, or even if you have, but haven't really looked into it, do yourself a favour and go find some pictures. It's amazing. There are thousands of soldiers, and they are unbelievably detailed. They are even life-sized, and if anything, they are a bit taller than most people. And there are horses. Qin Shi Huang must have seriously pissed off a lot of people if he thought he would need the protection of all that lot on the other side.

The Qin also put together an early version of the Great Wall of China. Big walls had been all the rage during the Warring States period, but Qin had them knocked down when he took over because they were splitting up his new country. Instead, he built walls on the edge of his territory. They were made to keep people like the Xiongnu out. The

Xiongnu were a nomadic group who dominated a lot of Central Asia, mostly around Mongolia. During this period, they had their own unification and set themselves up as a serious threat to the Chinese. Hence the walls.

Nevertheless, as impressive as they are, it's the next Chinese dynasty we want to talk about: the Han. The Han took over in 206 BC and lasted until 220 AD, so a lot of the period we are covering back in Europe. They were set up from a revolt against the Qin, and a bloke named Liu Bang, a peasant leader of the revolt, took over. He became known as Emperor Gaozu. It is known as the Han Dynasty because Gaozu had been from the Kingdom of Han, which was one of the states that Qin had unified.

The dynasty is usually split into two periods. The first is Western Han, which is because the capital city was in the west of the country. This capital was a city called, Xi'an, although it was known as Chang'an then. Incidentally, Xi'an and its surrounding area has a population of more than 12 million people, and this is the first time we have heard of it. It's safe to say that China is big. There was a gap in the dynasty after a revolt by someone called Wang Mang, who took over between 9 and 23 AD. This period is known as the Xin dynasty, which just means New Dynasty, which is apt since it never got the chance to get old. After that, from 23 AD to 220 AD, it's the Eastern Han period. You will be surprised that it got its name from its capital being based in the east of the country. It was now in Luoyang, a tiny city with a mere 6 million people living around it. So you don't have to feel too bad about not having heard of that one.

The Han are an important group in history because they came at a time when the idea of being Chinese was properly solidifying. The period, and the dynasty, gave their name to what is now the largest ethnic group in China. It was also during this period that a lot of the development of Chinese writing happened, and Chinese characters are known as Han characters. It's not as simple as we make it sound but, today, people who are classed as belonging to the

Han ethnic group account for somewhere between 15 and 20% of the world population. Obviously, they are congregated in China and surrounding nations, but anything that has had an impact on that group is globally significant.

Britain After Boudicca

Last time we were in Britain we saw the end of Boudicca's revolt. That was pretty exciting and was a very short space of time where there was a lot to talk about. Things got a bit quieter in Britain for a while after that. Not silent, but quieter. You can assume that the Britons were keeping their heads down after Boudicca. Luckily for them, the Romans spent the end of the 60s with bigger problems than the Britons. Don't worry, though Britain makes sure it got involved.

In this chapter, we ask ourselves, is it wise to leave Britons unattended? Do you think Tacitus was OK? And can you really think of a worse married couple than Cartimandua and Venutius?

All Quiet On The British Front

As we mentioned, after the revolt was put down in 61, Suetonius went in swinging with some brutal reprisals for the Britons. He was recalled, presumably to avoid encouraging the Britons to find a second Boudicca. 62 saw his replacement as governor, Petronius Turpilianus, turn up. As you will see, the sources are a bit quieter in the years 61-69, but it looked like Turpilianus did his job. Or at least he didn't cause any more trouble.

That means Britain had a conciliatory governor, who

hasn't done anything that involves the death of loads of non-Romans. Guess which Roman historian didn't like him. Tacitus' view of his governorship was:

'Petronius neither challenged the enemy nor was himself molested, and veiled this tame inaction under the honourable name of peace'

As in, he didn't have a go at the Britons, and in return they left him alone. He called this doing nothing a 'peace.'

Luckily for fans of excessive death, Turpilianus wasn't in the job for very long, and in 63 we get his replacement, Trebellius. Sadly for those horrible fans, Trebellius, if anything, came off worse in the eyes of Tacitus. Apparently, he was a:

'man whose sordid avarice made him an object of contempt and hatred to the army.'

As in, he was greedy, and the army hated him. Although, both the soldiers and Tacitus could have hated Trebellius for the perfectly reasonable attempt to not cause another rebellion. Tacitus hates that because he is all about continuous, violent expansion. The army might have been similarly annoyed because fighting means loot, which means profit.

As for the Britons, we don't have much idea of what they were thinking, but it seems reasonable to assume they weren't continuing the fight with the same rage that Boudicca and her mates had done. The Britons had taken a proper beating, and even for the tribes not directly involved, they had just seen a pretty sizable Briton force lose to the Romans. There was also the added disadvantage that when the people of your tribe are dead, replacements can only be found through the traditional biological route. Which brings with it certain time restrictions. The Romans, however, could lose a big chunk of a couple of legions and just replenish them with men from across the empire. So, while the tribes are scratching around trying to survive, the only long-term problem for the Romans was admin based. That meant the chance of more fighting and looting seemed a distant prospect for the legions in Britain. In fact, it was apparently quiet enough that at some point in the late 60s one of the four legions was sent elsewhere in the empire.

It is here that it's worth noting just how mental Britain was for the Romans. Britain was relatively new territory for Rome, and by 69, they had only been on the island, in force, for 26 years. Even so, it was taking up an unbelievable amount of resources. The size of the Roman army went up and down throughout Roman History. A bit earlier, when Tiberius was emperor, there were 25 legions, and it would peak at the beginning of the 3rd-century with 33 legions. Considering the size of the empire in 69, it must have been frustrating for everyone that Britain had needed four legions, just to keep a lid on Wales and most of England. Except they couldn't keep a lid on it, even with the four. Boudicca had just massively embarrassed them before finally getting beaten. However, clearly, it was calming down, if they had trimmed the army in Britain to three legions. We will see in a bit if having fewer soldiers in Britain was a good idea or not.

Rome Loses Their Minds, And Britain Helps Them On Their Way

This has all been leading up to the year 69. That year is notable in Roman history, and it's known as the Year of The Four Emperors. You can imagine why, and we will be going over what exactly happened in the next chapter, but for our purposes here is the summary:

Nero died, in 68, during the attempt of a bloke named Galba to become emperor. Which he did. For a bit. By the end of 69, we had seen another three emperors. As you can imagine, having four emperors in a year wasn't because an emperor-specific pandemic made three emperors too sick to keep the job. It was a story of assassinations and marching armies, like most Roman stories. However, the Romans in Britain, unlike other provinces, didn't put forward one of these emperors. Our island was very much, both literally and figuratively, on the edge of things. That's not to say we didn't get involved, although in this case, it wasn't the Britons of Britain, but the Romans in Britain who got stuck in.

It was in 69 that the army not liking Trebellius came to a head. Tacitus wasn't just having a go at a passive governor, Trebellius did have a big falling out with his legions. With three legions on the island, and nobody revolting or asking to be invaded, a bored army was an issue. If a Roman army was not visiting new exciting places and giving new and exciting people a kicking, then there is no loot, no opportunities for glory and advancement. The opportunity to change this came during the fight between the second and third emperors of 69. The third emperor was called Vitellius, and he had been governor of Germany when two of the legions there declared him emperor. A legion or two declaring you emperor was step one in nicking the imperial throne. He was then joined by the legions of France and Britain.

The sticking point in Britain was that it wasn't Trebellius' plan to back Vitellius. It was, however, the plan of the legionary legate, Roscius Coelius. A legionary legate was a commander of a legion, so presumably, when he said something, it was backed by a few thousand soldiers, and he needed listening to. The bored, skint army in Britain was well up for the chance of supporting a future emperor, and the potential rewards that could bring were clearly too enticing. Trebellius and Coelius's squabble ended with Trebellius fleeing Britain and the Romans of Britain declaring for Vitellius. Vitellius left Britain being run by the commanders of the legions. However, a civil war was a big event, so he needed soldiers, and they had to send 8000 men, or about half of the legionaries in Britain, to help Vitellius in his fight to be emperor number three.

A new emperor meant a new governor in Britain, Vettius Bolanus. He turned up with a seriously unpleasant sounding name and a new legion. That would have been handy for replenishing some of the men who had left the island recently.

The astute among you will have spotted we now have the Romans in Britain putting themselves behind the third emperor in a period called the Year of The Four Emperors. That sounds bad. The soldiers got their adventure, so full marks for the initiative, but 0/10 for long term planning. Oddly enough, though, it worked out OK in some respects for Bolanus and his soldiers. When the eventual fourth emperor, Vespasian, threw his hat in the ring, Vitellius (emperor no.3) called for reinforcements. Bolanus refused, which is a bit harsh since Vitellius just gave him a job. The refusal could have been Bolanus hedging his bets but was probably more to do with the troubles he was having back in Britain. In the end, Vespasian won and became the winner of Royal Rumble 69 (Imperial Rumble 69?)

As an aside, you might remember meeting Vespasian before. He was one of the commanders when Claudius and Plautius invaded Britain back in 43. When our Roman Britain alumnus was made emperor, Vespasian kept Bolanus as governor until 71. It looked like the hedging of bets was a good idea. Considering the possible outcome of backing a wrong emperor in a civil war, even if you do then pull out, keeping a governorship was pretty good going. Not that Bolanus would have enjoyed himself in Britain.

Marital and Martial Strife

This swapping of the men at the top, and the coming and going of whole legions, would be interesting enough on its own, but it also kicked off a bit of trouble for the Romans. Here we can get back to what the Year of The Four Emperors meant for the Britons, as well as the Romans in Britain.

It turned out, for some of them, it spelt opportunity. This time it was the Brigantes in the north who would be kicking up a fuss. The last time we saw the Brigantes, Queen Cartimandua was in charge of the tribe, which covered a fair bit of the northwest and northeast of England. Back in the 50s, Didius had chased her ex-husband, Venutius, out of Brigantian lands after he led a revolt.

The Romans spending a year fighting each other on the continent was a very tempting opportunity for anti-Roman Britons, like Venutius. One of the four legions had already left a few years earlier, and now the Romans were considerably weaker and more distracted than they had been in years. We couldn't find anything that would tell us how much a wannabe Brigantian king would know about the fighting around Rome, but, if he had any idea of what was going on, it would have been a safe bet that new legions wouldn't be turning up anytime soon. So Venutius jumped in, and his faction of the Brigantes attacked Cartimandua in an attempt to take over the tribe. Cartimandua's response was to turn to Boloanus for help, which makes sense since that tactic had worked with Didius. This time, however, Bolanus didn't leap to her defence with the same vigour. He was either too busy or too thick. We are told he did send some auxiliary troops, including some cavalry to sort it out. They had some scraps but didn't come up with any significant wins against Venutius. That doesn't sound like full-throated support of Cartimandua to us.

Whatever the reason, the Romans couldn't help Cartimandua properly, and instead, they opted to take her out of Brigantes territory, presumably meaning they could reinstate her when everyone calmed down. This sounds like sensible planning but was seriously optimistic. In effect, this was the Romans admitting defeat. Venutius took control of the Brigantes, and they carried on being a pain in the arse for the Romans for a few more years after this. We have no idea what happened to Cartimandua. It probably wasn't good, though. We are being flippant, but with hindsight, sacking off her husband to marry his armour bearer wasn't a smart move. Never mind 'a woman scorned' it seems like Venutius might have overreacted a bit to being given the elbow.

The World Is A Bit Calmer. Britain Is Still Annoyed

Bolanus remained as governor until 71 when he was replaced by Quintus Petillius Cerialis. This governor has been a part of our story before now. He was the commander of the legion who tried to save Colchester from Boudicca, only for most of it to be wiped out. Clearly, he was forgiven for that. His appointment was the start of another change in policy in Britain. There was to be none of this conciliatory approach. It was all attacking, all the time. Bolanus may have only been able to contain Venutius and his neighbours, but there was no way that party was going to last. Cerialis was fresh from crushing a revolt in the Rhineland (Germany), and he brought with him a new legion. He didn't hang around and headed north pretty quickly. As usual, we don't have a particularly clear picture of how exactly this all went down. However, we do know a Roman fort was built at Carlisle in around 73, so it looks like the action was in North West England. There are also suggestions of him making it to at least the Tyne up the east coast, as well as probably being in action around Southern Scotland. Get used to Roman's hanging around in Southern Scotland, it's going to be a feature.

It wouldn't be a new governor if we didn't get the view from Tacitus. As we know by now, Tacitus was only happy when Roman generals were ploughing their way through foreign soldiers, and he said:

'Petillius Cerialis at once struck the Britons with terror by attacking the state of the Brigantes, said to be the most populous in the province, and in many battles, some of them bloody, he conquered a great part of Brigantia.'

Considering they were the biggest tribe around, for Cerialis to have put them down in three years is pretty impressive. If there is anyone interested in the ongoing saga of Venutius and Cartimandua's marriage, I'm afraid we have already lost sight of Cartimandua, and we don't get a mention of Venutius either. Let's just say Hollywood isn't looking to turn their story into a romantic comedy.

Cerialis left Britain in 73, and he was made a consul in 74, so it looked like he wasn't sacked as much as promoted. His replacement was Sextus Julius Frontinus. We don't know much about Frontinus, apart from the undeniable fact that he had a very funny first name. What we do know is that he was in the same mould as Cerialis, including having come from fighting in the Rhineland. Frontinus' focus was more in Wales, and it was under his governorship that the Silures in South Wales were finally conquered, along with the Demetae being added under direct Roman rule. This was no mean feat considering Wales had been a pain in the arse for 30 years since Scapula tried to get them under control. Guess who was a fan of this? Our review of Frontinus, from Tacitus, was:

'Cerialis indeed would have overshadowed the administration and repute of any other successor, but Julius Frontinus, a man who reached the pinnacle of greatness that was then possible, shouldered and bore the burden. By force of arms he reduced the powerful and warlike tribe of the Silures, surmounting not only the valour of the enemy but also the difficulty of the terrain.'

As in, Cerlialis smashed it, but Frontinius lived up to it and hammered the Welsh Britons. We wanted to include that long quote because it's quite funny to hear Tacitus being a fan-boy.

Despite Frontinus, and his heroic achievements, the Welsh Britons weren't quite all tied up yet, and at the very least the Ordovices in Northern Wales were still being arsey. However, it looks like Frontinus finally broke the back of it.

We don't know much else for sure, but the odds are good he had to keep a close eye on Northern England, considering it's unlikely they just calmly sat back and accepted the defeat of the Brigantes under Cerialis.

Which brings us to 77, when we get the next governor, Agricola. We know quite a bit about him, and he got a lot done. That's something to look forward to in our next Roman Britain chapter.

So what have we learnt? Well, when the management is in disarray, everything goes wrong. The British might seem calm occasionally, but we will always be mardy. And if you want to get a longer mention in the history books of the future, you should try and have a funny name.

The Year Of The Four Emperors

The chapter on Britain after Boudicca was a bit heavy on Roman politics, but we want to double down on that and have a proper look at the 69 – the Year of the Four Emperors.

As a recap, it was kicked off by the death of Nero. We know all about him, and the fact that he had upset pretty much everyone. In 68 there was a serious revolt against him by Caius Julius Vindex, the governor of Gallia Lugdunensis, (a bit of Gaul). This was all the starting pistol that the posh men of the empire needed. When an emperor is clearly on the way out, it helps if there were one or two obvious candidates for his replacement. However, in this case, Nero had spent the last few years eliminating any proper rivals, so it was anybody's game.

We say anybody, but Vindex got the armed revolt equivalent of being subbed off after 5 minutes. The commander of a Roman army in Germania (Germany), Lucius Rufus, put Videx down quickly. After that sideshow, it was Galba, the governor of Hispania Tarraconensis (Northern Spain) that turned up as the proper candidate. He started marching towards Rome, from Spain, and the Praetorian Guard, who had enough of Nero so moved their support to Galba. Nero saw the way this was going and escaped the city before committed suicide, leaving the Senate to legitimately claim Galba as Emperor of Rome in June 68.

Emperor 1 - Galba

Galba had made it, he was top of the pile, cock of the walk, Billy big balls and king (emperor) of the world. And he immediately started messing it up. On his way from Spain to Rome, Galba was very unpleasant to people who didn't immediately accept him as emperor. He also didn't fancy paying the Praetorian Guard the rewards he had been promising to them. To be fair the promises were made by one of the supporters of Galba, rather than the man himself, so obviously felt he didn't owe them anything. Just to highlight how stupid, on the border of suicidal not paying up was, this was the same Praetorian Guard who were well-armed and trained to protect Galba and his household. The same guard, whose backing of Galba for the job of emperor, was a crucial factor in Nero now not being an emperor, but definitely being dead. This didn't happen in the deep and distant past; it had just happened. And Galba should know because it was partly his fault it happened at all.

It was ok though, Galba didn't need the support of the people between Spain and Rome, or his own Praetorian Guard. He could still count on the great and the good of Rome itself to support him politically. That was until, in a state of paranoia, the new emperor started executing people who he thought were conspiring against him - for example, senators (a.k.a. the great and good of Rome). Instead of trying to win support, he just killed off any dissenters to his rule. We have seen enough emperors come and go now to know how that ends.

To be honest, it's impressive how Galba managed to annoy everyone one he would have needed support from to keep being emperor. And alive. He even upset the people of Rome by putting in place austerity measures. Rome probably needed the measures, since Nero had pissed the treasure up the wall, but that sort of thing never goes down well. He could have given it five minutes. At least if the general public raised up against Galba, the Praetorian Guard would protect him. Oh, wait.

He also upset the Batavians in Germany. The Batavi were a small tribe, but what they lacked in size they made up for in being mental. Most of the Batavian males served in the Roman Army, and they were considered to be among the best warriors around. They were so impressive that Roman Emperors created the Imperial German Bodyguard from the best the Batavi had to offer. Sort of in the same pay as the Pope and his Swiss Guard. While the Praetorian Guard was a bigger force to protect the emperor, it was these Germanic Bodyguards who did the close personal protection. Like in American films, when the US President is walking around the place, he has aggressive-looking coppers everywhere, but the Secret Service, dressed in suits with earpieces in, are the ones standing next to him. The Germanic Guard was the Secret Service. Sort of.

There had been some rebellious actions from within the Batavi in the few years before 68/69. This was apparently reason enough for Galba to disband the Imperial German Bodyguard. If that hadn't been sufficient to upset them, then the real reason for the German Bodyguard being disbanded was that they had been loyal to Nero to the end. Annoying both sets of bodyguards and a whole Germanic tribe of people at the same time seems like a less than optimal play.

Speaking of Germany, that was where the real trouble started. Galba hadn't endeared himself to the army, and the legions in Germania were particularly displeased with him. Germany's legions had wanted to make Rufus emperor, but he had refused. A fat lot of good it did him though since Galba replaced him as general anyway. Then, on 1st of January 69, the Roman legions in Germania refused to pay allegiance to Galba. This was during a ceremony where soldiers were required to declare their loyalty to the current emperor. The legions on the Rhine decided they didn't fancy that and declared a bloke called Aulus Vitellius Germanicus Augustus as emperor. He was the governor of Germania Inferior (north-eastern Germany and the Low Countries), so he already had the support of the legions on the Rhine, and they were joined soon after by the legions of Britain, Spain, and Gaul.

This was bad news for the emperor, but it wasn't the legions which did for Galba. The annoyed person that broke the camel's back of his emperorship was Marcus Salvius Otho. He had been the governor of Portugal (Lusitania) and had travelled with Galba to Rome. Otho had himself down as the successor to Galba, and even all being well for Galba, Otho would have imagined that his turn as emperor would be pretty soon, as Galba was 70. Otho was, therefore, a bit disappointed when Galba decided to appoint someone else as his adopted son and successor. In what must have been one of the easiest coups in history, Otho got the support of the Praetorian Guard, and Galba was killed by a mob in the street. The Senate declared Otho emperor the same day.

Galba had been emperor from June 68 to January 69.

Emperor 2 - Otho

Otho might very well be the prime example of the dark shabby nature of high-end Roman politics. Back before all these new emperors started popping up, he had been a friend of Nero's, but Nero took a fancy to Otho's wife. Unsurprisingly, Nero got what he wanted, and Otho was divorced from his wife so she could marry the emperor. Presumably, to avoid any awkwardness, Nero then made Otho the governor of Portugal, which is notably quite far away from Rome. Ten years later Otho returned to Rome with fellow governor Galba, and we know what happened there.

It was a bit less his fault than it had been with Galba, but, when Otho became emperor, he was doomed. Once Otho had settled into his massive set of offices and started looking through the correspondence, he found out just how up in arms the provinces of Germania were. The natives weren't happy with the Romans and were now offended by the disbanding of the Imperial German Guard. On top of that, the legions had just refused to recognise Galba as emperor, choosing their own governor instead. It must have been like an incoming government, after months of campaigning about how the other lot had screwed the economy, finally getting into office, and opening the books. 'Holy shit....if we had thought it was quite this bad we wouldn't have tried quite so hard to take control of it.'

To be fair, he didn't make the same mistakes that Galba did. We doubt everyone was pro-Otho, but he paid up to the Praetorian Guard, and he sucked up to the Senate in the traditional way, so people were roughly on board.

The governor from Germany, Vitellius, was already on his way to Rome to claim the imperial throne even before Otho beat him to it. Regardless of what Vitellius thought of Otho, once you have an army marching, it must be difficult to turn it around just because somebody got there first. Otho did have some legions of this own, and they put up a bit of a fight, but Vitellius got the upper hand. Not waiting for Vitellius to outbid him for the loyalty of the Praetorian Guard, Otho, went the way of Nero and killed himself. According to Dio, before he died, he gave in speech, in which he said:

'I hate civil war, even though I conquer; and I love all Romans, even though they do not side with me. Let Vitellius be victor, since this has pleased the gods; and let the lives of his soldiers also be spared, since this pleases me.'

He told his soldiers to declare for Vitellius to avoid more civil war. If that's true, it's pretty cool. Not that it worked.

Otho had been emperor from January to April 69.

Emperor 3 - Vitellius

Anyone keeping count will have worked out Vitellius is the third of three Emperors in 69. What do you think the chances of the Romans needing a fourth emperor being the result of Vitellius dying of natural causes? Correct. Absolutely zero.

We are told that Vitellius was a horrendous bloke, but like with Caligula and Nero, we don't know how much of what he is supposed to have done is true. As a just flavour of what we are told; he killed his son before divorcing his first wife. It's that sort of level of bad emperor we are talking about.

It took him a few months to get from France down to Rome once Otho had committed suicide. When he did arrive, it's clear he had also learnt something from the Galba debacle. He pardoned the people who needed pardoning, he gave jobs to the people who had supported him, and the legions who had declared for Otho were sent back to their posts, mostly unharmed.

A lesson Vitellius hadn't quite picked up was the importance of making sure the army got paid what they thought was owed them. It sounds like Rome turned into a bit of a shambles as tens of thousands of extra soldiers had come down to Italy with Vitellius, and they were making the city rather unpleasant to be in. Especially when they reacted to not getting paid. It would not have been a good time to be living in the city.

However, it was from outside Rome where Vitellius had his problems, from the East, which keeps the story fresh at least. The next claimant to the throne was a bloke called Titus Flavius Vespasianus. He was in command of three legions in Judea, where he had been sent to sort out the Jewish Rebellion that had kicked off in 67. We have met Vespasian before when he was involved in the invasion of Britain in 43. So, he had been doing the rounds in the more violent bits of the empire for a while.

Vespasian was in a solid position. He had his three legions in Judea, and in the summer of 69 he got the support of the world-famous Bryanius Adamus - that is a lie we very much wish was true. Sorry. He was supported by the governors of Syria and Egypt, which got him another five legions to add to his own. He was also supported by the legions on the Danube, which was another six. In addition to his legions, it probably didn't hurt that his brother was the urban prefect of Rome (a sort of mayor).

It was looking bad for Vitellius, but he put up a fight, and the people of Rome seemed to side with him. In the end, Vespasian's legions swept down from the Danube and severely punished the people who got in their way - in a war crime kind of way. As a segue from horrific crimes against humanity, there is a slightly funny story about how one of these battles ended. One of Vespasian's legions had been in Syria, and as was the custom over there saluted the sun when it rose each morning. Vitellius forces assumed that they were greeting reinforcements coming from the east and gave up. Less funny is that this assumption let Vespasian's legions overrun the city of Cremona, in Northern Italy, and kill everyone.

In the end, Vespasian's forces made it to Rome, and Vitellius was found, killed and thrown in the River Tiber.

Vitellius had been emperor from April to December 69.

Emperor 4 - Vespasian

All this happened, from legions battling across Italy to Vitellius taking an unplanned dip, while Vespasian was still in Egypt. He was in no rush. In fact, he hung about and didn't make it to Rome until almost a year later. He was represented in Rome until then by his two sons, Titus and Domitian. They were joined by the governor of Syria, Mucianus, who had taken his armies to Rome, while Vespasian stayed in the East.

Hanging back was a very sensible approach for Vespasian. The people of Rome, and wider Italy, had been put through the wringer. It must have felt like an army pillaged their way through Northern Italy every few months. As for Rome, it didn't sound like they had much fun under Vitellius, and Vespasian's armies probably didn't add to the sense of safety about the place. The new emperor being on a different continent would have given him some distance from the actual suffering. Turning up later, meant he could be the bloke who arrived to rebuild everything from the smoking ruins - figuratively and occasionally literally.

And unlike the last three emperors, Vespasian had himself a decade to do that. Which must have been a relief for everyone involved. We mostly gave 69 so much airtime because it's interesting. However, it's a good example of the sort of thing the Britons were dealing with as part of this empire. And this was just a warmup.

The Parthian Empire

The Parthians, and their empire, get a few mentions in our Roman history. It's mad to us that the vast majority of folk in Britain won't have heard of them, as they were a pretty big deal. Not that we are judging, we hadn't either before all this. It's not like everyone can hear about everything, the world is a big place, and it's been around for a while. Nevertheless, the Parthians, and the other Persian empires, seem like a big one. And they are related to the Romans, so there is an obvious link for us European folks. We just feel they should get the odd mention, so here it is.

The Parthian Empire was a Persian Empire, which just means that geographically and culturally it was based around Iran. They were founded in 341, but they weren't the first big Persian Empire, in fact, they took over the region from the Seleucid Empire. The Seleucids had come out of the splitting up of Alexander the Great's empire in 323 BC. Even before that, Alexander had beaten the Achaemenid Empire, which dates back to 550 BC.

Oddly, it was a Parthian Empire but wasn't ruled by people you would traditionally call Parthians. Parthia had been a region of the Seleucid Empire, which was taken over by the Parni tribe, who took advantage of the Seleucid decline. The ruler of the Parni who first took over the Parthian region was called Arsaces I of Parthia. So you might see the Parthian Empire being called the Arsacid empire. Although we certainly can't use that excuse for not knowing who the

Parthians were, because we had never heard of him either.

In the 240s BC the Seleucids were busy scrapping with Ptolemaic Egypt, so the Parthians expanded into their territory. And they kept going until the Seleucids were done for, and the Parthian Empire reached a decent size. At its height, the empire covered territory from Turkey to Afghanistan. It was no Roman Empire, but it's safe to say they were a big player.

Being that widespread and taking over from the Sassanids, who had a Greek background, the Parthians were a fairly diverse group. The Parni tribe, who kicked off the Parthian Empire, took on Parthian as a language, but they also spoke Greek and Persian. Aramaic was also a common language spoken in the empire, which, we were surprised to learn, isn't a dead language. Modern versions of it are spoken by a few hundred thousand people around the Middle East. It was also the language of a little bloke called Jesus, who made a few headlines.

The Parthians were also varied in their religion. Obviously, early on in our period, there was no Jesus and no Mohammed, so Parthia wasn't Christian or Islamic. Like in Europe at this time, the Parthians were mostly Polytheistic, meaning a person would believe in more than one god. Think the Ancient Greeks with Zeus, Apollo and Athena rather than one Christian God or one Muslim Allah

The most interesting religion in the region was Zoroastrianism. This was kicked off by their prophet, Zoroaster, in the 500s BC. Zoroastrians aren't quite as dead set on monotheism. Still, they see their god, Ahura Mazda, as the one supreme being. They also have the usual good vs evil elements that you would expect for a religion from that region. To be honest, any quick description of any religion is going to be rubbish. They are complicated things that people study for years before they get a proper grasp of it. We mostly like the religion because it's got the best of all the religious symbols: the Faravahar. It's like a bird with a man on it - go and have a look, but it's loads better than a cross.

What makes Zoroastrianism the most fascinating is that it's still being practised by more than 100,000 people. You can find them in Iran, where it originated and in India. Freddie Mercury's family were Zoroastrians, and there is even a Zoroastrian temple in West London. We didn't think we would learn something about the UK from reading about a 2000-year-old Persian Empire.

Before we leave the Parthians, we should have a quick review of how they and the Romans fit together - they were around until 224 AD, so they are involved in a lot of our story. The relationship between the two Empires was very back and forth, and by no means did it all go the Romans way. There were plenty of full-on battles, but they also dabbled in some proxy warring. It was usually Armenia stuck between the two, with pro-Roman Armenians being a proxy for the Parthian's to fight and vice versa. And as always with someone stuck in the middle, it often went pretty badly for the Armenians, with neither the Romans nor the Parthian being above just killing an Armenian who preferred the other side. When you read through the details, there is a bit of a Cold War feel about it. Although before you feel too sorry for the Armenians, they were often in the mix themselves, causing a bit of grief.

To give a bit of context for the Parthian/Roman relationship at the start of our history of Roman Britain, we have the Battle of Carrhae, which was fought in 53 BC. The Romans invaded Parthian territory with about 40,000 men. The Parthians, under a general called Surena, met them with about 10,000 men in Southern Turkey. The Romans took a proper beating, with about 20,000 dead, 10,000 captured and the last 10,000 having ran off. This was the battle where Crassus, one of the First Triumvirate, was killed. That in itself made it a big deal, and this disaster was near the beginning of a full 250 years of scrapping. You can see why Britain might have been a bit of a sideshow back then.

Agricola - The Beginning Of Roman Rule Proper

We are now up to 77 in our story of Roman Britain, and it's a significant date because we have a new governor, Gnaeus Julius Agricola. Once we get to the end of his governorship, we are going to call that the end of the 41ish year-long Roman invasion of Britain. That's because Agricola gets as far as any Roman in taking over the whole of Britain. Don't get us wrong, the bit we have decided is no longer an 'invasion', but 'Roman rule' is still going to be mainly people kicking up a fuss. And fuss comes with all the associated Roman reprisals and more than a bit of Roman on Roman scrapping. But for now, sit back and enjoy the last bit of invasion chat.

In this chapter, we ask: is it a good idea to outshine your boss? Have the Scottish always been a bit aggressive? And is Britain an island?

Agricola: The Greatest Man Ever?

Agricola stands out in the early years of Roman Britain. For a start he was governor for a fair old while, from 77 to 83, so he had plenty of time to get on with things. He also had the advantage of being familiar with Britain before he got the job. Agricola had cut his teeth in the army under Suetonius, during the Boudicca revolt, which must have been a steep learning curve. Later on, he got sent back to Britain to replace Roscius Coelius, the legate who had mutinied against the governor, during the Year of The Four Emperors. So, again, he would be familiar with how Britain was full of nutters.

After the last couple of governors, Cerialis and Frontinius, it's clear that Emperor Vespasian wanted Britain conquering. Agricola took the same aggressive approach to the Britons, but he was going to take it up a level. Based on that, I think we all know what Tacitus was going to think of Agricola. However, in this case, we need a bit of context, or at least more than 'governor likes killing, so Tacitus is a fan.' In fact, Tacitus is the reason we know so much about Agricola, because he wrote a biography of him, and he was very much a fan.

We have been banging on about how hard it is to know what precisely was going on in Britain, and how anything we do know only comes from one or two writers. Tacitus and Agricola is the perfect example of why you have to be careful about taking too much at face value from those writers. Here's a hypothetical for you. Let's say in 1000 years a historian wanted to know what life was like in Britain at the beginning of the 21st century. They go looking for sources written at the time, and all they can find is a copy of The Guardian and a copy of The Daily Mail. According to those two sources, a historian will decide that either:

Britain has a small number of brave patriots, surrounded on all sides by Muslims of Asian descent and Marxists.

or

Britain is a cruel, capitalist dystopia, full of Islamophobes and elderly people who are trying to destroy the planet before they die.

Regardless of where you are on the political divide, you have to admit just reading one or the other, or even both, wouldn't be particularly useful. The book a historian would write from that wouldn't tell future readers much. It's a hypothetical, but let's be honest it's a relief we won't be around to see what the historians of the future write about us. It's not going to be complimentary.

What we are saying is that it's important to remember we don't know if Tacitus was more honest and even-handed than a modern journalist. In the case of Tacitus and Agricola, there is an added element of mistrust; Agricola was Tacticus' father-in-law. You might not like your in-laws, but you would need a massive pair of brass bollocks to write a whole book having a go at them. That makes us imagine it's a bit more complementary than it needed to be. Which makes sense when you read it because, as far as we can see, it claims that Agricola was the perfect man and may very well have been the second coming. That, in the 70s, would have been awkward, because the world was only just finishing up with the first coming.

As a side note, Tacitus was big on compliments, but he wasn't big on dates and places, which for historians is unbelievably annoying. We don't even know for sure the years of his governorship, but we like the guess of 77 to 84. Something we are clear on is that Agricola's big claim to fame is that he moved the Romans north. Now since we haven't really met anyone who lived above the Brigantes, before we carry on with the story of Agricola, let's have a look at the natives.

Who's Up There

Let's start in the North of England. We have been a bit misleading about the Brigantes in this region of Britain. The easy way of looking at it is that they controlled everything in Northern England from the Irish Sea to the North Sea. It makes it easier to talk about, but really that's too big a spot for one tribe to be properly in control of, not to mention it being split by the Pennines which would have made things difficult, admin wise. Historians usually see the area as being a sort of confederation of tribes, dominated by the Brigantes, who were based out of Yorkshire. We do have records of some of those other tribes, who might have been under Brigantian control. For example, we have the Parisii who were hanging around in north Humberside. The Gabrantovices were living in North Yorkshire, and the Carvetii were up in Northern Lancashire. They looked to be quite small, or maybe just subsets of the Brigantes, and they don't get the same coverage as the more significant tribes in Southern England and Wales.

Moving into Scotland, we are told the leading groups in Lowland Scotland were the Novantae, the Selgovae, the Votadini and the Dumnonii. A lot of what we know about who was where in Scotland comes from a bloke named Ptolemy. He lived in the 2nd-century, which is a bit after all this was kicking off, but he wrote a book called 'The Geography,' which is a description of the world as the Romans knew it. As ever, we do have to take what he says with a pinch of salt, as he was writing from around Egypt, and it's not like he had Google Maps to consult. You can't argue with a man trying something that hard nearly 2000 years ago, but if you want an idea of how he might not be 100% right, look up the 'Prima Europe Tabula.' It's a 15th-century copy of a map made by Ptolemy. The copy makes Devon and Cornwall about as big as the rest of England, and Northern Scotland goes off at a right angle to the rest of the island. You can kind of see what he was doing, but it's still odd to see. Even so, it's the info we have, so we are sticking with it.

The Votadini were a reasonably big tribe in Scotland, who were mostly based around Edinburgh. The Selgovae were probably based to the south of the Votadini down to the border between England and Scotland. However, there is some argument whether they were further west than this with the Votadini controlling land further south than Edinburgh. The Novantae were in the south-west, on the sticky-out bit around the Mull of Galloway, but they might have spread quite far east through Dumfries. To the north of the Novantae were the Dumnonii, who were knocking about where Glasgow now is.

It gets a little bit sketchier the further north you go, because, as we will see, the Romans had less to do with the folk up there. In the east were the Taexali, the Venicones and the Vacomagi. The west had the Epidii, the Creones, the Carnonacae and the Caereni. None of these really get a mention in Agricola's adventure. In fact, it was only really one name for a tribe which get a big shout: the Caledonians. They appear to have been right at the top surrounded by other tribes like the Cornovii, the Decantii, the Lugi and the Smertae.

No doubt the way of life varied across the island, but it seems consistent that, pre-Roman, the whole island was divided up into tribes. While it might be nice to imagine the whole of ancient Scotland rising up against the Romans, the story up there seemed very similar to the Romans in Wales and England, smaller tribes getting beaten a handful at a time. So now we have an idea of how everything looked up there, let's have a look at how Agricola got on.

Agricola Likes A March

Agricola arrived in Britain to the customary bad news which tends to meet new governors. A cavalry unit had been beaten up by the Ordovices in north west Wales. We know that Wales had been mostly put under control by previous governors, but clearly, it wasn't quite a done deal. We are told by Tacitus that the timing of this was an issue. Agricola had just turned up and was still organising his desk, and it was the end of the summer. As we know, fighting in winter wasn't ideal, and even less ideal when it is in harsh terrain like the hill and mountains of North Wales. The region might not be the most hostile environment in the world, nevertheless, attacking Wales during autumn going into winter almost 100% guarantees marching about in constant rain. That alone would have us staying at home. A lesser governor, or at least a governor less related to Tacitus, might have, like we would have, opted to keep a lid on what he had and defer the problem for a bit. Not Agricola, he grabbed up some men and ran headlong into the Ordovices. We aren't sure how significant the Ordovician resistance would have been, but Agricola had it wrapped up in the first year of campaigning. He even tacked on an attack on Anglesey (Mona). Suetonius had taken the island from the druids and their friends, back in 60, but he didn't have time to make himself comfy there. We are told Agricola's jaunt to the small island was impromptu, so there was no time for preparing for things like boats, and his soldiers needed to swim across to get to the Britons. That makes it sounds like Agricola was picking up Welsh territory like we grab a chocolate bar at a till in a shop, just because we fancy it.

In his second year as governor, he headed north to double down on the work that had been done in Northern England and edged into the Scottish Lowlands. This wasn't too flashy, and like with the Ordovices in Wales, this was just mopping up the work done by previous governors on the likes of the Brigantes. His third year was a push into Scotland, ending up at the Tay, which means he went past where Glasgow and Edinburgh are and stopped around modern Dundee. This was a lot flashier, because, as far as we know, the Romans hadn't spent a lot of time in what is now Scotland.

Marching north this quickly is unbelievable, and to us, non-military experts, it was a move that looked far too risky. We have seen what happens when the Romans spread themselves too thin across Britain. When Suetonius was in Wales, Boudicca went mad in East Anglia. When the Romans were fighting amongst themselves, Venutius had taken over the Brigantes. Despite knowing all this Agricola, having only recently finally put the unrest in Wales down, and having just gone through Northern England again, which itself had only just been added to Roman-controlled territory, he decided to mooch up to Dundee. That's a long way to have to travel if it kicked off in a different bit of the island, say in Wales. Just to show just how flashy this was, the distance between Gretna, which is just inside Scotland, to the Tay is 161 miles as the crow flies. That would be 161 miles marching through a territory full of people who didn't want them there. Not only that, but there wasn't exactly an endless supply of manpower available. It's estimated that Agricola had 30,000+ soldiers, which is a significant chunk of what Rome had to offer, so it's not like Agricola was charging into Scotland on his own. However, in the early 80s, soldiers were being taken from Britain to solve problems over in Germany. That means he was losing soldiers while he was doing this. Madness.

While recent history suggests it was a bit brave to be dragging men further north and leaving England and Wales exposed, Tacitus does give us a couple of suggestions as to why this was possible. So that's three reasons if you include the obviously incredible self-confidence of Agricola.

Firstly, is the nice reason given for why the natives in the south stayed quiet during Agricola's Scottish holiday. Apparently, Agricola made life a bit easier for the Britons there. This seemed to focus on making taxes a bit fairer and making the actual job of paying them simpler. It makes sense that Agricola might pay attention to this sort of admin, as he would have learnt from Suetonius' mistakes with Boudicca. Although we aren't sure why the Romans needed telling that upsetting people who were hundreds of miles from your main army was a bad idea.

Secondly, a reason why nobody kicked up a fuss when Agricola took his men further north was that a lot of the people who might have started trouble were busy being dead. Later on, in his description of events, Tacitus invents a speech from a leader of the Caledonians. This leader apparently says:

'They make a desolation, and they call it peace.'

As in, the Romans, under Agricola and the previous governors, ruined a place to the point where nobody had the means to fight back and then, because nobody can fight back, it means there is now peace. Clearly, it worked, but it's not an approach that's going to win anyone a Nobel Peace Prize.

Whatever the reason, Agricola was doing fine heading north, but his fourth year was a bit less adventurous. He set up forts along the Forth–Clyde isthmus, which is a fancy way of saying the thin bit of Scotland between Glasgow and Edinburgh. He also built up the roads in Southern Scotland, which is a very Roman thing to do, and would have allowed legions to get to trouble spots quicker. His fifth year saw him back on the offensive but focusing on taking control in South West Scotland. This included naval action around the coast, which must have been a different experience for any Romans who were used to the Mediterranean Sea. It is worth mentioning at this point, while Agricola was standing on the west coast of Scotland, he sent back to Rome to recommend invading Ireland. They didn't go for it, but how ambitious would that have been? Britain had been an angry, seething mess of Britons for a big part of the 40 odd years the Romans had been there. I'm not sure Ireland would have taken it any better. That's before you even take in the fact that the Romans were nowhere near finished with Britain. Agricola had his line of forts around Glasgow and Edinburgh but have a quick look on a map. The north of Scotland, with its Highlands and whatnot, wouldn't have been the most populated part of the world, but have you seen how much Scotland there is north of Dundee, never mind north of Glasgow-Edinburgh? The man was mental. Luckily for the Irish, and any Romans who would have been involved, the Romans didn't take up Agricola on his suggestion and instead, he carried on north.

The problem with the western coast of Scotland is that, if you head north up it, you hit the Highlands. We are not military tacticians of any note, but it is generally not a good idea to attack a people on their home turf when that home turf is whacking, great, big mountains. You would be asking for guerrilla warfare, of the sort that the Romans had already struggled with in Wales and Northern England. So, it makes sense that Agricola's sixth year involved moving up the east coast by land and sea, culminating in a pretty impressive seventh year.

In 83, before being recalled to Rome in 84, Agricola fought the battle of Mons Graupius. He had made his way up the east coast and had a fight with the Caledonians. Tacitus fails to mention exactly where this battle was, but we know it was in the far northeast of Scotland. The proposed spots are often in places around Aberdeenshire, but a lot of historians seem to put a lot of faith in it being around Inverness. Anywhere around there shows just how far Agricola went. We might not know where it was, but we do have a name for the leader of the Caledonians, Calgacus, the one who Tacitus invented the 'peace' speech for. Every now and again, we are struck by how weird it is that we can write about this stuff. We are talking about a man, who was originally from the South of France, fighting for an empire based in Italy, having a scrap with a bloke from Northern Scotland. And all this happened nearly 2000 years ago. It's weird.

The Roman's problem in Scotland is one we have mentioned over and over again. The natives had no need to fight the Romans in an open battle, and they could hide in their mountains. And since we are talking about the Highlands now, they had some proper mountains to be hiding in. Not that the Caledonians were always in hiding, and it sounds like they spent quite a bit of time raiding Agricola's camps. In an attempt to get a hold of some of them, Agricola split his army into three. Clearly, he hadn't watched a lot of horror films and had no idea that splitting up was a bad idea. One of those three groups took a beating in a night attack by the Caledonians. It was turning into a bit of a massacre when Agricola marched his legion over to rescue them. However, the Caledonians survived the reinforcements of the Romans because they could leg it away across terrible terrain into forests and up into mountains, where Agricola had no chance of following.

In the end, the Romans managed to meet the Caledonians in the sort of open battle they like best. The story of the fight, as told by Tacitus, was that it was a massive Roman win. Calgacus and his fellow Caledonians formed up on the side of a hill, and Agricola sent in his auxiliaries to attack them, while his Roman legions hung back in reserve. The auxiliaries were apparently made up of Batavians and Tungrians from what is now Germany and around Belgium, so they might not have been legionaries, but they were familiar with fighting. As we know from the initial invasions of Britain, the Romans didn't enjoy the Britons use of chariots, so Agricola sent some cavalry to attack the chariots and then swing in behind Calgacus. Trapped between the infantry and cavalry, the Caledonians got hammered. The official score was 10,000 dead barbarians for 360 heroic Romans. Not that you can trust Taciticus to get that right.

The remaining Caledonians escaped into the mountains and Agricola didn't follow them, presumably because, with such a significant death toll, they weren't worth chasing. The battle sounded like a last-ditch effort from the Caledonians, which makes a bit of sense since they had been chased so far north. There wasn't much Scotland left to hide in. We aren't too sure about the negotiations after the battle, but we do know that Agricola ended up with hostages. After all this was over, Agricola was able to send a ship up around the top of Scotland to prove that it was possible to circumnavigate the island, something the Romans hadn't done before.

As always, what happened in the following years is a bit uncertain. We have the year of Mons Graupius down as 83, and in that winter Agricola marched south to set up his army's winter living arrangements. By 84 he had been recalled to Rome, and, according to Tacitus, left the next governor a peaceful province. A seven/eight-year run as a governor in Britain is pretty impressive, most of them didn't last anywhere near that. And obviously, nobody had got anywhere near that much of the island covered before.

What's more impressive is that he was doing this while there were three different emperors in Rome. Vespasian was the one who gave him the job, he was replaced by his son, Titus, in 79, who was then replaced by his brother Domitian in 81. Rome was a lot calmer under these emperors than they had been for a while. Although, since they followed The Year of The Four Emperors, you would hope so. However, to survive three changes of management is something not a lot of people manage in ordinary jobs, let alone as a governor on the edge of the known world, fighting mad natives.

What happened after his governorship wasn't good for either Agricola or the Romans in Scotland. Agricola was an absolute beast of a governor. In his seven campaigns, he had pacified Northern Wales, consolidated Northern England, and went far enough into Scotland to beat tribes no Roman had even properly fought before. His reward? Nothing. He got no job. It's generally thought that this was because the emperor at the time, Domitian, wasn't a fan of Agricola. Hard as it is to attribute motives to people from a couple of thousand years ago, it's usually thought it was jealousy. Agricola was tearing it up at the northern edge of the empire and overshadowing what Domitian himself was doing. It's always a good idea to be second best in a competition with a megalomaniac emperor. What comes next for the Romans in Britain would be pulling further and further out of Scotland, but there will be more on that in the next British history chapter.

And there you have it, we are declaring the conquest of Britain as complete. Or at least about as complete as it would ever be. Don't worry, though, it keeps being exciting (with some periods of having no idea what was going on). It also is the point where we start to talk even less about 'Britons.' From now on most of the chat will be about Romans in Britain, with the line between the two getting blurry. The Briton nobles were becoming more Romanised, something which Agricola encouraged. They were taught Latin and started wearing togas, which as far as we are concerned are hallmarks of going full Roman.

We have also been calling the place Britain so far, and while we are still going to be talking about Britain, we are going to start calling it Britannia to mean the province the Romans had under control. There is no official date on when a part of Britain was made into a proper province. The obvious date would be in 43, in the year of the invasion. Whenever it was, it would have been early doors, which means they would have meant Southern England and Wales at a push.

It's not particularly important at this point, but while we are talking about provinces; Britain was an imperial province, not a public one. The difference was that a public province had their governor appointed by the Senate and imperial provinces had governors chosen by the emperor. Mostly, the imperial provinces were at the edge of the empire, where all the armies were posted. That way, the emperor didn't have to risk giving the control of legions to a man who might be loyal to the Senate rather than him, and as we know, Britannia needed legions. We doubt it was significant to the Britons, but it shows how the Romans viewed Britannia.

So, what have we learnt? Well, the Scottish have always been angry at folk from the south sticking their nose in their business. The Romans took a keen interest in what was going on at the edges of their empire. And it took 40 years for the Romans to get up to Aberdeen, which means they must have gone by coach.

Flavians

After the Year of The Four Emperors, we have moved from one dynasty of emperors to another. Before Nero died, all the emperors had been in the Julio-Claudian dynasty. Now, with Vespasian taking the job, we are beginning the Flavian dynasty. It's easy to think all emperors=bad because they aren't elected leaders like we have these days. However, Vespasian represents some changes, which, even us modern folk, can get behind:

He wasn't really, really posh. His grandad had been a centurion under Pompey The Great. On his mother's side, they were a bit posher, which is how Vespasian had reached the Senate, but not emperor level posh.

Not being quite that posh meant he hadn't had the same family baggage - i.e. his mam/wife/brother/cousin had not tried to have him assassinated at regular intervals.

There is a chance he got the top job on some kind of merit. Which you can't say for the likes of Caligula and Nero.

The Winner Takes The Big Job

If you read our last Roman history chapter, you will have some idea about the absolute shit-show Vespasian was going to have to deal with managing an empire. You have to assume there will have been quite a bit of ill-feeling about the place. Rome was knackered, and his own soldiers roaming about causing havoc in the region won't have helped. In the East, there was the Judean Revolt that was still going off. Although Vespasian couldn't complain too much about that. He had been the one Nero had sent to end it. Then you have the usual issues with annoyed tribes, especially along the Danube and the Rhine. All that will definitely have been made loads easier by the fact that Nero had slashed the treasure up the nearest wall. With the rest being spent by the three wannabes that followed him in 69.

Vespasian seemed to take a sensible approach to solve his cash flow problem. One thing he did was turn a few client kingdoms into proper provinces, which would have meant a nice bump in direct cash. Although there was more to it than that. Some of these reorganised kingdoms/provinces were on the Euphrates, the river that runs through Syria and Iraq. Having direct control over the region and putting a few extra legions over there was probably more about expanding Roman influence, rather than just earning a few quid.

A more definitely financial move was increasing the tax on the people of Alexandria, Egypt. This did not go down well, and he picked up a new nickname over it, 'Cybiosactes,' which was the same nickname given to an old king of theirs who had been notoriously stingy. Another move, which also birthed a nickname, was the taxation of piss collected at public toilets. The ammonia in urine was important in the treating of cloth, so it was collected and sold to folk in that industry. In this case, it wasn't Vespasian who picked up the nickname, but instead, the urinals got a new name; vespasiani. We are told that outdoor urinals are still called vespasienne in France. Whether or not that is what the French youth of today would call them, it's still quite a thought that a 21st-century loo could be named after a 1st-century emperor.

The methods he used to raise money seemed to annoy some folk, and Suetonius seemed particularly, if not annoyed, then disappointed in the emperor. He gives a lot of anecdotes for how stingy he was including this exchange with his son Titus about the piss tax:

> 'When Titus found fault with him for contriving a tax upon public conveniences, he held a piece of money from the first payment to his son's nose, asking whether its odour was offensive to him. When Titus said "No," he replied, "Yet it comes from urine."

A less funny tax which was raised by Vespasian was the taxing of all the Jews in the empire. Obviously, he had been in the East fighting the Judean Revolt, so it's perhaps unsurprising he had an axe to grind. That would undoubtedly have made recovering from the revolt in the East a bit harder for the population there.

The Judean Revolt ended in 73, and we know that Vespasian reorganised the territories over there and put a few more legions about the place. However, it wasn't just the East where his issues would be. It all went a bit wrong in Germania when a Batavian leader got involved. Julius Civilis, as well as being a leader of the Batavians, had been an auxiliary in the Roman army and had got himself Roman citizenship. He saw an opportunity during the Year of Four Emperors and joined the fighting on Vespasian's side. However, when the Romans stopped fighting each other, Civilis carried on fighting Romans. He clearly didn't much care for Roman politics, and just wanted to be handing out a beating to Romans.

It wasn't just the Batavians that got involved, Civilis was joined by other tribes, like the Treveri and Lingone, from northwest France/Belgium, with tribesmen deserting from the auxiliaries. They declared themselves as a Gallic Empire, or Empire of Gaul, which must have been a bit annoying (or galling we suppose) for Vespasian. They didn't last too long, but they did manage to overrun nearly all the legionary camps along the Rhine. Luckily for Vespasian, not all the Gallic tribes were on the side of Civilis, and some of them joined in against him. Presumably for a mixture of the rewards from Rome and settling old scores between tribes. In the end, Civilis was finished off when Vespasian sent Petillius Cerialis, who we have met in Britain with Boudicca and later as governor, to sort it out.

Not to be left out, the tribes along the Danube also fancied a bit, and the Romans suffered from raids by the Sarmatian tribes. Vespasian, being ever the practical man got rid of the immediate problem and reinforced the Rhine and the Danube frontiers. Not that this was a lasting solution. We will be revisiting those two rivers and the people that lived along them continuously for the rest of our story.

We quite like the sound of Vespasian, after the last lot, he seemed very sensible, and he kept his madness to a minimum. However, do you know what his most sensible move was as far as we can tell? He decided to treat the army right. For a start, he paid up to his soldiers when he became emperor. That was a lesson that seemed to take a while for emperors to get to grips with. Probably as important as that was making his son Titus, the Prefect of the Praetorian Guard. As we have seen, as soon as the Praetorian Guard decide they are done with an emperor, it would be quicker if they just throw their imperial selves in the river. Presumably, Vespasian felt he could trust his son more than some other bloke.

He also fixed up the broken top end of Roman society. As Suetonius put it:

'He reformed the two great orders, reduced by a series of murders and sullied by long-standing neglect, and added to their numbers, holding a review of the senate and the knights, expelling those who least deserved the honour and enrolling the most distinguished of the Italians and provincials.'

It makes sense that a lot of the senatorial class, and the class beneath them, the equestrians (knights), were no longer with the living. It would also be unsurprising to hear that a lot of the senators who were left were arseholes. So, he cleaned house and promoted some blokes he liked from outside Rome to fill the positions. This was the same thing that Claudis had done, making the Senate a bit less of a Roman boy's club, and having it a bit more on his side than it might have been.

All in all, Vespasian was a very sensible man who managed to be emperor for ten years before he died of natural causes at the age of 69. That's no mean feat at this point.

Disasters Galore

Our next emperor Titus gets off to a good start in our eyes. There were some rumours that he poisoned his dad to become emperor in 79, but generally, it's thought that he didn't. For a Roman emperor, only a vague disbelieved rumour of patricide is a decent start.

In fact, the overall impression of Titus as an emperor is a good one. Not that everyone was loving Titus, you can assume that the Jewish world had a few choice words for him. Before he was emperor, he was heavily involved in the Judean Revolt, both when his dad was there, and later when he was put in charge of the whole thing. There are some very graphic details on how brutal it was.

We want to pause here and talk about a writer from the period, Josephus. It's him that we get a lot of the information about the Middle East, and the history of the Jews in the 1st century. He was actually a friend of Vespasian and Titus, despite having fought against them in the Judean Revolt. How that came to be is either a load of bollocks, the biggest example of 'if you can't beat them, join them' or the worst case of Stockholm Syndrome in history. In 67, Vespasian and Titus were closing in on Josephus and his friends, so 40 of them, including Josephus, hid in a cave.

As the Jewish writer tells it, he persuaded everyone to kill themselves rather than surrender. They drew straws for who should kill who, and eventually, it came down to Josephus and one other. He then persuaded the other person to join him in surrendering to the Romans. After a couple years imprisonment, he came out as a supporter of Vespasian, and later on travelled to Rome with Titus and became a Roman citizen.

So, Josephus literally organised the death of 38-odd of his fellow Jews, decided against joining them and then became a Roman. And he told this story himself - did he not realise how badly he comes off in that. You would definitely come up with something better than that.

Titus' rule was only short, but you will be more than familiar with two big events in his two short years as emperor. The first was the inaugural events at the newly built Colosseum. The building had been started by Vespasian a decade earlier, but it was completed under Titus. The Colosseum is still a massively impressive building, so it must have been ridiculous back then, with its capacity of 50,000 people. Titus opened the place with 100 days of ludicrously lavish games, involving sport and gladiator fights. According to Dio, they might have even flooded it and held mock sea battles. Although, boringly, historians tend to doubt that.

On the less positive side, Titus managed to squeeze in some fairly sizable natural disasters into his two years as emperor. In 80, Rome suffered from both a fire, smaller than Nero's, but big enough that we know about it and a plague. Titus put his hand in his pocket and paid for repairs out of the imperial treasury. Although to be fair, that's what Nero did as well. The difference is that Titus didn't rope off a bit of the damaged area and build himself a new palace with a whacking great big statue of himself in it.

The real disaster that happened during his reign was the eruption of Vesuvius and the destruction of Pompeii. In 79 Mount Vesuvius erupted and destroyed Pompeii,

Herculaneum and anything around them. Actually, that's not true the eruption threw hot ash and molten rock out, which killed everyone nearby, but preserved the towns. The volcanic activity lasted a few days, and in the end, left Pompeii under about 6 meters (20 feet) of debris. It means historians have been able to find out all sorts of specific things about things which might have been hard to discover otherwise. Food, the arrangement of homes and election posters were all there, still to be found in modern excavations. Which we are sure would be the smallest fragment, of a hint, of a silver lining for the people who were there.

Titus apparently did pretty well in the case of this humanitarian crisis, and devoted funds towards fixing the place up. Obviously, they didn't rebuild the lost towns, since they stayed under all the ash, but the region recovered, and Titus gets a bit of credit for that.

To finish on Vesuvius, if you want to get an immediate sense of concern, crack open a search engine, type in 'Vesuvius', find it on a map, have a look at where Pompeii and Herculaneum are/were and then have a look at Naples. A city with a population of just shy of 1 million. Still, it hasn't gone off since 1944. So it's probably fine.

Overall, Titus seemed like a pretty reasonable bloke. Dio wasn't a big fan of him, but even he has nice things to say about him. Including how he didn't have anyone executed. Which is a bit rare. He also got rid of the rule banning people from insulting the emperor, and put in place a double jeopardy law, meaning you couldn't be tried twice for one crime.

Dio, as part of his not being a big fan, did say that Titus:

'ruled with mildness and died at the height of his glory, whereas, if he had lived a long time, it might have been shown that he owes his present fame more to good fortune than to merit.'

So Titus was like a rock star dying at the height of their

fame and talent before they can get old and annoy everyone with their questionable politics. Dio reckons Titus' reputation benefits from only being emperor from 79 to 81. Titus died of a fever, but the details of that are best saved for our next emperor...

<u>Finally, Another Dickhead Emperor</u>

Titus only lasted a couple of years, when he died of a fever which came on suddenly. He was only 41 when he died, and there are some strong suggestions that he was killed by his brother, and next emperor, Domitian. One of the rumours, which we get from Dio, is that when Titus was sick, Domitian locked him in a chest full of snow to make him sicker. That's a bit out there, and it's just one of the deaths of an emperor where we will never know what happened. It's always possible that Titus just died. It does happen. On the other hand, as we are about to see Domitian was a proper shitbag, so maybe he did kill his brother.

Before we lay into the man, it's worth pointing out that he actually did ok as an emperor, as far as we can tell. For a start, his military victories seemed decent. We know that he had pulled back in Britain, but he had successful scraps elsewhere. He fought, and beat, a Germanic tribe called the Chatti, who were from central Germany. We get info on this from Tacitus, who as we know was upset with Domitian, so isn't the most balanced of sources. According to Tacitus he outright made up beating the Chatti, claiming that, when he was celebrating his win, the 'captured Chatti' were really slaves who had been taught to sound German. Other Roman historians, like Frontus, were quite impressed with the win against the German tribe, so we can probably assume it happened. The other claim is that Domitian wasn't justified in fighting the Chatti at all, and he was just looking for a cheap win. In fact, Domitian was proud enough of the fight against the Chatti that he gave himself the title of Germanicus - like when Claudius gave himself the Britannicus title.

So, he must have been involved enough not to make that embarrassing.

A fake fight and a big fuss would make sense because he might have had a bit of an inferiority complex. His dad had been fighting all across Europe and the Middle East, and he did well enough that he won an emperorship out of it. His brother had been involved in the Judean Revolt, which was no small thing. Domitian, on the other hand, didn't have that pedigree.

As well as the Chatti over on the Rhine, Domitian also had some issues on the Danube. Both the Dacians from Romania and the Sarmatians from around Ukraine decided to kick off. This wasn't a little scuffle, and the Dacians killed a governor of the province of Moesia (in the Balkans, around Serbia). It took a few years, but eventually, everyone was put back in their box. The Rhine and the Danube region would be a problem for a very long time, and Domitian keeping control of it seems like decent work to us.

In fact, Domitian must have been popular with quite a lot of the army. For a start, they got the first military pay raise since Augustus, which had been the best part of a century earlier. The raise was an increase of a third, so no token effort of 1-2% most of us hope the best for each year. He was also involved in the actual campaigns. Not precisely fighting face to face with mad barbarians, but, nearby at least.

Not that every bit of the army liked Domitian. The governor of Germania Superior, (think south-west Germany and a bit of Switzerland and France) decided to revolt. This governor, Saturninus, had himself the support of four legions, so it wasn't a little affair, but all the same, it wasn't a very well thought through plan. As well as his legions, Saturninus also had the support of some the Germanic barbarian tribes. Unfortunately for him, as Domitian's legions marched up there to sort it out, the Rhine thawed, and the barbarians couldn't cross the river to join Saturninus, so he took a beating. Again, it looks like Domitian had a handle on the military stuff.

On a more domestic front, Domitian also seemed to do some decent things. He was apparently good at handling the economy and didn't go too hard on throwing money about in a Caligula/Nero fashion. He did, however, do a bit of building in Rome. A lot of which was fixing the place up after the fire that caused damage under Titus. He also put a few finishing touches on the Colosseum, which we are grateful for, because as we said, it's a proper cool building.

However, it was on this domestic front, which Dometians personality does, unfortunately, show through. Apparently, Domitian didn't like a lot of delegation, and he relied on a close set of his friends as advisors. A lot of the men he gave jobs to weren't from the old crowd, and he relied quite a lot on the people from outside of the city, including equestrians of lower social standing. That meant the top-end posh folk not only saw a drop in the amount of influence they could personally wield, but they had to share it with some slightly less posh folk—something which wouldn't have gone down well in the Senate.

We are told by Suetonius, that as a younger man Domitian was quite a nice bloke, who didn't want to harm anyone, but that changed later on. Suetonius reckons a lot of the change happened after the scrap with Saturninus. And quite the change it was as well, by all accounts. He executed eleven high ranking senators, as well as countless other folks. It all went a bit Caligula, from the sounds of it.

As we often say with these sorts of unpopular emperors, our view of Domitian is probably worse than it should be because the writers from the time were sticking the boot in. Either because they hated him, or maybe because they wanted to suck up to the next set of emperors. However, there is usually one thing which tips us over the edge into deciding that an emperor is, in fact, a shitbag. In Domitian's case, it is the fact/potentially true story that he only allowed statues to be erected of him if they were in gold and silver. As a distasteful bonus fact, he apparently renamed the months of September and October, 'Germanicus' and 'Domitianus' after himself. What sort of megalomaniac does that?

We all know what happens to emperors who act like that, especially when they start to make people scared for their own safety. That's right they die of sharp and unnatural causes. Often when an emperor dies, there are rumours of assassination. Not this one. There is no doubt about it, Domitian was stabbed to death. The actual stabbing of the emperor was done by a member of his household, Stephanus. However, the list of the conspirators runs to include, both the Praetorian Prefects (standard), a lot of senators (typical), his friend and replacement, Nerva (predictable) and his wife (harsh). A few of those groups/people getting involved isn't out of the ordinary for these sorts of things. To have all four of them join in suggests it had gone badly wrong. That is not the end of an emperor who has things under control.

After Domitian's death no there was no great state funeral, he was just cremated without any ceremony. The Senate declared a Damnatio Memoriae, which means a condemnation of memory. It was supposed to lead to the wiping out of Domitian, from the public record. So, statues were to be taken down, coins melted, and records struck off. Mostly it wasn't followed, because that sounds like effort, but even suggesting it should happen shows the Senate weren't exactly torn up that Domitian had been stabbed to death.

And with the end of the Flavians, all three of them, that's your lot. From a pretty cinematic beginning, with the Year of the Four Emperors, to an ignominious death, that's the Flavians.

Teotihuacán

Over in the Western Hemisphere, people were busy building civilisations entirely unconnected to Rome, or any other Eurasian peoples. A lot of the more exciting civilisations from our period come from the Mesoamerica region. This is the part of North and Central America between Southern Mexico, down through Guatemala, Belize, El Salvador, Honduras and into Nicaragua and Costa Rica.

These civilisations were often pretty sizable and involved the building of cities that supported a significant number of people. The one we want to mention here is Teotihuacán, as it was the biggest city in that part of the world until the Aztecs built bigger ones more than 1000 years later. The city, or at least its remains, is in Mexico and it's about 30 miles (50 km) from Mexico City. People had been living in the area for a few hundred years before the building started in earnest around 100 BC. This was no little settlement, and it was large enough for about 200,000 people. That's not Rome big, but it's big. Estimates for the population of Rome have been high as one million, but it's possible the figure was really as low as 450,000. 200,000 people would put Teotihuacán at roughly around the same size as Newcastle. That's a reasonable effort.

The architecture of the city is crazy. The centre of it is dominated by a large straight road called the Avenue of the Dead. It's a 40 meter (130 ft) wide road that's 1.5 miles (2.4 km) long. At one end of the avenue is the Pyramid of the Moon, a massive 43 meter (140 ft) stepped pyramid. Nearby of the Pyramid of the Sun, which is even bigger standing at 66 meters (216 ft). That must have been unbelievably imposing for the people living there. Just looking at the photos now and it looks pretty imposing. You certainly wouldn't want to be wandering through at night. There are some serious spooky vibes.

As is typical for cultures during this period, religion was important, and the people of Teotihuacán had a few different gods. There was a Great Goddess, among others, but the one that's most interesting to us is the Feathered Serpent. This particular deity had its own temple, called the Pyramid of the Feathered Serpent, and there are statues of it as a snake coming out of the walls, with a sort of headdress looking thing at the back of it, and they look very cool. Especially considering they were carved thousands of years ago. As you can see, we like the Feathered Serpent because of its cool statues, rather than its religious significance. To be fair to the big snake, it was significant, and you might have actually heard of this god before. It's usually known as, Quetzalcoatl, which is a bit of a mouth full. It's one of the better-known gods of the region because the Aztecs adopted it as well.

A part of a lot of Mesoamerican cultures, that often gets mentioned because to be fair it does stand out, is human sacrifice. The Teotihuacán dabbled in that as well. Both humans and animals have been found buried under the pyramids of the city. And it's safe to say they didn't all have a pleasant time before they were buried there. For a start not, it's possible not everyone was dead when they were buried there.

It's worth noting that we have been referring to the Pyramids of the Moon and Sun, and the Avenue of the Dead, but that wasn't what the people of Teotihuacán would have called them. We get these names from the Aztecs who live centuries later in the same area. The ruins were pretty impressive, so obviously the Aztecs had some time for the ancient city, and it's from them we get those names. You can see why the Aztecs were fans. They were a civilisation that kicked off properly in the 14th-century, so Teotihuacán was even older to them than the Aztec cities are to us, so they would have found everything just as cool.

It's a bit after our period, but the end of the city came in the 700s when its people disappeared, and historians don't quite know why. They do know that at some point the city had a lot of the buildings in the city got burnt. Historians see this as part of an internal revolt rather than the city being attacked by other people. It's mad to us that we can have a city of such a big size, that still has some massive buildings standing, and we know so little about the place. We do love a pyramid, though.

Hadrian Knocks Up A Wall

Now for something most of us will have heard of before: Hadrian's Wall

We have called it that the Roman invasion of Britain has ended, and we are now properly into Roman Britain. It's a bit arbitrary, but we are going with it. Governor Agricola got about as far north into Scotland as the Romans ever would. England was mostly under control, and the Welsh weren't being a big issue anymore. You don't like to see a people being ruled from somewhere else, and it's not as if the Roman were particularly nice. However, it must have been pleasant for the Britons to stop being killed by the Romans for a bit.

For us, on the other hand, fighting in Britain meant people writing about Britain, so, after Agricola, there is a bit of a gap where we don't really know what was going on. For some reason, no Romans wanted to spend time documenting effective administrative activities.

Agricola had been the governor until 84, but he was recalled by Emperor Domitian, who was himself was replaced by Emperor Nerva in 96, who was then replaced by Trajan a couple of years later in 98. It was under Trajan that the Roman Empire was the biggest it would ever be, but that didn't include expanding in Britain. In fact, he was so busy elsewhere that Roman-controlled Britannia shrank a bit. However, after Trajan, we have Hadrian, who took an interest in our island in the 120s, which means we have something to talk about. Quite a big thing.

In this chapter, we ask ourselves, why bother with a big wall? Who was on the wall? And what was going on between Agricola being governor and Hadrian building this wall?

What Was Going On Before Hadrian Turned Up?

This book so far owes a lot to Tacitus, the mad bloodthirsty Roman that he was. Without him, it's not likely that we would know all that much about the Romans march north. The last Roman Britain chapter would have been some chat about some bloke called Agricola who we think was a governor, and a load of Roman forts dotted about Scotland. Unfortunately, Tacitus doesn't write quite as much after Agricola, probably because he died in 120. So, we don't have a handy book that describes what happens next, and it's a bit vague between 84 and 117, when Hadrian was made emperor. This was an important period for the Romans, with Trajan expanding their control to its greatest extent. However, that meant he was busy elsewhere to much care about Britain.

We don't even know the name of the bloke who replaced Agricola as governor. We do, however, know the general theme of his orders, again thanks to Tacitus. Everyone's favourite aggressive general was a big fan of Agricola and a bigger fan of the conquering of people. You can imagine the tone he used to describe the post-Agricola Roman policy when he wrote:

'Britain was conquered and immediately let go.'

It was a bit of a stretch to say that Britain had been conquered. Agricola had got as near as makes no difference to the top of the island. Which means he had passed most tribes to get there, whether they wanted him to or not. We suppose Tacitus means 'conquered' in the same way that Claudius conquered Britain (or at least the South East). Agricola had given the folk in Scotland a proper beating, and if the Romans had stayed there, it would probably have gone the way of England and Wales. A few revolts, followed by brutal oppression, rinse, and repeat until you have an actually suppressed territory.

Tacitus' overall view on this seems to be that it comes from Emperor Domitian's jealousy. Not only did he call Agricola back to Rome because he was doing too well and showing him up, but Domitian rolled back the territory in Scotland to make it look like Agricola hadn't really done anything. To be fair to Domitian, he was having some trouble with the Dacians, a group from Romania. A quick look at a map would show why a Roman emperor would be more concerned by the angry people from around the Danube than the people in the top half of Britain. No doubt the tribes of Scotland were very angry, but, even if they were the angriest Scotland had ever been, they weren't a threat to Rome.

We aren't exactly sure when the Romans pulled back from Northern Scotland. Tacitus makes it sound as if, when Agricola travelled south back to Rome, he was followed close behind by thousands of legionaries being chased by angry pre-Scotsmen. It wasn't quite that quick, but there are some clues it wasn't far wrong. Archaeologists often follow the money when it comes to the Romans, and they can use coins to roughly date certain things. There was a big Roman fort at Inchtuthil, which is just north of Dundee and Perth. Coins have been found here, and in some other forts that far north, dated 86, but there aren't any coins from the years that followed that. If that's the last year the fort was used, then that means the Romans had sacked off Northern Scotland a year or two after Agricola left.

That particular fort wasn't a small outpost to keep an eye on the entry to a glen, it was a proper headquarters and was big enough, at 53 acres (214,483 sq. meters), to be a base for a whole legion. So that suggests it was a massive withdrawal when they left, but it doesn't look like that they were chased out by angry Britons. Ever the organised, the Romans demolished and packed up the whole thing, so it was a planned withdrawal, rather than a forced one.

When Domitian's reign ended (badly) in 96, there were three legions in Britain, which is a bit short from the four we had previously seen. Even so, the Romans did keep themselves in Southern Scotland for a while longer. It looks like it was somewhere around 103 - 105 that the Romans pulled back to the Stanegate (a.k.a. The Stone Road), which ran across Northern England, roughly from Newcastle to Carlisle. This doesn't mean they didn't get involved further north, but it seems like this was the cut-off where everything south of it was definitely Roman, and everything north was a bit more fluid than that. How fluid would probably depend on if you asked a Briton or a Roman.

Interestingly, the last manoeuvre south might not have been 100% voluntary. As we said with the Inchtuthil fort, when the Romans left a fort, in what is effectively enemy territory, they tended to tidy up, strip it of useful stuff and then burn what was left so nobody else could use it. Some of the forts in Southern Scotland might not have been abandoned all that orderly, and it might be that the Romans were forced out. At a fort near Melrose, there is evidence of broken equipment and pits with human remains in them. To be honest, it doesn't sound like anyone can really date this evidence of destruction, or even tell if it is really evidence of destruction in the first place. The best we could find was some folk saying that maybe it meant the Romans were forced out. It sounds as if we shouldn't read too much into it (as much as you can downplay a pit of dead people). Still, it's a flash of something interesting in a period where we don't really know what was going on.

The Emperors Remember Britannia

Hadrian was made emperor in 117, and he was very different from Trajan. Trajan was your classic Tacitus style emperor. He was all about giving people a kicking and taking more territory. Hadrian was the builder emperor, and not just his wall, which we will get to in a minute. England and Wales had been going through some renovations from the beginning of the century. The whole place was starting to look like a proper Roman province. It seems like they had decided on three main bases for their legions, and they began to rebuild them in stone. These forts were at Carnforth (South Wales near Newport), Chester (on the Welsh Border, south of Liverpool) and York (North Yorkshire).

Three new stone forts aren't all that exciting, but we do get some clues as to what was going on from it. Firstly, England and Wales were settled enough that permanent forts could be made. You wouldn't do that if there was a chance you would have to abandon them, like the wooden ones in Scotland. Secondly, it must have been decided that Britannia needed three legions. Lastly, Southern England didn't need a base for a legion in it, with none of these three forts being anywhere near the South East. Maybe the choice of the areas was just convenient because that's where the legions had been for a while, but it seems significant that one was in South Wales, one was between North Wales and North West England, and the last was in Yorkshire in the north-eastern bit of England.

It wasn't just the army getting upgrades. The Romans had been putting up civic buildings since they got to the island and by now England and Wales were dotted with Roman settlements and buildings. There were the baths in Bath (oddly enough), Chester had an amphitheatre, and there was a palace at Fishbourne, in Sussex, to name but a few. The Fishbourne Palace was even started really early on, in the 70s. These weren't buildings you would knock up if you through some Boudicca tribute act was going to sweep the nation and burn it all down. Although to be fair, the Romans had built some stuff pre-Boudicca, which she did burn down, so that might have been a bit optimistic. What we are saying was Britannia was being Romanised nicely, and Hadrian seemed happy to add to that.

The surge in interior decorating makes Britannia sound like it was now a nice place to be for the Romans. Hadrian found out early on in his reign that it wasn't the case. We think. Something went down in Britain, probably between 117 and 119, although it might have been in the 120s. As far as we can tell the trouble was both from outside and inside the province.

The whole thing is seriously vague. Something we do have is a mention of some argy-bargy in a letter. This letter was written by a bloke called Fronto to Emperor Marcus Aurelius, who would get the top job in two emperors time, after Hadrian. In this letter Fronto was consoling Marcus Aurelius, who had just had loads of men killed in the east, saying it was OK because his grandad, Hadrian, had lost loads of men as well, in Judea and Britannia. This Judea uprising was a pretty significant bit of grief from the Jewish population in the Middle East, and it cost the Romans a fair old bit. So for Britannia to be mentioned in the same breath suggests it might have been a big one. Also, it must have a decent bit of fight for it to be getting a mention a couple of emperors down the line. Luckily, that's not the only evidence we have. We also have a coin, minted in 119, being released with a personified Britannia on the back. Some historians claim this could be after a victory, or at least to celebrate a new peace. Or it was just a cool design, like when we put Paddington Bear on the back of a 50p. Who knows?

If you will allow us to just have a bit of a guess of what happened, the clever money is that it was an attack from Southern Scotland, with the Selgovae generally being pegged as being a bit unfriendly to the Romans. They might have had some help, including from some folk from the Brigantes. If that's the case, it would have been a big problem for the Romans, but that's just a semi-educated guess taken from what historians generally say happened.

If you want some evidence that Britannia was at least of importance to the Romans, if not proof that it was all kicking off again, how about the fact that Hadrian himself turned up in 122. Hadrian spent a long time travelling the empire, including trips to North Africa, the Middle East and across Europe, including Greece, Spain, and Britain. Even if it was just part of his world tour, a visit from an emperor is significant for Roman Britain. It was on this visit, bringing along a new governor for Britannia, Aulus Platorius Nepos, that Hadrian's Wall was started.

The Wall

So first, where is this wall? Well, it goes along the line that the Romans had already settled on defending. This line was a road that ran from the River Tyne to the Solway Firth, or Newcastle to Carlisle. It's worth pointing out that this isn't the current border between England and Scotland. It's pretty close at the Carlisle end, but Newcastle to Bewick-upon-Tweed, which is the English town just south of the border, are about 60 miles apart. So, people making jokes about keeping folk on the other side of Hadrian's Wall hit the double whammy of being both boring and wrong.

The reason for the wall being built here is reasonably obvious when you see it on a map. It's a bit like the bit of Scotland between Glasgow and Edinburgh that Agricola had fortified on his Scottish adventure. A handy skinny bit of the island, which makes it easier to defend. Even bearing in mind that it's probably the shortest line to defend that Hadrian could have picked, the wall is still 73 miles (117 km) long. That's a long way to walk, never mind build a wall along, and this wasn't just a crappy token effort. This was a proper bit of wall.

The length of a wall is important, but if you are building a barrier between you and a pack of mad Britons, you are going to be pretty interested in the height as well. The best guess seems to be that the wall topped out at 4.6 meters tall, which is 15 feet. Meaning it wasn't something you could hop over. And because we are always thorough about these things, and have a very short attention span, we had a look at the high jump world record. Currently, that record is a mere 2.45 meters. So, nobody is jumping that 4.6 meter high wall. The pole vault record, however, is 6.18 meters. So, assuming the Romans put out a load of padded mats, I think we can all imagine how the angry, ancient scots got over that particular obstacle. Or ladders, maybe.

The least exciting dimension of this wall was always going to be width, but bear with us, because it does show us something interesting. There were different widths along its length. In fact, it also had different materials. In the east, the wall was made of stone and was 3 meters (10ft) wide. The last 30 miles of the wall in the west was made of turf and was 6 meters (20ft) wide. That was the plan anyway, and it was thinned out a bit mid-construction to 2.4 meters (7.8ft) That suggests they wanted to speed things up a bit. Even in the thinner bits, the wall would have been wide enough for a Roman to walk along, presumably making patrols a bit easier. Not that we know if it had a walkway along the top, but it's nice to picture it like that. Maybe with some crenulations along the top, like a medieval castle - crenulations are the up and down bits you get on the top of turrets.

It wasn't just the thickness of that wall which changed, there was quite a lot of changes to the original plan, made after they had started building the thing. The major one was the inclusion of forts. There were already some forts along the Stanegate, and three forts were built north of the wall in the east, as forward positions into Briton territory. The Romans weren't happy with that feeble level of defence. So, in addition to those, more forts were built into the wall itself at intervals of just over 7 miles (11km).

All in all, there were 17 full-sized forts along the wall. These weren't the only fortifications, however, and in between these forts were mini forts at mile intervals all along the wall. These mini forts are creatively called milecastles.

Hadrian's Wall is 73 miles long, so there should be 73 milecastles. However, a Roman mile was shorter than a modern mile. The word comes from the Latin phrase 'mille passus' or 'thousand paces.' That means, for the Romans, a mile was about 1418 meters compared to our 1609 meters. That all means, to a Roman, the wall was 80 miles long, so there are 80 milecastles. The Romans were nothing if not thorough, so the 17 forts (20 if you include the outposts) and 80 milecastles weren't enough. In between each one was two towers, to keep an eye out. That means, assuming it was fully manned along its length, there would have been a Roman standing roughly every third of a mile, or about every 500 meters. Nobody was sneaking over that.

These 17 forts and 80 milecastles are just Hadrian's Wall itself. The defence actually stretched a bit further than that, although without an actual wall. The defensive stretched down the west coast all the way down to Maryport. That's about another 30 miles. It makes sense to have a bit of defence down the coast. There is no point in building a massive wall if the people you are trying to keep out can just sail around the edge.

As annoying it must have been for the blokes building it to change the plans after they had already started, it's assumed that the change of plan was to do with ease of movement. The forts in the wall had three entrances from the north, each with two doors. This means it had six times as many doors leading north as one of the milecastles had, which would make it much quicker to get a legion or two marching north. It sounds like someone at some point asked, 'so what happens if we want to campaign in the north again?'

We assume that was followed by a lot of finger-pointing and a redesign.

Something else you might take from the plans is that the Romans were more worried about the west than they were the east. Those three forts on the north side of the wall, show they wanted an extra presence up there. They were all quite close to Carlise, at Bewcastle, Netherby and Birrens. Or maybe they were part of a future plan for moving into Scotland. With the milecastles down to Maryport, it looks like something was going on over on that side.

However, before we go on about future plans, we haven't finished with the wall yet. Hadrian and his mates weren't playing. In front of the wall, to the north was a big ditch that was up to 10 meters (32ft) wide, except where they didn't need it because natural defences, like cliffs, did the job. We've checked again, and the long jump world record is 8.95 meters, so the Romans were safe behind that.

A big ditch in front of a wall makes absolute sense. Putting something in front of your big wall is classic fortification basics. Less classic is the feature placed to the south of the wall, on the Roman-controlled side; The Vallum. This was another big ditch, about 6 meters (20 feet) wide and 3 meters (10 feet) deep. On either side of the ditch, there was a mound of earth which was about 2 meters (7 feet) tall. The Vallum ran pretty near to the wall, occasionally drifting to 700 meters away when the ground nearer the wall was a bit too rocky to dig into.

If you want to be petty, calling the Vallum, the Vallum, is wrong, because the Romans used the term to mean to wall itself. But be warned, that sort of thing is straying into 'erm actually, the doctor was called Frankenstein' territory, and that's no way to make friends.

So, what was the point of this? Why dig a massive ditch the length of a country when you have already built a gigantic wall and loads of forts? Our first thought was that it would be the second line of defence if some angry Britons got over the wall. It turns out this isn't what historians reckon it was for, and to be fair if you can't defend a huge wall, a ditch isn't going to be much use to you. Instead, the Vallum might have been used as a marker for the Britons living to the south. Over the past few decades, Northern England hadn't always been pro-Roman in their outlook, and Agricola getting control over them hadn't been all that long ago. And then we have that rebellion we don't know anything about in around 117, which was really recent and could have easily taken place in what was now south of the wall.

If the Vallum was a southern border to the wall zone, it would have been a handy line to stop Britons getting too close while the Romans were busy watching the north. Presumably, if you were hanging around near the wall you had better have yourself a good reason. It's hard to have a lot of sympathy for invaders and occupiers, but you have to feel a bit sorry for the individual Romans. You have been sent from the other side of the empire, into a strange land, where the people in the north are so mental you had to build an absolutely massive wall across the whole island. Not only that, but you have to put up defences against the people in the south. Even though those people are living in a Roman province. It must have felt like a permanent siege.

Another similar theory for the Vallum was is that it protected land that was meant to be used by the soldiers posted to the wall. They used the area to grow crops to feed themselves, and maybe cattle were living on the gap between the wall and the Vallum. One of the forts, Chesters, which is in the east, near Hexham, housed a cavalry unit, and they would have had to find somewhere to graze their horses. So, as well as perhaps stopping Britons attacking the Romans from the south, the Vallum was to stop the local Britons nicking the Roman's stuff.

The People & The Point of the Wall

The wall is clearly an impressive bit of building, but another bonus for us is that we get some information about the people who were involved in it. That's something you don't always get with the Romans in Britain.

So, who made this wall? Well, it started construction in 122, and it took about 10 years to build, which sounds pretty quick considering how long it is and it's not like they had cranes and lorries and whatnot. A 73-mile long wall, of any height, being built in 10 years would need a fair few people involved, and it's estimated more than 15,000 men worked on it.

It was started under the governor Aulus Platorius Nepos. But 122 was also the year that Hadrian was in Britannia. He was big on the building, and he loved himself a wall, so the assumption is that he was involved in the design of it himself, which is pretty cool. Like any big construction job in the Roman Empire, the actual work was done by legionaries. There were three legions in Britannia at the time, not to mention any attached auxiliaries and all three legions were involved in the building. They were also helped by the navy in Britain (the 'classis Britannica')

Once the thing was built, who exactly were the soldiers who ended up posted at Hadrian's Wall? The answer to that is quite impressive. While the legions constructed the wall, it looks like the manning of the wall was often left to the auxiliary units, meaning the non-Roman citizen bit of the army. Most of these men would have been from Northern Europe, so they were mostly from Germanic tribes. However, there were men from further afield, like Asturians, from modern Spain and Dacians from Romania. Even more exotic than that, at one point there was a unit from Mauritania (Morocco), stationed in a fort near Carlisle. There were also a group of Syrians posted at the

Housesteads fort, which is near Hexham. We can all agree that would have been quite the change of scenery for those blokes. We shouldn't really be surprised by this since we know the empire was massive, but it still sounds odd to us. It would be strange to hear there was a big group of Moroccans living in Carlisle now, let alone 2000 odd years ago.

We want to end our bit about the wall by making sure we are clear on what the point might have been. It was a massive undertaking and not the sort of thing you knock up on a whim.

Let's start with the obvious. It was a defensive wall against the people north of the wall. You can't deny it was a military structure. You don't put forts along a big line, and man it with soldiers, if it's not meant to be defended. Given that the 80 years of Roman rule on the island up to that point had involved constant fighting, and some not little revolts, it makes sense that Hadrian and his friends couldn't just leave the tribes in the north to freely wonder about. That was a recipe for permanent warfare.

A not so obvious reason behind the construction could be it was handy for admin. Following on from Trajan and his very fighty activities, Hadrian was all about keeping what he had. He set up proper borders all around the empire. On the continent, he used the Rhine and the Danube for most of his borders. Where the Roman-controlled land didn't neatly match up with the rivers, there was a line of forts and wooden walls. These already existed before Hadrian, but he beefed it up a bit. In the south, he set up another series of walls to mark out what was the Roman's territory in North Africa. All of these structures gave out a clear message. 'This is ours, and that is, for the time being at least, yours'. Keeping other people out of your territory is useful, but it was also a handy line where you could tax any goods for trade going in or out. War is all very well and good, but the Romans were also partial to some profitable trade. Managing who was taking things in and out of the province would have been easier using the gates to the forts and milecastles than trying to police 73 miles of open space. It was a pre-EU, European based, trade zone. Very modern.

A third reason for the building of the wall is one we have brought up quite a few times with different important Romans, and it just goes to show how cynical we are. You can't help but notice the whole giant wall thing was some impressive dick swinging. Hadrian wasn't planning any big wars, but he still had to impress back home in Rome. The building of a giant 73-mile long wall, in what was still a hostile territory, is going to get a mention. It also has the benefit of being impressive military-themed, without actually being a war. There is also the prestige in a more local sense. If the natives had been kicking off, nothing says 'this is mine, and you are too puny to do anything about it' than a giant wall in a period when the locals still lived in small communities. Think back to Caractacus and his wondering why people who live in Rome would care about the Britons and their crappy tents. We imagine the sight of the wall made folk think twice before getting stuck in.

And that's it. As we will see, the Romans didn't settle on Hadrian's Wall as the border between them and the barbarians of the north. However, it was manned for most of the rest of the Roman Britain period. In fact, for a fair chunk of the time, it was the most heavily fortified border in the empire. Now that's an impressive wall.

So, what have we learnt? Folk in Scotland have always been a pain. Donald Trump isn't all that original in his thinking. And Romans didn't mess about when they built a wall.

From Nerva To Hadrian

Our history of Britain pretty much jumped from Agricola being recalled by Domitian to Hadrian throwing up a wall across Northern England. A history of the Roman Empire which did that would be a bit odd, and you would miss one important bloke and one old man who didn't do too much before you got to Hadrian.

Nerva

Nerva got the job when Domitian was bumped off. He was selected by the Senate, and it smells of a decision being made to put off having to make an actual decision. He was from a fancy enough family to be at home in the Senate, without being from a top-end family who would have had uncomfortable relationships with the previous madder emperors. He had also been a mate of Vespasian and had been given the consulship under both him and Domitian. So, he was qualified, presumably unthreatening and old enough that he wasn't going to be around forever. He also had no children to make for a messy succession when the time came. It had all the hallmarks of a non-decision.

To be fair, we are talking like he was 100 years old and on death's door. He was in his 60's, but he lasted two years in the job before he died, of natural causes. If you feel we are being mean to the elderly, we do get this picture of a frail old man from Dio:

> 'Now Nerva was so old and so feeble in health (he always, for instance, had to vomit up his food) that he was rather weak.'

It sounds like Nerva was a decent ruler, and Dio, even after that jibe, does list a few bits of good work he did. He ended the spate of executions that Domitian embarked on. Domitian had particularly taken a dislike to Jews, so Nerva was good news for them at least. He also gave back property that Domitian had taken from people and gave grants to the poorest Romans. He even sold some imperial property when cash was low. Dio makes him sound like a lovely, kind grandad.

However, unlike your kind old grandad, there were plots to kill Nerva. A bloke named Crassus, ran a conspiracy to kill him, and according to Dio again, Nerva's response was cinematic:

> 'he caused them to sit beside him at a spectacle (they were still ignorant of the fact that they had been informed upon) and gave them swords, ostensibly to inspect and see if they were sharp (as was often done), but really in order to show that he did not care even if he died then and there.'

And that was that. The emperor banished Crassus, but he decided not to execute his way through the upper echelons of Roman society like a lot of emperors would have.

There was a more serious plot soon after when the Praetorians went for him. This time, while Nerva didn't get the chop, he had to give in to some demands, which must have been embarrassing. Once you don't have the Praetorian Guard in your corner, you are done for. Although he made it through without being murdered. Not that winning by dying of natural causes seems like much of a win. He did, however, manage to sort out a successor: Trajan.

Trajan Of Column Fame

Trajan was interesting mainly because it was during his reign that the Roman Empire got to its largest size.

He had got the job after his adopted dad, Nerva, died in January 98, but he didn't make it to Rome until 99. Instead, Trajan hung about in the Danube. A lot of legions were posted in that region, and the barbarians across the river were a worry. The Dacians, in Romania, had particularly been taking the piss in recent years. Including the wiping out of a Roman legion in 86, while Domitian was in charge. Trajan was having none of that and took the opportunity to shore things up, doing stuff like rebuilding fortresses in stone rather than wood. He also had a walkway carved into a cliff, to give Roman soldiers better access to the Dacian territory. The man was not messing about.

Trajan definitely called it right about that tribe, and he ended up back over that way when those pesky Dacians kicked off again in 101. They had been a pain in the arse for a long time from their stronghold in Romania. This time Trajan gathered troops from around Europe and dove right into their territory and wrecked them, attacking their capital, Sarmizegetusa, and bringing them to peace. He let their king, Decabalus, keep his job, but Dacia was now a client kingdom.

The peace lasted until 105 when Decalabus had another go, or at least he pissed off Trajan by ignoring the terms of their peace/client kingdom arrangement. Trajan was straight in again with his legions. Presumably, it was even easier to do this time because the Romans had broken a lot of Dacian fortifications the first time around, but also because a lot of Dacians didn't really fancy the second go, and he joined the Romans instead. That meant the Dacian's second attempt didn't last long, and in 106 it ended with Decalabus committing suicide. Although before he did that, he tried to finish the whole thing by having Trajan assassinated. By all accounts, this Decalabus was a hard man.

This whole war was massive for the Dacians in the region. There is evidence that the approach that Trajan took to the natives was on the border of genocide, with the population being replaced by Roman colonists. It's probably telling that Dacia, is now best known as a budget Romanian car manufacturer, and the region is now in a country called Romania. You won't need a big leap of imagination to decide on where that name came from.

Trajan was pretty proud of this conquest, and he gave himself the title Dacicus (the Dacian version of Britannicus) and built the Trajan Column. You can still see that in Rome, and there is a cast of it in the V&A museum in London. They are both very cool and worth a look if you are ever in either city. It's a 200 meter (650 ft) tall column with a spiralling scene, telling the story of Trajan's win in Dacia. It's like a massive Roman comic strip.

At the same sort of time was happening, in 106, the Romans also picked up a new province in Arabia. The Nabataean Kingdom was based around modern Jordan, with its capital at Petra. It was a client kingdom of the Romans, nestled between the major provinces of Egypt and Syria. Their king, Rabbel II, died and the Romans decided it was theirs now, and without a lot of fuss, he just made it into the Arabian Province. Not exciting, but it has to be included as it was part of what made Trajan the emperor while Rome was its biggest.

More impressive than the Arabian Province, was Trajan's work in the Parthian Empire, when he dove headfirst into the Roman squabbles in the east. The Parthians had been a pain in the Roman behind for a long time. Ever since Rome was a republic, in fact, and the situation had been tense for a while by the time Tajan walked his size nines all over them. The Parthians were an Iranian/Persian empire and were based mostly in Iran and Iraq, with the capital being Ctesiphon, in Iraq on the Tigris.

The Parthians were no joke, and generally, when they and the Romans weren't fighting, they used buffer kingdoms to make a bit of space between them. Armenia was one of these buffer kingdoms, and the general rule was that whoever ruled there had to be acceptable to everyone. Trajan got a bit upset when the Parthian king, King Osroes I, decided to put his brother Parthamasiris on the throne of Armenia without the Romans giving him the nod.

Trajan, and his army of about 80,000 men, set off for the Middle East. When he got as far as Athens, Osroes sent envoys to try and organise a peace, but Trajan didn't fancy that. He arrived in Armenia in January 114 and turned the kingdom into a Roman province. So, no more buffer state and no more making sure everyone was happy. It was all Roman now. From there he kicked on straight into Parthian territory, taking the major cities of Ctesiphon and Babylon, before reaching near Kuwait on the Persian Gulf. And that's as far as he got.

It is worth saying that while Trajan was knocking about as far as the Persian Gulf, it's not like he made the area into proper 100% Roman-controlled provinces. It was a bit nearer to what Agricola achieved in Scotland than that. The Romans were that deep into Mesopotamia for longer than Agricola, and the Romans, were in Scotland, but not by a lot. Part of the problem is people kicking off behind Trajan back in the Roman provinces.

This time the problem was again the Jewish population of the Roman Empire. The uprisings earlier in the century, which were put down by Vespasian and Titus, had ended. However, there was still ill-feeling there, not least because of the way the uprisings had been dealt with and the discrimination they faced from subsequent emperors. Oddly enough, the problems didn't come from Judea, or anywhere in that region. Instead, it kicked off in the province of Cyrenaica, which is a part of Libya in North Africa and goes to show how widespread Judaism was.

The revolt spread from there to Egypt and up the Middle Eastern provinces. The sources are a bit sketchy on this conflict, known as the Second Jewish-Roman War, or Kitos War, named after one of the Roman generals who fought it. The problem is that the Romans weren't fans of the Jews, and they wrote the sources we have. We have always quite liked the way Dio writes about things, but he does show flashes of things which make you more than a bit less inclined to enjoy his writing. In this case, he said of the Jews involved:

'They would eat the flesh of their victims, make belts for themselves of their entrails, anoint themselves with their blood and wear their skins for clothing; many they sawed in two, from the head downwards'

That description is hard to buy, but its undoubtedly true that it was a brutal fight. The numbers of non-Jews who died during the revolt is put in the hundreds of thousands, with more than 200,000 dying just in Cyrenaica. On the Jewish side, they didn't fare a lot better, since they obviously lost. Hundreds of thousands were dead, and you can assume the ill-feeling between both sides carried on for a bit after.

This all happened between 115-116, and in 117 Trajan died in Turkey, travelling back from the Middle East to Rome. He cast a pretty long shadow on history, and the sources from the time were falling over themselves to tell us how great he was. He even managed to secure a nice tidy succession...maybe.

Hadrian

We all know Hadrian, he of whacking great wall fame. Luckily for this chapter, he did a bit more than that during his 21-year reign, from 117 to 138. We did say that Trajan secured a smooth succession for Hadrian, but that might not be true. It's possible that Trajan didn't adopt Hadrian as a son until he was on his deathbed. There is also a story that he didn't even do that. In this version, Trajan's wife, Pompeia Plotina, hid the fact that Trajan had died for a few days to give her time to forge some documents that declared Trajan's intention for Hadrian to be emperor. Dio certainly reckoned the story that Trajan wanted Hadrian to be emperor was a load of old bollocks. However, we like that Trajan's wife might have been part of a conspiracy while being called Plotina.

Hadrian was in Syria, where he was governor, while everyone was trying to organise Trajan's succession. We have seen enough of these to know that a questionable succession, with the leading candidate not being either in Rome, or where the recently dead emperor was, is a recipe for at best some assassinations, and at worst a civil war that wrecked the whole empire.

Luckily for Hadrian, Syria had more than its fair share of legions, so when the army there declared Hadrian emperor it was pretty much a done deal.

If we were going to summarise Hadrian, he was the geek to Trajan's all guns blazing classic Roman emperor. We know that he set up Hadrian's Wall as an obvious limit to Roman expansion, but that was the least of it. Right at the beginning of his reign, he pulled back in the east. Trajan had got to the Persian Gulf, but Hadrian pulled back to the Euphrates River, which put a serious dent in the Roman gains. He also pulled back to the Danube, not in Dacia, but on the lower Danube, and set up defences all along his border there.

It's a bit boring but considering the effort (and money) the Romans had been spending on these borders in Eastern Europe and the Middle East, you can't fault it. Something else you can't criticise is his approach to his empire. He saw a lot of it and travelled about more than the sons and daughters of a tech millionaire in their gap year. Hadrian's first big trip was in 121, only four years after he got the job. He travelled up through Central Europe (through Slovenia, Austria) into Germany and France, before stopping in Britain in 122, and heading back down to Spain. Then he was off to Greece and Turkey, before stopping back home in Rome in 125. Another trip took in North Africa, the Middle East and Greece again before returning to Rome. Again, there was another trip through the Middle East, Greece and Eastern Europe, before getting back to Rome in 132. This was not normal for emperors. Even Trajan only usually travelled when someone needed a kicking. Hadrian wasn't fighting anyone; he was just having a look about the place.

His actual itinerary is a bit vague, but you can follow the bloke about by all the buildings he left behind. Roads, aqueducts, temples, walls (obviously), he had a lot of stuff built, so his name is on things all over the place. One building of his we particularly like, the wall apart, is the Pantheon. It's a temple built in the middle of Rome, with a great big circular hole in the ceiling. Now, that is a crap description for a seriously impressive building. We are sure if you have been to Rome, you will have been in, but if you ever visit, put it on your todo list. Trust us, it's not just a room with a leaky ceiling.

Hadrian really was a massive geek, with his sensible borders, impressive architecture, and love of the Greeks with their fancy philosophy. He did, however, get himself into some classically Roman military scraps. He had been the governor of Syria at the time Trajan was fighting the uprisings of the Second Jewish-Roman War, so he wasn't exactly a complete stranger to Roman warfare. Apparently, a major part of his tours was taken up with inspecting defences and spending time with the army. He also wasn't a stranger to the anger the Jewish population had to the empire. Which makes his approach to the region around Jerusalem, more than a bit odd.

On one of his tours around the Middle East, he decided the best way of solving the issues between Romans and

Jews was to Hellenize the Jewish. Meaning he wanted to make them more Greek - the Greeks call Greece, Hellas, or the Hellenic Republic. This was in 131, so not a very long time since the significant uprising in 115-117. Hadrian's new policy towards the Jewish involved rebuilding Jerusalem, which had been wrecked since the Great Jewish Revolt in 66-73. That would be a good idea usually, but obviously, Hadrian would want it done in his own style as a Roman colony. That included a new name, Aelia Capitolina, with a temple to Jupiter (the Roman god, who the planet is named after) where the Temple of Solomon was (an incredibly significant Jewish temple). He also banned circumcision and put a Roman legions insignia on one of the gates in the city. That last one would presumably have been fine if the insignia hadn't been a boar. Pork isn't kosher, and the symbolism wouldn't have been lost to the people in the region. Although, it's possible that it wasn't true and instead Hadrian wasn't using the symbol of a legion, and he put up a statue of a pig specifically to mug off the Jews of the city. You get the impression that if Hadrian had been born 2000 years later, he would have added swastikas to the decorations. Why is it every time we find an emperor we start to quite like, they either turn out to be massive anti-Semites or marry very close relatives?

You will never guess what happened after this very kind attempt to rebuild a city. The people that Hadrian was specifically targeting, and insulting got angry and kicked off another revolt in 132. Obviously. This was known as The Bar Kokhba Revolt. Named after the Jewish leader Simeon Bar Kokhba. It was no little uprising, and it involved Hadrian calling one of his top generals, Sextus Julius Severus, from Britain to Judea. The fighting was guerrilla fighting, rather than open battles, which makes sense from the Jewish perspective, as not many could beat the Romans at their own game. The fighting lasted the best part of four years and sounded as brutal as all the Roman-Jewish conflicts were. According to Dio:

'Five hundred and eighty thousand men were slain in the

various raids and battles, and the number of those that perished by famine, disease and fire was past finding out.'

The Romans liked inflated numbers, but either way, you can assume the death toll was massive, and the Romans didn't come out of it lightly either. It ended with Judea, the province, being renamed Syria-Palaestina, and Jews being kicked out of the area.

From a Roman point of view (and very much not from a Jewish point of view), Hadrian's reign must have been relatively calm. I reckon he would have been one of the better emperors to live under, certainly nowhere near the worst. Still, he wasn't always popular. As Dio says:

'Hadrian, though he ruled with the greatest mildness, was nevertheless severely criticised for slaying several of the best men in the beginning of his reign and again near the end of his life'

The slayings early on included some important men, who had plotted his assassination, presumably because he was busy undoing the work or Trojan, who everyone was a big fan of. Hadrian also used the trick of promoting men outside of the top echelons of society. This no doubt made for a smoother running of the empire but will have pissed the Senate off no end.

For proof over how pissed off the Senate was, is how they dealt with his death. The succession was nice and smooth. Hadrian had no sons, and while he picked a few heirs who he outlived, he ended up choosing fellow wall fan, Antoninus. So, no civil wars, no burning down of Rome. And yet, when Hadrian died, the Senate voted for 'damnatio memoriae', as in damning his memory, and having the records of him removed. Antoninus fought to avoid that kind of thing and even got Hadrian deified, as happened with most of the emperors. We quite like that not only did Hadrian not end up with a bad name, or indeed have it wiped from the record, but his name is, in Britain at least, scrawled across maps in big letters.

We aren't sure he was a nice bloke. For a start, even for the time, he was wildly over the top antisemitic. However, he probably rounded off the last three emperors quite nicely - the sensible old man, put in place to stop the madness, the mad empire-building military man, and the geeky builder. For Rome, and the ancient world, there had been plenty worse before, and a lot worse to come.

Ireland

Something you might have noticed for far in this book, so far, is that there had been sod all mention of Ireland. That does feel like a weird omission will admit, but you can blame the Romans. For most of British history, Great Britain (the island with England, Wales and Scotland on it) has been tied up with Ireland (the island with The Republic of Ireland and Northern Ireland on it) It's not typically been in a mutually beneficial way, but linked we are. In this case, however, when Britain got dragged kicking and screaming out of prehistory and into history, Ireland got left alone. The Romans never invaded Ireland, which we suppose does make some sense, as they have struggled to get hold of the whole of Britain, so they probably didn't need to add angry Irishmen into their problems.

That's not to say that the Romans never got to Ireland. It was an empire that never missed a trick when it came to making a few quid from trade, so they didn't completely ignore the island. At the end of the 1st century, Tacitus gives the Irish a mention:

'the interior parts are little known, but through commercial intercourse and the merchants there is better knowledge of the harbours and approaches'

Then there is Agricola, the governor of Britain, who reckoned that it would be a piece of piss to take and hold Ireland. We know he was a beast of a general but considering just how long it took to get half of Britain under control, it's hard to see Ireland being a lot easier. So, the Romans were at least thinking about it.

We have previously mentioned the Roman geographer Ptolemy, who drew a 'world map' in the 2nd-century. It's a hell of a map, as far as we can see from the reproductions we still have, and luckily it includes Ireland. And to be fair to Ptolemy, he does a decent job of the outline of the island. Quite a bit better than with Britain, although it does look a bit like someone has squeezed it a bit. For someone to have such a clear idea of what Ireland was shaped like, the Romans must have been used to sailing around it.

As with Britain, Ptolemy lists the tribes in Ireland at the time. The whole setup was very similar to the tribes we have already met on the other side of the Irish sea. Although, these tribes/small kingdoms were known as tuatha. It wasn't until much later that tribes started to amalgamate into larger groups, which eventually led to a united Ireland centuries later.

The Celts of Pre-Roman Britain and the Celts of Ireland shared a lot of the same sort of characteristics. For example, like a lot of Europe before the Romans, both islands spoke Celtic, but the Celtic languages of the British Isles developed separately from the continental versions. British Isles Celtic is known as 'Insular.'

Other similarities in the British Isles include the living arrangements. Roundhouses were the standard type of house over here, whereas the continent tended to go for more standard looking rectangle efforts. We also both built a lot of hillforts. These are roughly what they sound like. They were defensive structures that were usually built on a hill, and they were handy for keeping safe in when dodgy folk were about. This wasn't just a British Isle thing, but it's safe to say we really liked a hillfort over here. The remains of some of these are very, very cool. For a good example of an Irish hillfort, have a search of Dún Aonghasa. Our favourite one, because we are now the sort of person who has a favourite Iron Age hillfort, is Maiden Castle in Dorset. It's absolutely massive.

If the concept of Iron Age hillforts has piqued your interest, then Oxford University, along with Edinburgh and Cork, have created an online atlas showing all the hillforts that have been discovered in both Britain and Ireland. It's worth a look - search 'online hillforts atlas oxford' to find it. What it shows is that, if you are in either Britain or Ireland, you are almost certainly near a hillfort that you probably didn't even know about.

Ireland would remain a bit more mysterious than Britain until things from the island started to get written down. This happened when Christianity started being widespread in Ireland, in the 5th-century. Monks loved to jot stuff down, which is a massive win for modern historians. The new religion spread to Ireland a lot slower than in Britain because it had been the Roman Empire doing the spreading. The story goes that it was St Patrick who introduced Christianity to the Irish, but he was probably a bit later. In 431 a Bishop from Gaul, who had been reposted to Britain, was sent to Ireland by Pope Celestine I, so it seems like Ireland was getting Christianity and more written records, just as the Romans were leaving Britain.

It's a bit of a shame to boil down prehistoric Ireland down to, 'they had houses that were round, and hillforts are cool,' but it's all we have space for here. Also, hillforts really are cool.

Antoninus – Two Walls Are Better than One

Emperor Hadrian died in 138. While he was a good man to know if you needed a wall knocking up, he hadn't made many friends among the posh and influential Romans during his 21-year reign. Even so, it's something we haven't been able to say too many times, but Hadrian died of natural causes. Generally, an unpopular emperor dies of Praetorian Guard, or from the scheming of a close relative. So well done Hadrian.

His replacement was Antoninus Pius, who can look a bit like a Hadrian tribute act at times. You would think after an unpopular emperor who was known for consolidating territory, the next bloke would dive in all guns blazing, just to be different. No, Antonius was pretty calm, and he didn't go in much for military action. There were, however, a few exceptions to that, and luckily for us that included another crack at Scotland. For anyone who really enjoyed the in-depth wall chat in the Hadrian chapter, we have something you might like in a bit.

In this chapter, we ask, isn't it time to just leave Scotland alone? When will emperors stop trying to look hard in front of their mates? What's the worst ever decision you have made that you have had to go back on

The Romans Back In Scotland

This is a period where we get annoyingly little information on the goings-on in Britain. There is a handy book, written by a later Roman Historian, called Historia Augusta (Augustan History), which is a history of the Emperors from 117 to 284. We should say that this particular book, even in a field of questionably accurate sources, is generally seen as more somewhere between really sketchy and absolute bollocks. However, it's occasionally all we have, so we need to trust it a bit. The Historia Augusta tells us that one of the governors in Britannia under Antoninus was a bloke called Lollius Urbicus. We know this because apparently, Antoninus:

'defeated the Britons through his legate Lollius Urbicus, and having driven back the barbarians, he built another wall, of turf.'

What the book doesn't tell us is why or how, but we can have an educated guess as to roughly what went down. Since we are now all wall experts, let's go straight to that bit. There was indeed a new wall built, and this is called the Antonine Wall. It lacks creativity, but at least you know what you are dealing with, with a name like that. This wall also stretches across Britain from east to west, but this time it is in the narrow bit between Glasgow and Edinburgh.

Construction was started in 142, which suggests that the Romans had a decent amount of control of the Britons living between Hadrian's Wall and where the new wall was going to be. To build a wall across a country, you must be pretty confident in what's behind you. In this case, behind the legions sent north to build a new wall, were all the tribes in England and Wales, as well as the tribes of Southern Scotland. That means the Novantae, the Selgovae, the Votadini and the Dumnonii were now behind the Romans and living in Roman-controlled territory. We imagine the legions preferred it when they were on the other side of Hadrian's Wall. So will have the tribes no doubt. Considering the whole history of the Romans in Britain, let alone in Scotland, it's hard to imagine many of them rolled over without at least some fighting.

We know that the Romans had been this far north before, under Agricola. It's also true that the Romans were already mooching about further north than Hadrian's Wall before this new march north. There were the forts built and manned in Southern Scotland, so Antoninus was just pushing further up on this. Plenty more forts were made in this period, and they were dotted all around Southern Scotland on both the east and west sides. They were mostly small affairs, rather than full legionary forts, holding a century of soldiers, of about 80 blokes. There was a lot to keep an eye on, and these forts popped up all over the shop, along trade routes and the like. You don't build a new wall and set up forts around the place if you aren't pretty committed to a bit of conquering. It was quite the statement of intent.

The reinvasion of Southern Scotland already sounds like hard work, but the governor of Britannia didn't get an extra legion to do this with, which means that they had to drag soldiers north. Obviously, they could stop manning Hadrian's Wall and those soldiers could be moved up, but they also emptied the small forts around Northern England. Again, you don't do that if you thought the natives would be rising up again soon. That suggests that the area below Hadrian's Wall was a bit calmer these days, or at least that the Romans thought it was worth the risk.

They also had to break Hadrian's Wall a bit because it was getting in the way. The Romans had all their cool stuff in Britannia, but all their soldiers were in the north, waiting for the cool stuff. All along the Vallum, the big ditch to the south of the wall, bits were filled in making it easier for soldiers to march north. Not that the whole set up was abandoned. The forts along the coast near Carlisle were kept up and running, which presumably means they were still worried about folk sneaking around the wall to the west.

That's honestly about it. We don't have info on big battles or which tribes were fighting back. Just that, one day the Romans were relaxing on their big wall, and then they decided to make a new wall to relax on much further north.

Why Bother?

When Hadrian built his big wall, there was at least a hint of why. A big uprising sometime before 121 meant the locals needed slapping down, at least to stop the spread of the madness going south. There's no real clue as to why Antoninus felt the need to head north and build his version. So, in place of being told the real reasons for a wall up at Glasgow, here are our guesses.

Firstly, maybe Antoninus was just making things neater. He did something similar in Germany, which was the other really dodgy border of Roman territory. There wasn't a wall like Hadrian's, mostly because that would have been an unbelievable distance to build along. The Limes Germanicus (German Frontier) stretched from the North Sea, where the Rhine flows out, down to near Regensburg in Southern Germany. That's about 350 miles long, so instead of one lone wall, it was fortified using rivers where possible and ditches with watchtowers elsewhere. Antoninus pushed this frontier out westwards, making a new version with new fortifications. We don't have a good reason for this, but it looks like it was done to make the messy line a bit neater and easier to manage.

It could be that Antoninus was pleased about making his German lines look smarter, and one day he was sitting in Rome and noticed that in Britain, about 100 miles north of their border wall, there was a much shorter gap to hold the Britons behind. Logically, it would need fewer soldiers to man a wall that was 39 miles long between Glasgow and Edinburgh than the 73 miles between Carlisle and Newcastle. Anyone who has worked in an office will recognise this style of management logic. Yes, on paper it might make sense, but the people doing the actual work, i.e. the legions in Britain/office workers, no doubt took one look it and said something like:

'Well, yeah. It is shorter, but there are the 100 miles of angry Britons who are going to fight us all the way up. Not to mention the equally angry folk, which we will have just moved in next door to. They are probably going to want to have words with us as well.'

But that doesn't matter because someone more important than them had a bright idea. We are just guessing, and it might be complete bollocks. The whole concept might just be us projecting some personal issues back 1881 years.

Another reason for moving north was to solve the problem of Britain. It sounds like the province of Britannia was as calm as it has ever been. We haven't heard anything from Wales or Southern England for ages, not since Agricola was marching about in the 80s. Even Northern England seemed a bit quieter than it had been, except for that potential revolt during Hadrian's reign. Maybe Antoninus thought that hiding behind Hadrian's Wall was just prolonging the amount of fighting in Britain. If he could move the border of Britannia north, it would be a good steppingstone to taking the whole island. That would be no bad thing. It's the same logic Julius used to invade in 55 BC when the Britons were helping the Gauls of Northern France keep up the fight.

A third reason for the move north could be one we have mentioned a few times; internal Roman politics and the need to look hard. Antoninus was no military man, and that wasn't what the ideal Roman emperor was like. Like Julius and Claudius before him, if Antoninus could give the heathens in the far north of the known world a beating, he would look well hard. We have no doubt that Antoninus really oversold the achievement of moving up to the Glasgow-Edinburgh line.

What Was This Wall Like?

What was the Antonine Wall like compared to its far more famous southern cousin? (if you can describe walls as being cousins?) It was pretty similar, mainly because there is a limit to how different two really long walls can be? We know Antoninus' wall was shorter, being 37 miles (59 km) long. Which makes sense because it's a narrower bit of Britain. It was about 3 meters (10ft) tall, although that will have varied along its length. It also had a ditch in front of it, just like Hadrian's Wall, which was up to 5 meters (16ft) deep, with a defensive mound next to it. It also had a road that ran along its south, but it doesn't look like there was anything like the Vallum which they had built at Hadrian's Wall.

One similarity between Hadrian and Antoninus' walls was that it looked like the plans changed after it was started. Initially, there were six forts built along the wall, with some of them being constructed before the wall was. Later on, more were added, to make seventeen of them of varying sizes. These forts were a bit smaller than the standard Roman forts, including those on Hadrian's Wall. All told, the seventeen of them could hold the 6000-7000 soldiers that were stationed there. So, they were small, but not that small. All this was built by the legions in Britain, with soldiers from all three of the legions being involved. As the wall was shorter than Hadrian's and used a lot less stone, it would have taken them about three to four years to build the majority of it. Clearly, we are less impressed by this wall than Hadrian's effort, but we should take a minute to acknowledge how impressive that is. The legions established a 37 miles long wall, with accompanying forts and a ditch, in four years. It took us nearly five years to replace Wembley Stadium. Admittedly, we didn't draft in the army, but the Romans didn't get to use cranes and diggers and things. Those Romans got shit done.

So why, exactly, is this wall so much less famous than Hadrian's? It's similar-sounding, and it was even built deeper in enemy territory, making it all the cooler. That's if you are the sort of person who can find 2nd-century walls 'cool' (hello). Well, one reason would be that Hadrian's Wall was used for pretty much the whole time the Romans were in Britain, whereas the Antonine Wall was abandoned in around 158. Since it had only been started in 142, it was only used by the Romans for about sixteen years. Probably the bigger reason for it not being quite as famous is that it's mostly gone. Hadrian's Wall was built in stone, or at least rebuilt in stone soon after bits of it were constructed in turf. On the Antonine Wall the forts were built in stone, but the wall itself was made of turf. That means if you go looking for it today, it mostly looks like a little, weirdly long hill, whereas you can still see the remains of a lot of Hadrian's Wall.

Back To England - Antonius Makes A Saving With A Return Ticket

As we have said, the Antonine Wall was abandoned by around 158. That is a surprisingly short time after it was started in 142. In fact, if you take it from 139, when Lollius Urbicus turned up as governor of Britannia, to 158, when the Romans went back to Hadrian's Wall, the whole jaunt into Southern Scotland lasted less than 20 years. This is longer than Agricola had, and he made it all the way to the top of Scotland. So maybe 20 years shows there was a good attempt, but it just didn't work. What makes abandoning Scotland again seem even stranger is that Agricola's gains were started under Emperor Vespasian, continued under Emperor Titus, and rolled back by Emperor Domitian. The Antonine Wall jaunt was started under Antoninus, completed under Antoninus and abandoned by Antoninus. That rules out another emperor just undoing someone else's work to make themselves look good. Antonine basically admitted the defeat of his own plan. It's a good job he was the emperor of the biggest empire in the world, and he would be made into a god when he was dead. Or people might have laughed at him.

In 158 the governor of Britannia was Julius Verus, and he started repairing Hadrian's Wall, as well as some of the forts around the Pennines, in Northern England. That makes sense, the legions were going to be moving back in, and bits of it wouldn't have been used for more than a decade. Some of it had even been broken to make it easier to march soldiers north. One thing that had been broken but wasn't fixed again was the Vallum. A lot of that had been filled in, so soldiers could get across it, but it was left alone on the march back south. Maybe Versus thought there was no point in fixing it if there was a chance the next emperor was just going to march everyone north again. That meant there was no real barrier to the south of Hadrian's Wall, to keep the natives out. In fact, the Britons were so far from being kept out, you can find the remains of a Briton village between the wall and the Vallum, at a place called Milking Gap, which is about halfway between Newcastle and Carlisle. That makes the situation in Northern England seem a bit cosier, doesn't it?

So why was the wall, and Southern Scotland, abandoned?

Before we have a crack at answering that, it's worth pointing out just how unsure historians are over all of this. At one point it was thought that the Romans held the Antonine Wall for three different periods between 142 and the 180s, with them running off back to Hadrian's Wall in the gaps. Then it was decided that it was actually two different periods that they held the wall, with the first one starting in 142 and the second one running from the mid-150s to 163.

Now it's believed it was one continuous period of Romans mooching about on the Antonine Wall from 142 to 158.

With that level of uncertainty, feel free to take what we are about to say with a massive pinch of salt, and pick the reason you like the best.

You would assume the abandonment would be because of the relentless onslaught of the Britons from beyond the wall. Or maybe because of problems from the recently beaten-down Britons living between Hadrian's Wall and the Antonine Wall. Being sandwiched between two sets of angry Britons would be a reasonable excuse to run back south. However, it doesn't look exactly like that was the case, or at least it probably wasn't because the Romans were literally chased out. The forts along the Antonine Wall seemed to be neatly dismantled and packed away, which you wouldn't bother doing if screaming Britons were running at you with swords.

There are a few hints that maybe the problem was back further south in Northern England. This would presumably have been a revolt by the Brigantes in the 150s. Something like that would make having a big chunk of your soldiers all the way up in Scotland seem a bit risky. This theory mostly comes from a reference to the Brigantes being deprived of some Genounian territory after an attack. Although historians don't take this to mean much anymore. To start with the Brigantine territory was all in Britannia, so there wouldn't have been an opportunity to give or take away land they didn't really have. Also, we don't really know what Genounian territory would even be in Britain, so the view currently is that this was talking about somewhere in Germany instead.

There is another hint that something had kicked off in Britain around that time. And, as usual, it's a coin. This coin, minted in the 150s, included an image of a subdued Britannia - a female representation, not the actual island. It's the sort of thing you might make following a big victory.

Even if that is the case, it doesn't mean the problem was in Northern England. It could have been that the Romans won a big fight up in Scotland.

The more likely reason for moving back down to the safer Hadrian's Wall is far more boring. It was kicking off over in Germany and soldiers were being pulled from elsewhere to fortify the Rhine. That might have included soldiers for Britain, which would mean fewer men to manage everything south of the Antonine Wall. We want it to be something more exciting than that, but it probably wasn't.

Not that Britannia was suddenly a pleasant, but boring, part of the empire. The 150s might not have had a big revolt, but it looks like there was some grief shortly after that. Antoninus died in 161 and was replaced by Marcus Aurelius. He was emperor from 161 to 180, and he probably had some problems in Britannia. The Historia Augusta claims that soon after Antoninus died a new governor was sent to Britannia, Calpurnius Agricola (that's obviously not the same as the real Agricola, this one is, at best, a tribute act). Apparently, he was sent to Britain to sort out some hostilities which had broken out. We know that he was knocking about the Lake District and around Lancashire, in North West England, along with some cavalry he had brought with him from Germany. That suggests that any grief was centred around there, which isn't too surprising. However, there isn't any proper evidence for this being a real thing. Or even, if there was a revolt, how big it was. It could have just been a small group of Britons roaming about causing trouble.

There was a similar story in the 70s when some extra soldiers were sent over. Marcus Aurelius had some severe problems in the east, and along the Danube, however, he still felt the need to send 5500 Sarmatian cavalrymen from around the Danube to Britain. We aren't exactly sure where they were immediately posted when they got to Britain, but we do know some of them were, at one point, in a place called Ribchester, which is in Lancashire, near Blackburn.

That could mean that there was a big problem in Britain that needed solving. However, historians are keen to put a dampener on that. These Sarmatian soldiers had been drafted into the Roman army from the region around the Danube. That was where the real trouble was, so it might have been convenient to send them a long way from home, where they couldn't join in with any anti-Roman scrapping.

If we could pause again for a second to just look at these Sarmatian cavalrymen. Sarmatians were people of Iranian origin who, over hundreds of years, had migrated west from Central Asia through Russia and were now causing the Romans problems around what is now Bulgaria and Romania. 5500 of them had been sent to Britain for a bit, to hang about in Blackburn. Obviously, that happened across centuries, but it's still crazy to think how connected all those areas were considering how long ago it was. That stuff continues to blow my mind.

This whole period is a bit disappointingly vague, and, considering it involved heading up into Scotland and back, it was missing a certain spiciness we have come to expect with Roman Britain. Don't worry, though, it all kicks off again from 180, as we will see in the next Roman Britain chapter.

So, what have we learnt? Just because the cool kids are building walls, doesn't mean you should. Building out of stone is better than building out of mud, which is a solid tip for any little piggies reading this. And the Romans really needed to let go of the idea of conquering Scotland.

Antoninus & Aurelius

We have spent some time with Antoninus and his wall. This particular chapter is a bit of a mixed bag, as we move from one of the most boring emperors of the Roman Empire and straight into a couple of full on co-emperors.

Antoninus

We said in the previous Roman history chapter that Hadrian was geeky (boring) compared to the warmongering Trajan. However, the next emperor, Antoninus, who ruled from 138 to 161, made Hadrian look like a rock star. A rock star who moonlights as a stuntman. It seems almost traditional for history books to start chapters about him by saying how boring he was. Which was quite annoying, but honestly there isn't a massive amount else to say.

He became emperor smoothly, without even a hint of a scandal of forged papers, or angry senators. We know he had a go at expanding in Britain and built his wall, but that was close to the sum total of the military shenanigans we know about. He ruled for 23 years, so were some hints of trouble, like in North Africa and the Middle East, but nothing even close to what you would expect to see.

Apparently, Antoninus was also sensible with his money. He supported people during problems, like when another fire happened in Rome. He also was very particular about not putting too much of a tax burden on the provinces. You can't fault that, generally people are much less likely to join an armed insurrection that kills hundreds of thousands if they have a few quid in their pocket.

He is even called Antoninus Pius. A name he picked up from his loyalty to Hadrian in the face of the Senate wanting to rubbish his memory. His wife, Faustina the Elder, died in 140 and Antoninus seemed to be really upset by that, having her deified and building a temple in her name. He didn't remarry after that, although he did live with a woman. Most emperors have had a couple of wives before they even get the top job. Not Antoninus. There's nary a sniff of matricide, fratricide, or patricide - in fact, there was no dead relatives, assassination plots or anything. No genocides, no back to back treason trials. None of it. Just solid fiscal planning and sensible building programmes. We are starting to think he would have had to have a lie down after even thinking about ordering troops into Scotland.

Even his succession was all sorted. Hadrian had given him the job, on the basis that Antoninus adopted two lads, called Lucius and Marcus, as his sons and heirs. Antoninus was 52 when he got the job, so it made sense to have the next generation lined up. Although it probably wasn't necessary, as Antoninus lived until 74 when he died of natural causes. Which, in itself, is crazy. Pretty much every other emperor, who had two young, ambitious young men in the queue behind him, would have been poisoned well before he was that old.

What can we say, Antoninus was almost definitely the best emperor so far to live under, but he doesn't give you a lot of wiggle room when writing a history of him 1859 years later.

Lucius and Marcus - BFFs?

If you missed all the standard emperor activities with Antoninus, don't worry, Lucius and Marcus get involved in all that stuff. These two took over the emperorship as co-emperors, although it's fair to say that Marcus Aurelius Antoninus was the head emperor. He was nine years older than Lucius and was 40 when he got the job. Although Dio makes him sounds a lot older than that:

'Marcus Antoninus, the philosopher, upon obtaining the throne at the death of Antoninus, his adoptive father, had immediately taken to share his power Lucius Verus, the son of Lucius Commodus. For he was frail in body himself and devoted the greater part of his time to letters.'

Whatever the reason, Marcus demanded that Lucius got all the trappings of being an emperor along with him. And as Dio suggests the split was that Marcus was the numbers man and Lucius was the military man. Dio wasn't just being kind to Aurelius, he was literally a philosopher. His book, Meditations, is a classic text on Stoicism and covers Marcus' view on how to live life. No doubt he was a clever bloke.

In the split between the pen and the sword, luckily for our new military-style emperor, the world woke up, and Lucius had some fighting to do. In fact, it was a bit of a return to form for the Romans after the calm Antoninus year. It kicked off both along the Danube and in the East.

The problem to the East was Armenia again. The Parthian king, Vologases III, had invaded and installed his own bloke as in charge, which is very deja vu. So, in 162, Lucius was sent over that way with some legions to sort things out. And sort it out he did. In fact, Lucius pulled a bit of a Trajan and kicked the Parthians out of Armenia and Syria, before following them into Iraq. He attacked and destroyed the major settlement of Seleucia, which is near Baghdad. He then went one step further and made it into Media, which is a region in north-western Iran. That is a pretty decent achievement for a Roman emperor, and he got the title Medicus (like Britannicus in Britain)

The problems back in Europe kicked off while all this happened and were probably more concerning to the co-emperors. Tribes from further east had been migrating into Ukraine, Poland, and Russia. This was causing problems for the tribes that were stuck between these tribes moving west and the Roman Empire. Being caught between a rock and a hard place, a lot of tribes decided to take advantage of the Romans legions being as far away as Iraq and started moving over the Danube. They went as far as attacking Northern Italy and having a go at Venice, which must have been far too close for comfort for the Romans.

This kerfuffle over the Danube kicked off in 166 and is called the Marcomannic Wars, after one of the Germanic tribes involved. You would imagine that the Romans would channel their inner Trajan and give them all a kicking. There was a slight problem with that, in the shape of a plague. This plague was a particularly bad one, and the famous Roman doctor/philosopher, Galan described the symptoms as including diarrhoea, high fever, and pustules. And death, in a lot of cases. It's generally assumed this plague was smallpox. The death toll may have been in the millions, and it completely ruined a lot of towns, cities, and crucially, the Roman army. You would assume an army marching back from Asia to Eastern Europe in the 2nd-century wouldn't be the most hygienic of groups. The plague lasted 15 years or more and could have wiped out as much as 10% of the Roman Empire.

Plague and barbarians weren't the only problems Marcus and Lucius had. In 186 the co-emperors met up to take on the Germanic tribes, but Lucius got ill and died. He was only 38. It's possible he got the plague or was just ill, but there is a claim that he was poisoned by Marcus, or maybe by Faustina, Marcus' wife and Lucius' mother-in-law. There we go. That's the stuff we are expecting. It's almost comforting. To be honest, it's all rumours, but you can see why it would happen. You have the head emperor, a philosophical, well-educated bloke, in Rome, writing books and being nice and competent. While Lucius was in the East smashing up Rome's enemies, picking up a reputation as a bit of a party animal. You can certainly see a world in which the Romans decide they prefer the fun soldier over the philosopher. So maybe he had to go.

Which leaves us with Marcus Aurelius as the sole emperor of Rome from 169, and it's not fair to have him down as a boring philosopher. His reign lasted until 80, so he had plenty of time on his Todd, and he spent a lot of that scrapping. That year he was straight back up north to deal with those pesky Germanic tribes.

It wasn't a simple fight because there were numerous tribes causing problems. The Romans certainly had some setbacks, like losing 20,000 soldiers in the offensive of 170. It's not important to the fate of the empire, but there is a really weird story about the running of one of these battles. The Romans, following the advice of a prophet, released two lions into the Danube. Apparently, according to this prophet, that would result in a victory in an upcoming fight. Unfortunately, the lions were clubbed to death by barbarians when they reached the other side of the river. The Romans proceeded to get hammered by the tribes in the battle. The prophet managed to escape the punishment he was obviously due by claiming that he hadn't specified which side would win. There is a man who would if he were alive now, have a premium rate phone number.

Despite that mental attempt at winning, Marcus did see some gains in the war. The Marcomanni tribe, who the whole set of wars was named after, accepted peace, and Marcus got himself the title Germanicus. There were still plenty of other tribes causing trouble, but Marcus was forced to take his eye off the ball when it went wrong in the East again.

This time, however, you can't blame the Parthians for Rome's eastern problems, and it was the Romans kicking up a fuss. In 175, a bloke named Avidius Cassius popped up and had himself declared emperor. Apparently, a rumour went around that Marcus had died, and Cassius decided to jump the gun. It was a move that was potentially very bad for Marcus. Cassius had been the man who had done a lot of the legwork for Lucius in the war against the Parthians, so he was no slouch. Marcus had put him in charge of the whole of the eastern provinces, including the crucial province of Egypt. That meant Cassius had a serious number of legions under him.

In the end, Cassius' revolt came to nothing. Marcus set off to put him down, but luckily before he got there one of Cassius' own soldiers killed him. For some more juicy Roman imperial rumours, it has been suggested that Marcus' wife, Faustina, was involved in the rebellion. The same Faustina who was implicated in Lucius death. She died while Marcus was travelling east to fight the revolt, and the rumours are that she committed suicide when she heard Cassius' was dead. Historians generally assume that it's a load of old bollocks, but after Antoninus, we want to get stuck into that sort of stuff.

It was around this time that Marcus started including his son, Commodus, in his activities, and he put a lot of effort into making sure the army liked him since he was the heir. Commodus was made co-emperor in 177, at the age of 16.

The end of Marcus' reign was filled up with the problems on the Danube, with hostilities properly kicking off again. In the end, he was doing ok against them and was pushing his armies back into barbarian territory. However, he died in 180 before he could finish the job, and he left the place in the care of his son Commodus, who is our next emperor.

The end of Marcus Aurelius was the end of the Five Good Emperors - Nerva, Trajan, Hadrian, Antoninus and Marcus Aurelius. To be fair to the five of them, the empire had done very well, and they really put a limit on the insanity you come to expect from Roman emperors. The general view of the Roman Empire is that the death of Marcus Aurelius was a bit of a watershed, and it was all downhill from here. The Roman writers of the time certainly fell over themselves to tell everyone how great Marcus Aurelius. The end of those sensible emperors was a bugger for the Romans but is good for us because there is some absolutely mad shit on the way.

The Kushan Empire

One region that was just a little bit too far for the Romans to threaten was the region of Northern India, Pakistan, and Afghanistan. It was around this time, in that region, that the Kushan Empire was at its peak, under their great king, Kaniska. There are some arguments about it, but historians reckon he became king in either 78 or 127. Either way, he was pretty influential.

The Kushan were descendants of the Yuezhi, a group who had dominated Central Asia in the 2nd century BC. They had settled down in the region, and one of the kingdoms they split into became the Kushan, who went on to do very well for themselves. They made a lot of money based on where they were in the world. There were the Persians next door, with the Romans and the Greeks further west than that, and to the east, they had the Chinese. In fact, the Kushan seemed to be relatively open culturally, which makes sense if they were surrounded by that lot. We can get an idea of their influences from their coins which have been found to include all sorts of gods on them: Roman, Greek, Iranian, Hindu, and Buddhist.

Of those sorts of gods, one of the sets you will be most familiar with will be Hindus. Hinduism had been up and running in the Indian subcontinent for a couple of thousand years by this point. It's not what we want to talk about but, considering this is a religion followed by as many as a billion people, it's mad how old it is.

However, what we wanted to talk about was Buddhism. Buddhism is a religion that most people in the UK have a vague idea of, but not the specifics, and almost certainly not the history. It's probably because we are much more likely to know a Christian, or Hindu, or Muslim, but most of us won't know a Buddhist. Saying that, we are sure you have a fair image of what a typical Buddhist is. In our mind, it would be a Chinese or Thai person, certainly someone from that part of the world. Odds are that is right, but Buddhism actually started in India.

The Buddha, whose teachings Buddhism are based on, was from Nepal, just north of India, and he lived sometime around 500 BC. By the time of Kaniska and his Kushan Empire, Buddhism had spread across the whole of India and was drifting further out. The main reason we have called Kaniska influential was because of his role in moving the religion out much quicker to the east. Kaniska was a big supporter of Buddhism, having convened one of the big Buddhist councils to get all the big thinkers of the religion in one place.

Like a lot of famous secular leaders of nations who were big into religion, Kaniska and his Kushan did also dabble in the more practical side of empire building. Meaning they were also typical ancient peoples, which meant war and conquering. To that end, he took control over city-states between northern India and China, including the city of Yarkand which is in modern China. Between this and the extensive trade between India and China, Buddhism spread out and reached China sometime in the 2nd-century. Kaniska is credited with a lot of that, and in that way, an empire most people haven't even heard of influenced one of the world's major religions. We think that's worth a little mention.

Romans In Britain Go Mad & Join In With Wizard Wars

In our last few Roman Britain chapters, we have had the Romans go in and out of Scotland, a couple of big walls and some vague suggestions of the Britons kicking off again. Now we have reached 180 and Commodus was now the sole emperor, after being made co-emperor with Marcus Aurelius in 177. You might have come across Commodus before. Even if you don't remember him, you might recognise someone he knew; Maximus Decimus Meridius. Maximus was a father to a murdered son, husband to a murdered wife. No? Well, he was going to have his vengeance, in this life or the next, which turned out to involve seeing off Commodus.

Gladiator. It was a good film, but definitely fiction rather than a documentary, so you can ignore all that.

In this chapter, we are asking ourselves; how often do you actually feel sorry for management? Was there ever a problem that Roman Britain didn't want a piece of? And would ancient history be better if everyone was a wizard?

More war in Britain?

Sometime around 180, it kicked off in Britain. Exactly when that was is a bit of a mystery. Again. I suppose we are lucky that there are sources which talk about it at all, but they are annoyingly vague. Cassius Dio claimed that, for Commodus, his...

> 'greatest struggle was the one with the Britons. When the tribes in that island, crossing the wall that separated them from the Roman legions, proceeded to do much mischief and cut down a general together with his troops, Commodus became alarmed but sent Ulpius Marcellus against them.'

Considering how vague a lot of Roman comments about Britain are, that's a pretty handy quote. We know the Britons were a pain in the arse for Commodus, which almost goes without saying at this point. We also know that the problem was the Britons living on the other side of the wall. We can assume that's Hadrian's Wall, but the Romans still had forts north of that so it could have been the Antonine Wall. Either way, the problem came from the Britons in Scotland. We know a Roman general was killed, so the Britons weren't messing about, and that Britannia got a new governor who was sent to sort them out.

So, what's our problem? Well, it's with the new governor Ulpius Marcellus. He was definitely the man who gave the Britons a beating after the killing of a general. But we also know that he was the governor of Britannia in 174, which is before all this. The theory is that he was governor of Britannia in the 70s and then went somewhere else for a bit, before being sent back to deal with this problem. There were coins minted celebrating a big win in Britain from 184-85, so that timeline makes the most sense. We will never again look down our noses at the stupid commemorative 50p coins the Royal Mint puts out. Clearly, occasion-based coins are really handy.

Along with our quotes and coins, we have the fact that Commodus took the title Britannicus, which is the same title Claudius gave himself when he invaded back in 43. That suggests that the win was at least impressive enough that the emperor wanted to show off with it.

We get a lot of our info on this period from Dio, and while he didn't fancy letting us know precisely what went on with Ulpius Marcellus in Britain, he had plenty to say about the man himself. He starts by saying that Marcellus was 'temperate and frugal.' That doesn't exactly make him sound fun, but there's nothing wrong with being sensible. The more Dio talks about the man, however, the more that Marcellus sounds like an amalgamation of every arsehole CEO that the more aggressive corner of Linkedin dribbles over. We are told that he didn't sleep much, which is a trope you get for politicians as well, like Thatcher, and we all know how calm she was. Dio claims that this was a natural 'ability,' which was presumably some sort of insomnia, but Dio also claimed that Marcellus trained himself for it. One way he did that was too fast, and he would never eat until he was full. This included sending for his bread from Rome. Not because he missed his mother's cooking, but because by the time it got to Britain it was stale, so he wouldn't fancy eating much of it. The man sounds like a psychopath, and like any good psychopath, it wasn't about 'bettering' himself, it was about making other folks' lives miserable. The move that really made us dislike this man, from more than 1800 years ago, was his nighttime' prank.' This involved the writing of twelve tablets, which he got his aides to deliver to different people throughout the night. Not only did it make it look like he was up and working all night, but it ruined the sleep of the people working for him. Arsehole. We have no idea why we are laying it on so hard for Marcellus, but that story upset us.

This lunatic governor (go with it) is important because it nicely sets the background for the Roman legions in Britannia getting a bit 'bolshie' with their higher-ups. For a start they mutinied against Ulpius Marcellus, presumably getting sick of feeling tired, after not being able to sleep all night, and queasy from watching a man try to eat mouldy bread. As was standard for annoyed Roman soldiers, they decided to declare one of their generals as emperor. This would have been an absolute nightmare for Priscus, the general in question. No doubt the idea of being emperor appealed to him, certainly more than marching up to Scotland to fight yet another set of angry Britons. However, his problem was that when you are going for an emperorship, a swing and a miss means being dead. It's not like missing out on a job after a bad interview and spending another weekend rewriting your CV. The emperor you tried to replace is unlikely to be forgiving. So instead, Priscus took the equally risky move of saying:

'I am no more emperor than you are soldiers'

It feels like he missed the opportunity to politely decline. Instead, he took the 'insult all these heavily armed, and already annoyed, men' route. Bold.

Priscus, and the rest of the generals, were recalled to Rome and no doubt they were given a kicking for their inability to keep control of the legions in Britain. Although we would like to think Priscus got away with it after his grandstanding. Ulpius Marcellus was also recalled to Rome and put on trial. Presumably, these charges were legalese for 'being a massive twat, unnecessarily.' He wasn't condemned, probably because he had just won that victory in Britain which we don't know much about. And because the world is cruel. People like Marcellus, usually get away with it. That's the last dig at the man, I think we are over it now.

Understandably, the leaders of Britannia got shafted over the whole mutiny thing, but what about the soldiers? We have no doubt they were given a telling off, and things wouldn't have been too comfortable over there. Luckily for the writing of this chapter, they did not learn their lesson. The officers in Britannia were still annoyed, and they chose 1,500 soldiers who were sent marching to Rome to complain to the manager. That's mental, but what's more mental is the result of it. The soldiers were met outside of Rome by Commodus, and when he asked what was wrong, they told him that they wanted to complain about a bloke called Perennis. Being a Praetorian Prefect, Perennis was a powerful man. The Praetorian Prefects developed out of the Praetorian Guard and ended up being a high-end advisor to the emperors. Not only that, but Perennis was also a favourite of Commodus and had taken a lot of power for himself. The Romans from Britain grassed him up for plotting against Commodus and claimed that they were annoyed with him because he had been appointing equestrians instead of senators to command legions. Why the Romans marched to Rome from Britannia, and why they cared how posh their commanders were, isn't 100% clear, but they definitely got lucky. Commodus executed Perennis. Actually, executed isn't quite the right term for it. That suggests a hanging or beheading, or that kind of thing. Instead, Perennis was given over to the soldiers, who killed him, along with his family. Dio takes a dim view of this, saying that Commodus:

'had not the courage to scorn fifteen hundred men, though he had many times that number of Praetorians ... Thus Perennis was slain, though he deserved a far different fate, both on his own account and in the interest of the entire Roman empire.'

So at least Dio thought Perennis didn't deserve it and that Commodus didn't have to give in to a mere 1500 men. He did have control over quite a few legions after all.

Honestly, in all the reading we have done on the Romans, this is one of the most confusing stories we came across. We really don't get what was going on here, and it happened relatively quickly. The Roman legions in Britain fell out with their governor. They then declared one of their generals as emperor, which is a dig at the governor, but also very definitely a dig at the actual emperor. The leaders in Britannia are changed, for obvious reasons, but after that, 1,500 soldiers travel to Rome. When they get there, they complain about one of the most powerful men in the whole empire. That didn't end with the 1,500 soldiers being brutally dealt with. Instead, the same emperor, who had just been mugged off, hands over the powerful man so he and his family could be killed. The legions in Britannia had lost their minds. And nobody seemed to care all that much.

As you can see, by now the Roman legions in Britain had gotten away with quite a lot of very obviously rebellious behaviour, so when a new governor, called Pertinax, arrived in 185 he was tasked with calming them down. He did not. Although to be fair, that's not entirely true. Dio did claim that he 'quelled them,' which suggests a certain level of calm, at first at least.

We know a bit about Pertinax. He has his own bit of the Historia Augusta because he ended up being an emperor. We know that he only lasted as governor in Britannia until 187, and he had been recalled at his own request because the legions didn't like him. Apparently, 'he had been strict in his discipline.' However, unlike Ulpius Marcellus, his harsh, disciplinarian ways were probably justified.

In the beginning, the Romans in Britain quite liked Pertinax, so much so that when they, again, decided to declare someone other than Commodus emperor, they picked him. Like with Priscus, who had the same thing done to him by the legions a couple of years before, Pertinax declined. This time the legions don't appear to have taken it quite as well. So much so that they kicked off, and, in the ensuing riot, Pertinax was left for dead. Unfortunately for the legions, he wasn't really dead. So, the 'strict discipline' that followed that was probably on the aggressive end of the scale. You can forgive a general being a bit tetchy with the soldiers who just tried to kill him. At the very least, some legionaries were going to have to sit through some very awkward annual reviews. In the end, Pertinax asked to be given a different job. Which was probably the best for everyone.

This whole period was just full of insane behaviour from

the legions in Britannia. Just to hammer it home again, in the space of a few years they had:

- Declared their general emperor to get rid of their governor.

- Sent a delegation of 1,500 men to encourage the execution of one of the most powerful men in Rome.

- Declared their new governor emperor and then tried to kill him, but without actually killing him.

It looks like spending so much time in Britain wasn't healthy for the Romans. The Romans might have spent more than a century Romanising most of the island, but it also looks like the Romans had caught some crazy from the natives. Having multiple cracks at the current emperor was the legion version of a tribe of Britons lining up against the Romans in a pitched battle. Just not sensible. The end of this run of mad legion behaviour looks particularly bad in hindsight when you fast-forward a few years to when Commodus was dead and Pertinax was made emperor. There must have been some worried-looking legionaries around when the news of that imperial coronation got to the north. However, it looks like Britain's Romans mostly got away with it. Honestly, this whole thing has us baffled, and we can't help but assume we've misunderstood somewhere.

By this point, the rank and file of the legions had calmed down but wasn't the end of the Romans in Britain kicking up a fuss. This time it came from the governor. This next section is a bit more Roman Empire politics than Roman Britain history, so we will give you the details in the Roman History chapter. For now, a summary will do.

When Pertinax was made emperor, he didn't live up to the expectations of the men who put him there. Mostly because he was too big into discipline, which tends to upset people. Although, they should have known he was into that by now. What followed has a sort of Year of The Four Emperors vibe, except with five emperors. Pertinax, who replaced the assassinated Commodus, was emperor from January to March 193, until he got murdered as well. He was replaced by Didius Julianus, who lasted from that March all the way up to June. Didius getting the job annoyed a lot of people and three other blokes threw their hat in the ring to be the one to overthrow him. The three candidates were: Septimius Severus, who was the governor of Pannonia, which is around Hungry, Austria, Serbia, Pescennius Niger, who was based over in Syria, and finally, Clodius Albinus, who was the governor of Britannia.

It's essential to stop at this point and discuss a significant point. Have you ever heard of three people who sounded more like characters from Harry Potter? Septimius, Pescennius and Clodius Albinus? This was less the 'Year of the Five Emperors' and more the 'Wizard Wars.' Unfortunately, it's not likely that name will be catching on with proper historians.

Our Britannia candidate, Albinus had been governor since around 192. So, he had been around for a couple of years while this madness was unfolding. All three governors who had thrown their hat in the ring were in relatively strong positions, but Severus had the edge. He was nearer to Rome, so he got there first. Since Severus had snapped up the support in Rome, his strategy was to make friends with Albinus while he fought against Niger. In order to make friends, an agreement was made to make Albinus a caesar, while he took the title of augustus. Augustus was a title used by the Roman emperors, taken from Augustus (the bloke who was the first proper emperor). Caesar was used similarly, but it became a title for the junior member of a partnership and the 'emperor designate'. Think of it like augustus = the Queen and ceasar = Prince of Wales. Albinus was happy with this, it meant he had some power, and he was next in line. He was also able to mint his own coins and put up statues of himself, which seemed to be a major perk of being an emperor. He was content to stay at home in Britannia and wait for his turn. That left Severus free to beat

Niger in 194, before making himself comfortable in Rome.

Unfortunately, it became increasingly evident that Albinus had been taken for a mug, and that the next emperor was going to be a son of Severus. Despite that, Severus was definitely worried about Albinus. Not only were the legions in Britannia a decent force, but Albinus was from a posh senatorial family, so he would have support in the Senate. Unfortunately, that made it harder to get rid of him, and Severus had no good excuse to kick off a war since Albinus had bought the pretence that he was a proper Caesar. We are told by Herodian that Severus' plan was to send some messengers to Albinus, who would either stab or poison him if they got the chance. Albinus was a bit suspicious, so he arrested the messengers and had them tortured until they told him about the plot. The Romans really were unpleasant.

The whole assassination thing soured relations a bit, so in 196 Albinus started calling himself augustus on his coins, got his legions together, and sailed over to France. Albinus had waited for so long, it meant that Severus had tied up the support of the crucial legions, and the governor from Britannia was only joined by a legion from Northern Spain (Tarraconensis). While Albinus was marching about, the governor of Lower Germany tried to stop Albinus, but he didn't manage it. Albinus winning that battle didn't do him any good, and he only got as far as Lyon before Severus beat him at the Battle of Lugdunum in 197.

We started this chapter with the Britons causing the Romans some grief and, as a nice symmetry, we will end it with some more Briton shenanigans to bookend the Romans being mad in the middle. It's another period when there is less information than you might like, but we can guess where the problems started. Albinus taking his legions over to France would have made Britannia far too tempting for the folk above Hadrian's Wall. The new governor was called Lupus, and he was probably the same boke who had been governor of Lower Germany who had been beaten by Albinus. Lupus was made governor straight away after Albinus got defeated by Severus, and it sounds like he turned up to find the traditional Britannia turmoil.

There had been a bit of a change north of Hadrian's Wall. According to Dio, the tribes had formed into two larger federations, with the Maeatae being the Britons just north of the Romans and the Caledonians living north of them. Exactly where they were is up for debate, and we assume the wall we are told they live beyond was Hadrian's, but it could have been the Antonine Wall.

Wherever they were, it looks like the Maeatae had been causing the Romans some problems. The Romans had spent a few years fighting amongst themselves, and the legions had left Britannia with Albinus and probably didn't come back with as many men as left. That meant Lupus was in a bit of trouble. Dio says:

'Because the Caledonians had not kept their promises and were preparing to assist the Maeatae, and because Severus was attending to the Parthian war, Lupus was forced to buy peace from the Maeatae for a large sum, in return receiving some prisoners.'

Which suggests that the Romans had some sort of agreement with the Caledonians to make them leave the Romans alone. It also shows what that kind of arrangement was worth, and how Lupus had to buy a bit of peace. After Lupus, there were another couple of governors, Valerius Pudens and Alfenus Senecio. We aren't exactly sure what dates they were governors, but we do know there was quite a lot of building done during the first few years of the 3rd century, so we have their names from inscriptions on buildings.

This brings us to 208, which is a pretty significant date for Roman Britain. According to Herodian, a Roman historian writing quite soon after these events, the governor of Britannia wrote to Emperor Severus and asked for more troops to help keep the natives in check. This, and for some other reasons, which we will explore in our next Roman Britain chapter, led to Severus himself turning up on our little island in person. Which is exciting.

So, what have we learnt? Well, you can't take your eye off Britain for a second. If you want to make trouble, you need to go so big that you don't even get punished. And Gladiator is a good film, but not useful when you want to know what was going on in 2nd-century Britain.

Commodus & Three To Five Other Emperors

Marcus Aurelius was the last of the Five Good Emperors, and what followed was a bit of a shitshow. Although, only in comparison to what we have seen so far. Compared to what goes on later in our story, the blokes running things in this chapter were model leaders.

Commodus

We have seen the back of Marcus Aurelius in 180, and now 19-year-old Commodus was emperor. A teenage emperor should set some alarm bells ringing. That's a lot of power for someone so young, and we have seen what can happen with Nero.

Commodus started his emperorship by stopping the offensive across the Danube and calling a peace with the Germanic tribes. That was the start of a reign which doesn't have all the usual military aspects you would usually see from the Romans. Don't worry though he more than made up for that with his domestic politics.

Commodus seemed to be pretty popular with the average Roman. He threw money about a bit, and he loved holding events, especially gladiator fights. Even took part in them, which must have been a bit of a spectacle. When it came to the view of the Senate and other posh Romans, they were a bit less impressed. For a start, they probably weren't too happy about the peace with the tribes, especially as by the time Marcus Aurelius died, the Romans were on top.

According to Dio, Commodus was:

'not naturally wicked, but, on the contrary, as guileless as any man that ever lived. His great simplicity, however, together with his cowardice, made him the slave of his companions'

Which meant he was led astray by his friends. He did seem to have a group of favourites and had them run the place, while Commodus took it easy. These favourites were mostly not 'the right sort of people.' which would have upset the senators no end. The first imperial best friend was a Greek called Saoterus. He didn't last long though, as he fell victim to the first big conspiracy against Commodus. There was an attempt to have the emperor assassinated that came from his older sister, Lucilla. She got someone to jump Commodus in the Coliseum, but the amateur assassin messed it up, which meant executions all-round, including for Lucilla.

We have already met the next bloke who took control of things, Perennis. He was the one who got the axe when the legions in Britain sent 1,500 soldiers over to Rome to complain about him. Perennis was followed up by Cleander, who was cock of the walk until 190. He made sure he did very well for himself, and seriously upset the posh folk of Rome, especially considering he wasn't 'one of them.'

In 187 there was another attempt on Commodus. A mutineer from the army tried to kill him, by dressing as a Praetorian Guard and sneaking upon him. If that sounds implausible, you aren't the only one who thinks that. A lot of historians reckon this was a load of old bollocks, and it is only mentioned by one Roman writer, Herodian.

The end of Cleander came in 190 during a protest against him. The people of Rome were angry about a famine that was impacting Rome, which is probably fair enough. Commodus gave in to the mob and Cleander's head chopped off and displayed to the angry crowd. Just to keep everyone happy. That's the second time Commodus had killed off one of his 'friends' to appease a mob.

In fact, Commodus was more than free with the executions. As Dio days:

'I should render my narrative very tedious were I to give a detailed report of all the persons put to death by Commodus, of all those whom he made away with as the result of false accusations or unjustified suspicions or because of their conspicuous wealth, distinguished family, unusual learning, or some other point of excellence..'

As in, he had a lot of people executed for all sorts of bullshit reasons. By all accounts, Commodus was a full-on megalomaniac. Here are the titles that Dio says he used when addressing the Senate:

'The Emperor Caesar Lucius Aelius Aurelius Commodus Augustus Pius Felix Sarmaticus Germanicus Maximus Britannicus, Pacifier of the Whole Earth, Invincible, the Roman Hercules, Pontifex Maximus, Holder of the Tribunician Authority for the eighteenth time, Imperator for the eighth time, Consul for the seventh time, Father of his Country, to consuls, praetors, tribunes, and the fortunate Commodian senate, Greeting'

We imagine he worked hard to fit a reference to penis size in there but didn't have the time. The mad emperor also had a literal god complex and referred to himself as Hercules. He had a load of statues built with him dressed up as the Greek hero, and son of Jupiter, which lacks subtlety.

He also renamed all twelve months of the year after himself and renamed Rome, Colony of Commodus (Colonia Commodiana). This is another example of a bloke who historians struggle against the temptation to diagnose. We still don't like doing that, but, in this case, you have to assume there was something wrong with the bloke that went well past just being a twat.

Before we finish up with Commodus, it's worth mentioning the gladiator film again. The film is obviously bollocks, Hollywood has always had a loose relationship with historical accuracy - but that's probably fine if you are just trying to make a good film. However, the thing that must have piqued their interest was real. Commodus really did lean into the Herculean heroic thing. Something which involved fighting in gladiatorial contests and putting on displays. Saying that, we 100% doubt they were competitive gladiatorial fights. For a modern equivalent of how it must have gone, find your search engine of choice and type in 'Putin ice hockey match.' We aren't joking. Do it, it's very funny.

We have quoted Dio a few times so far, and he is particularly useful for Commodus reign because he was there. Here is a quote from the man about an event he was at:

'Having killed an ostrich and cut off his head, he came up to where we were sitting, holding the head in his left hand and in his right hand raising aloft his bloody sword; and though he spoke not a word, yet he wagged his head with a grin, indicating that he would treat us in the same way.'

You will no doubt know where this is going. Anyone who upsets senators, and has them living in fear, is not going to die in his bed surrounded by family. Unless it's family members who are stabbing him in his sleep. According to Dio, he had started to really worry the people of Rome, and not just the senators, with his mad displays of cruelty. Dio claims that rumours were going around that Commodus was looking to start shooting spectators at his events. For fun. He also says that these rumours were easy to believe because:

'he had once got together all the men in the city who had lost their feet as the result of disease or some accident, and then, after fastening about their knees some likenesses of serpents' bodies, and giving them sponges to throw instead of stones, had killed them with blows of a club, pretending that they were giants'

If that happened, as Dio claimed, that is full-on crazy. Even the fact that Dio could reasonably claim it shows what people thought of him.

The end for Commodus came when the consuls of the year 193 heard he was going to have them killed. To avoid that happening they worked with one of Commodus concubines, Marcia, to poison him. When that didn't work because Commodus threw up the poison, they sent someone to strangle him to death. And that was the end of Commodus, in 192.

The Year of The Five Emperors - Severus Wins Wizard Wars

We went over the basics of what happened after Commodus died, in the Roman Britain chapter. It's crazy (if you will excuse the term) how similar the end of the megalomaniac Commodus' reign was to the end of Nero's. If ever there were two blokes to show inherited power is not the winner's choice, those two are it.

We have had the general gist of the fight after Commodus was killed, but let's go through it step by step.

Pertinax

Pertinax got the nod for the emperorship after Commodus died. He had been the Praefectus Urbis (a sort of mayor) in Rome, and he was offered the top job by the two consuls who had narrowly avoided being killed by Commodus. It looks like Pertinax might not have actually been involved in the plot, and he was just given the job afterwards. His first port of call was to head out and get the Praetorian Guard to support him, before heading to the Senate to get the job officially. The Senate was probably just glad to have got rid of Commodus. They claimed the dead emperor damnatio memoriae, so they could go about taking down his statues and calling him names without getting into trouble. Getting the Praetorians to back him was essential, as we know, and money goes a long way with that lot.

In the end, Pertinax lasted three months in the job. The Senate was still fans of his. He treated them quite respectfully and didn't raise 'unsuitable' friends above them as Commodus had. Pertinax's problem was that while he had got the Praetorian guard onside initially, they weren't really feeling his approach. Pertinax was still the same stickler for rules and discipline he had been in Britain, which meant less fun and money for the soldiers. They immediately tried to replace him with a senator called Falco. Pertinax got away with it, and even though he caught them all red-handed, he didn't execute Falco. He did execute a few Praetorians, which is only fair. Clearly, Pertinax was a man with a death wish when it comes to this sort of thing. Did he learn nothing from the legions in Britain?

In the end, Pertinax was killed when hundreds of Praetorians stormed his house and killed him. Once again, the Praetorians proved they were just about the most important people around.

__Didius__

The Praetorians had always been a bit barefaced when it came to them making a profit. When a new emperor got the throne, he gave them a 'donative', which was usually a payment of a sizable chunk of cash for each man. It was basically a shakedown, and part of Pertinax's problem was that the figure he gave the Praetorians was too low - 12000 sestertii vs 20,000 when Marus and Lucius got the job.

What happened when Pertinax died tipped this donative from extortion wrapped in tradition into full-blown profiteering from a whole empire. While the Praetorians were busy parading the head of Pertinax on a spear, two blokes claimed they wanted to be emperor. What the Praetorians did with that was hold an auction, and the one who paid them the most money got the job. Apparently, Didus offered 25,000 sestertii for each man, while the other bloke only went up to 20,000.

Money Bags Didius only lasted from the end of March to the start of June 193. His problem was that, while the support of the Praetorian Guard was vital if you wanted to survive, if everyone else thinks you are a twat you are still in trouble.

As we know, three men threw their hat in the ring to replace Didius. Pescennius Niger, who was over in Syria, Clodius Albinus, in Britain, and Septimius Severus, a governor in Pannonia, around Austria/Hungary. The people of Rome made it clear they were up for a quick change of emperor, and the Senate were in some agreement. The Senate was helped along by the fact that Didius was clearly going to lose to someone. Severus, the nearest to Rome, had 16 legions from around the Rhine and Danube, so he was going to arrive sooner or later. In the end, before Severus even got to Rome, the Senate voted to execute Didius and have Severus declared as emperor.

Severus

Severus arrived in Rome a few days later and set about fixing things. Pertinax's assassins were executed, and the Praetorian Guard were all sacked to be replaced with his own men. Which is so much cleverer than bribing them.

The newly minted emperor didn't waste too much time and decided that his biggest threat was Niger out in the east. Niger had six legions, which is a notable amount, but Servus had the sixteen he had pulled from around the Rhine and

Danube. The fight was a bit mismatched, and by the middle of the 194, Niger was beaten at a battle in Turkey, caught and executed. By Dio's telling, this last battle at Issus was pretty impressive. Niger's soldiers were doing very well and had the beating of Severus, but as they were looking like winning a storm whipped up:

'They would have been completely victorious had it not been for the fact that clouds gathered out of a clear sky, a wind sprang up after a calm, and there followed heavy thunderclaps, sharp lightnings, and a violent rain-storm, all of which they had to face. This did not trouble Severus' troops, as it was at their backs; but it caused great confusion to Niger's men, since it was directly in their faces'

Dio was not particularly complimentary about our first vanquished wizardly sounding Roman emperor wannabe. Apparently, Niger:

'was remarkable for nothing either good or bad, so that one could neither praise nor censure him very much'

That wasn't the end of Severus trouble in the east, as not everyone over that way was up for giving up and having Severus as emperor. The city of Istanbul (Byzantium) took about a year to finally give in. While the siege of that city was going on, Severus entertained himself by pushing further east to have a go at the Parthian peoples who had supported Niger. He crossed the Euphrates and into Mesopotamia, to hand out a bit of a kicking.

He also handed out a beating to the Roman supporters of Niger. Although, sensibly, he didn't execute any senators, again giving off the impression he was on their side, to an extent. Instead, he just took their stuff, which would have been annoying, but better than getting killed. He also made claims that he was Marcus Aurelius' heir, which he absolutely wasn't and a descendant of Nerva. That was two emperors who were well thought of by the Romans, and certainly by the senators, so it makes sense to associate himself with them.

This tactical overture to the important Romans doesn't mean he had finished scrapping with all of them. We know that Clodius Albinus was the last remaining wizardly sounding governor who wanted power. He had been bought off with the title of caesar, but we know how that went. When Severus gave the same title to his son, Caracalla, the cat was firmly out of the bag that Albinus had been played.

After trying the failed assassination attempt on Albinus, it was war, especially since Albinus had declared himself as an augustus. The Governor of Britannia did have his three legions, and he had some support in the Senate, despite Severus' careful handling of the men there. However, three legions vs the rest of the empire was no real contest, and in February 197 Albinus was beaten at Lyon (Lugdunum).

This time Severus did go in a bit heavy-handed, and he executed about 30 senators who had supported Albinus. Which must have put a damper on the relationships there. He also started giving out more power to the equestrian class. For example, he raised three more legions and gave them to equestrian commanders, rather than senatorial one. Severus also gave the important jobs in the east, where Niger had been based, to equestrians. That kind of thing would never go down well in the Senate. However, the Senate was only one group that was important to have onside, so Severus threw a bit of love at the other two. Plenty of cash found its way to the urban poor, and he put on the events that the people of Rome loved. That was the unwashed masses sorted, but what about the most critical group? Since they had put him in the job in the first place, Severus needed the support of the army. He already had the Praetorian Guard filled with his own men, but the legions got a little something as well. Their pay was raised, and he removed the restrictions on them getting married, which is a nice touch. Although no doubt some men had been using that restriction as an excuse for a while.

From Severus declaring himself emperor to Albinus getting a beating, took four years, so it moved quickly since the scrap took in pretty much the whole width of the empire. His armies weren't done yet, however, and in 197 Severus headed back east. Where the Parthian king Vologases IV, hadn't taken kindly to Severus nipping over the Euphrates a few years earlier. The Parthians had responded by taking the border town of Nisibis, which is in Eastern Turkey. Severus took that back and sailed himself and his legions down the Euphrates and, following Trajan's example, took Ctesiphon, down near the Persian Gulf. As with Trajan and Lucius, Severus didn't keep all the territory they had won down there. Instead, the Romans just pillaged it and left most of it. However, the province of Mesopotamia was re-established, although smaller than the one Trajan had won, and Hadrian had abandoned. The Severan version was just the northern bit around Southern Turkey and Syria.

Back home, Severus did have a few problems. He gave a lot of power to one of his mates, Plautianus, who it turns out was a wrong'un. Plautianus married Severus' daughter and had designs on being emperor himself. He dabbled in a lot of persecution of important people in Rome and even started having a go at Severus' wife, Julis Domna, and his son Caracalla. Eventually, Severus had him executed and replaced with a saner man; a legal type called Papinian.

One of the hallmarks of Severus' reign was improvements to the legal system, and he spent a lot of effort putting law and order back in place, with a particular focus on the 'moral virtues' of the empire. He was a bit of a prude. We mention this because a lot of historians credit Severus' reign with a lot of the basis of Roman law, which eventually got taken on in later European periods, and is the basis for a lot of the ways we do things now. Notably, it was another thing that Severus took away from senatorial control, which must have been annoying. Historically administering the law has been very profitable for people.

We are going to end there, but we will be seeing Severus

again soon, as he is a big feature of our next Roman Britain chapter.

Samarkand

For this 'rest of the world' chapter, we are going to visit Uzbekistan, although to be honest, it's just an excuse to segue into a topic we like. Samarkand is a city in Uzbekistan, that is still there, and has a population of about 500,000. It's in a part of Central Asia that was both convenient and inconvenient for the settlement. Sitting above Afghanistan and on the way from China and Europe, via Turkey, it was in the ideal spot to make some money from trading. However, it also meant that whenever a nearby empire was growing, it was on the list to get nabbed. It is one of the oldest cities in the region and was founded in the 7th-century BC. It belonged to the ancient nation of Sogdia and became a region of the Achaemenid Empire, which was the first big Persian Empire. The Achaemenid Empire got snatched up by Alexander the Great, who took Samarkand in 329 BC. Later on, the city would be controlled by the Kushan and Seleucid Empires, and eventually became part of the Sassanid Empire. Everyone wanted a piece.

The city really was central to the goings-on in the region. UNESCO says about the city that it was the 'crossroad and melting pot of the world's cultures.' That's a touch grand, but you see where they are coming from. Part of this being a crossroads meant that the city was on a famous trade route travelling from east to west: The Silk Road. And that is what we really want to bring up here.

The Silk Road is something you might have heard of

before. It was basically a route that connected China, through Central Asia, Afghanistan, into the Middle East through Syria and connecting to Europe across the Mediterranean and through Turkey. Clearly, the idea of someone starting in Istanbul and taking something to sell all the way to China along a 4000 miles route, is a bit much. Really what happened would be someone in China would take something, like silk, to the next stop along the route. Then they would trade for something else there, and then the silk would move along the route, being passed along by different traders. This way, silk got to Europe from China, and things like wool and gold made it the other way. There have been discoveries of glassware, that was made in the Mediterranean in the 4th-5th century, in Korea. It's estimated that something made in Istanbul could be found on sale in Korea as soon as six months later.

The Silk Road wasn't exactly an official thing, but an established trade route across Eurasia. There were clearly offshoots, like the one from China to Korea at one end. The other obvious addition is goods, like spices, coming up routes from Indian and joining the main Silk Road before heading east and west. We have already seen how contact between India and China had helped spread Buddhism, so the links along the Silk Road are clearly more important than just silk and wool.

We are told that in 166 AD, around the time Marcus Aurelius was the Roman Emperor, a group of Romans arrived in China. This could have been just traders who decided to do the whole length, but some historians see it as more of an official embassy. The idea of an official political relationship between Italy and China in the 2nd-century is mental. It's things like that which make just reading about British history a bit limiting. During the period of Roman Britain, there was a connection that ran from us, at one end of the Roman Empire, all the way to the furthest reaches of Chinese merchants. Lovely stuff.

Severus Visits Britain

We have made it all the way to 208, the year of a significant event in Britain. Emperor Severus had decided to visit our little island for a rainy holiday. By our count, Britain now had been visited by three Roman emperors. Obviously, there were a few more if you count the blokes who came to Britain to do some fighting and then went off to be emperor later. The weather might be crap, but it was a decent place to make a name for yourself in the army. In this chapter, we ask ourselves: who is the worst pair of brothers ever to see Britain? Will Scotland ever be the solution to an emperor's problems? And where in Britain would make a quality setting for an ancient horror film?

Why Bother?

Like with all the other imperial visits to Britain, as well as a couple of outings by pre-imperial Julius, we can think of a few reasons for Severus to head over. As ever these reasons come in both official and ulterior forms. The official reason given was that the governor of Britannia, Alfenus Senecio, wrote a letter asking for more troops to help keep the Britons at bay. Presumably, this was the Britons above Hadrian's Wall. We can only imagine what Senecio felt when Severus decided to come himself. 'No, no. I just need some more soldiers. You don't need to come and check on us.'

There is a little bit of scepticism about this request, and it might have been a handy excuse to avoid admitting the real reasons. Dio gives us our first realistic sounding reason. Apparently, Severus was:

> 'angry at the thought that though he was winning the wars in Britain through others, yet he himself had proved no match for a robber in Italy'

The Italian robber was a bloke called Bulla, who spent a couple of years mugging off the Romans, mooching about Italy with a big group of slaves and other unfortunate folks. Severus was sick of losing in Italy and being made to look stupid. So, nipping to Britain to slap the natives about was an excellent opportunity to look hard. We can't imagine Severus needed help in that department. He had already beaten two other Roman emperor wannabes, Niger, and Albinus, to become emperor, during the Wizard Wars (a.k.a. the civil war in the Year of the Five Emperors). Still, maybe Bulla had made him look really, really stupid and going to Britain was a way to remind people of what he could do.

Beating up the Britons in Scotland might seem petty and not all that impressive on the scale of the Roman Empire, but it's worth remembering that it had been seen as a big achievement. It's easy to forget, especially for those of us living in England, that modern-day Scotland might only account for about 8% of the population of the UK, but it's pretty big. As Dio points out, the Romans only had control of half of the island. We checked, and the South Coast to Hadrian's Wall (Brighton to Wallsend) is about 473 miles and Hadrian's Wall to the North of Scotland (Wallsend to Thurso) is 417 miles. It's not quite half, but there was still plenty of the island the Romans didn't have, so taking it would make Severus look well hard. Or maybe he just liked winning wars. Either way, it could be that he was up for a bit of self-aggrandisement.

The other non-official reason for Severus packing up and heading to Britain was his sons were being stereotypical uber-rich young men. Both Herodian and Dio claim that at least part of the reason for the northern tour was that he had to take his two sons, Caracalla and Geta, away from Rome. Dio's quote on the subject of the sons is a touch damning:

'They outraged women and abused boys, they embezzled money, and made gladiators and charioteers their boon companions, emulating each other in the similarity of their deeds, but full of strife in their rivalries; for if the one attached himself to a certain faction, the other would be sure to choose the opposite side.'

Anyone who has a brother or sister will have some empathy for that last part, but if you have taken it to the levels of Caracalla and Geta, then you should seek help. The sons of an emperor misbehaving would have been embarrassing, and these two were top tier. You will see later what sort of blokes the sons were, but as a bit of a spoiler, Dio might have had a point, they were clearly colossal arseholes.

Whatever his reasons in 208, Severus packed up his family and his armies and marched to Britannia.

Severus' Great Northern Tour

In 208 Severus arrived in Britannia with around an estimated 40,000 soldiers. We imagine Roman emperors didn't travel light, and they certainly wouldn't drag themselves across Europe, from near enough bottom to top, without a few blokes. So that many soldiers being gathered isn't too surprising, but clearly, they meant business. Dio claims that the aim of the expedition wasn't just to put down the angry Britons in the north, but he wanted to conquer and occupy the whole island. Given how many soldiers were now in Britannia, this would be the largest force the Romans had sent against the people living above Glasgow and Edinburgh. Severus had come to get properly involved, and he was playing to win.

It looks like Severus and his army first went to London, which makes sense because it was a major settlement in the south of the province, and nearby where they would have landed. When he headed north, he left one of his sons, Geta, there to oversee a bit of imperial admin. Scotland was the aim, but they didn't go there directly, and the main base for the preparations was York (or Eboracum to the Romans). Which, again, makes sense as it was one of the more significant settlements on the way up to Scotland.

The preparations were extensive, and it looks like there had been quite a bit of construction activity in the build-up to this. While York was where the imperial family would be basing themselves, more work had to be done further north. In South Shields, at the mouth of the Tyne (Newcastle), there were twenty extra granaries built to go with the two that were already there. Obviously, if you have extra 40,000 men marching about, they are going to want to eat, so the granaries would come in handy for that. The Romans were getting good and set up.

Sadly, this is another occasion where the sources are a bit vague on the whole matter when it comes to what Severus actually did. We do know that this wasn't a quick blitzkrieg style attack. Severus was moving his army slowly in a massive show of force. Some Briton leaders even came to him before he got to Scotland to submit for peace, but they were told to bugger off.

Severus travelled up the east coast, following the same sort of route as Agricola had in the 80s. It makes perfect sense when you see it on a map. If you stay east, you miss a lot of mountains as you get towards the Highlands. Also, like Agricola, he used the navy to transport things northward along with the army, which is, again, a bit easier if you stay near the coast. There is evidence of the legions being around the forts on the Antonine Wall near Edinburgh. However, most of the excitement seemed to be around the Tay, near Dundee. A sizable fort at Carpow, between Dundee and Perth, was probably built at this point. That suggests the legions were comfy and weren't planning on going anywhere for a while. As with all these events, we also have a convenient coin. This one, from 209, has an image of a bridge made of boats being built across a river, with a Latin inscription saying 'crossing'. This commemorated the crossing of a British river, and it's probably the Tay, and since they bothered to make a coin, it must have been seen as a decent achievement.

So, what did Severus actually achieve? Well, he roughly matched what Agricola did in terms of distance. According to Dio he:

'did not desist until he approached the extremity of the island. Here he observed most accurately the variation of the sun's motion and the length of the days and the nights in summer and winter, respectively.'

That makes it sound like he was on holiday to see the Northern Lights, which sounds quite nice. But if this trip north was anything, it wasn't nice. Part of the reason that the sources don't give us a lot of information about the campaign was that there wasn't a lot of cool, exciting goings-on to report on. The Britons had finally put into practice what they had realised nearly 200 years previous. In England, Wales and Scotland, the natives had their best successes when they were fighting a guerrilla war, and they took their worst beatings in open battles with the Romans. This time Severus couldn't get anyone to fight fair, in a convenient Roman-style open battle, where he could march his legions about and devastate the Britons. This quote from Dio shows how the level of bad times the Romans were having:

'The enemy purposely put sheep and cattle in front of the soldiers for them to seize, in order that they might be lured on still further until they were worn out; for in fact, the water caused great suffering to the Romans, and when they became scattered, they would be attacked. Then, unable to walk, they would be slain by their own men, in or-

der to avoid capture, so that a full fifty thousand died.'

The terrain of Scotland was a bit of a pain for the Romans, and they spent a lot of time 'cutting down the forests, levelling the heights, filling up the swamps, and bridging the rivers.' But they couldn't do the Roman equivalent of paving over the whole of Scotland, so the Britons were clearly luring groups of Romans into dodgier terrain and picking off the stragglers. It's like a terrifying horror film. We have said this sort of thing before, but can you imagine being a bloke from somewhere like Bologna, in Northern Italy, and finding yourself more than 1000 miles from home, being hunted through a bog by an angry Briton? We should all be glad we weren't born 1800 years ago.

Even with the Romans losing men in such a horrendous way, Severus was able to claim a win. We are told that the Romans met the leaders of the Britons in the region and came to terms, which included the Romans getting more territory. This would have been land from around Edinburgh on the east coast, which meant territory taken from the Maeatae. That fort built at Carpow would have been the centre of Roman control in the new area they had claimed.

While we don't really know what Severus got up to during his campaign, we do know what he didn't do. He didn't build a wall. That would have been news to medieval historians though. Later Roman historians attributed the building of a wall across Britain to Severus, and that was taken as fact in the following centuries. It came from comments like this, from Hieronymus:

'There, in order to make the provinces he had recovered more secure against attack by the barbarians, he built a rampart for 132 miles from sea to sea.'

You can assume this is referring to either the Antonine Wall or Hadrian's Wall, which clearly Severus hadn't built. It's generally thought what really happened was that Severus sorted out a big renovation of Hadrian's Wall because it was a few years old by then and probably needed sprucing up. Despite those claims and the fact that Britain was on a run with massive showy walls, somehow Severus managed to restrain himself from adding a third.

After claiming a win, without even a new wall to help, Severus returned to York, but they weren't done yet. In 211 the Britons of the north kicked off again, despite the agreement the year before. This clearly upset Severus, whose orders were:

'Let no one escape sheer destruction,

No one our hands, not even the babe in the womb of the mother,

If it be male; let it nevertheless not escape sheer destruction.'

As in, 'kill them all.'

Dio reckons this less than subtle, genocidal approach united the Maeatae and Caledonians against the Romans. He also suggests that Severus go all the way to the top of Scotland, which would have had him face off against both groups of Britons. However, it was the lands of the Maeatae he had taken hold of and built forts all over. From that, it looks like the Maeatae got the party started and the Caledonians joined in when they heard about the extermination policy.

211 looked to be a bad year for the Britons of Scotland, but, for the second time, it seems like the people of ancient Scotland got lucky after initially losing to the Romans. The last time the Romans got all the way to the tip of our island, Agricola was recalled, and everyone was ordered to pull back southwards. This time the Romans' issue was that Severus died in February 211, while he was in York. The emperor hadn't been too well, and for a lot of the trip he had been carried about in a litter, so it wasn't a surprise when he died. His son Caracalla did head back north into Scotland,

but, as we will see in a bit, there were other things to do. Even if he had been bothered about properly conquering Scotland, according to Herodian, he couldn't get the army to support him as the new sole emperor. In the face of that, he came to terms again with the Britons, and the Romans pulled back south, eventually settling back at Hadrian's Wall.

The sources of the time sell this retreat from Scotland as pretty quick. It's a bit like the way they talked about Agricola. If you took it at face value, the Roman army was back on Hadrian's Wall while Severus was still warm. Historians generally reckon that Severus' sons left a general in charge to carry on securing the new Scottish lands they had claimed, and to fight off the, now extra angry, Maeatae and Caledonians. So, it looks like the Romans were up in at least the Scottish Lowlands for a while after this. Either way, the Romans did find themselves back in England before too long.

It always seems a bit odd that the Romans didn't take the rest of Britain at any point. Scotland pretty much always remained outside of the province of Britannia. It wasn't exactly all free, with the Romans having a sizable presence all the way up to Glasgow and Edinburgh for a lot of the time. However, it feels that long term, having the whole thing would have made the island easier to manage. The Romans struggled in other parts of the empire, not least around Germany, where they had near-constant issues from people at the borders of the empire. However, Germany isn't an island, so no matter how far east they pushed, at some point, the Romans would have to have set up defences against people to the east. The only other solution would have been to carry on pushing across Asia until they were eyeballing Japan, which doesn't seem reasonable. In Britain, they only had another 400 miles to go. Considering how much grief the rest of Britain had given them, maybe the Romans didn't think it was worth occupying, but surely it would have been better to do it. There was plenty to gain in Scotland, it's got lots of farmland, for example. It wasn't all swamps and mountains where you could get your legions horribly killed. You have to assume that's part of the reason the Romans had given it a really good go at least three times up to now, first with Agricola, then under Antonius and his wall and now with Severus. It's pointless to play 'what if' with history, but surely if the Romans had properly doubled down after Agricola or Severus, they could have cracked it, just like they did in Wales and Northern England. Clearly, they always just had better things to do. Speaking of which, what did the newly minted Emperor Caracalla have to do that was so important?

Unhappy Families

We have mentioned that Severus' sons were unpleasant people and that they had a big rivalry, with Dio putting it as:

'if the one attached himself to a certain faction, the other would be sure to choose the opposite side.'

This is an unbelievably mild reading of the situation. The younger son, Geta, had been left in the south while Severus and the elder son Caracalla marched north to Scotland. This was a sensible sounding division of imperial manpower. No doubt having the son of an emperor was useful for administering justice and organising things in the south. Having said that, the real reason for leaving Geta in London was that Caracalla was planning on killing him. Parents can over-react when it comes to their children, but this didn't appear to be a paternal worry that his sons' disagreements would escalate. It was an open fact that Caracalla was going to try and kill Geta, or, as Dio put it, Severus was worried about 'his evident intention to murder his brother if the chance should offer.' That's pretty chilling.

It's not important for the story, but if you are looking up this lunatic son, it's worth knowing that Caracalla's actual name was Marcus Aurelius Severus Antoninus Augustus.

Although, when he was born, he was called Lucius Septimius Bassianus. Given he had seven names to pick from, why do people call him Caracalla? It's a bit like Brazilian footballers. They have really long names, and for some of them, we just call them something else. Pele's name is Edson Arantes do Nascimento. So where did Caracalla come from? Apparently, it's a nickname he picked up after the name of a sort of cloak he started wearing. Daft as that sounds.

Fun little nicknames aside, Caracalla was a full-on psychopath. He didn't like his brother, enough that he was going to kill him, but he didn't much like his dad either. There is a borderline unbelievable story told by Dio that proves the point. To set the scene, Severus had just beaten the Britons in Scotland, and they were going to come to terms. Severus and Caracalla, along with a sizable group of influential Romans and soldiers, were riding out to meet the leaders of the Britons. Severus was out in front on his horse, as you would expect, and Caracalla rode up behind him with his sword drawn. The other Romans, spotting that he was about to stab his dad, kicked up a fuss and Caracalla didn't do it. Later on, Severus called a meeting with his son, and laid a sword between them and basically said 'go on then if you are going to do it.' And then nothing happened. Severus let Caracalla get on with being an emperor's son, an emperor's son who was already planning to kill his other son. That's some odd parenting.

When Severus died, the arrangement was that both his sons would be co-emperors. Having co-emperors was standard by this point. In fact, Caracalla had been made co-emperor with Severus in 198, and Geta got the same title in 209 - although it was very much a junior job that they had. You can see where this is going, but let's lay it out. The campaign in Scotland ended, and both Caracalla and his co-emperor, Geta, travelled back to Rome. According to Dio:

'After this Antoninus (Caracalla) assumed the entire

power; nominally, it is true, he shared it with his brother, but in reality, he ruled alone from the very outset.'

Now, the only surprising turn of events here is that Severus died in February 211 and Geta lived until December 211. We know that Caracalla was wanting to kill his brother, and Geta was a bit keen on getting in there first. Which meant that both took 'defensive measures.' It sounds like something from a film about a Mafia family going to the mattresses. With his brother guarded, Caracalla made the sneaky move of getting their mum to organise a reconciliation meeting, where Caracalla had his brother killed. That wasn't really in the spirit of reconciliation.

This wasn't all precisely about Roman Britain since the murder happened in Rome, but an important bit of it happened in Britain, so we are claiming it. It also goes to explain why the new 'co-emperors' were too busy to take advantage of their dad's gains in Scotland.

So, what have we learnt? Well, no matter how much you hate your family, it could be worse. The Romans really need to give up on Scotland. And there is such a thing as the right number of walls.

The Severan Dynasty

Severus was a decent emperor. He fought off some significant candidates for the job in the first place. Then, when Severus was in charge, he managed things well, with no major disasters. Unfortunately, he was a better emperor than he was a dad. That means we now have the rest of his dynasty, which was mostly a wall to wall disaster. Not that we are upset, that's the stuff we love.

Caracalla: 211-217

We know from our British history chapter that the two new emperors, Caracalla and Geta did not get on, and the disagreement between them ended quite quickly in Caracalla's favour. The picture of Caracalla we get from history is a bloke of the Commodus/Nero mould. He celebrated his win over his brother by getting rid of anyone even slightly associated with Geta, from the tea lady to close relatives. Incidentally, as they were brothers, that made them close relatives of Caracalla as well - a good reason not to play favourites within your family. We aren't talking about a little intimate purge, it's estimated that up to 20,000 people died during this, and the accompanying violence.

Outside his hobby of fratricide, during his reign, Caracalla fought the Germanic tribe, the Alamanni, around Southern Germany and Switzerland. This was early in his reign, and it's usually assumed that this was just him getting an early win under his belt, rather than fighting an actual threat. Apparently, it was during this that he started wearing the Germanic cape that gave him his name.

Caracalla shared all the traits from past bad emperors. He had already killed off family members, Nero style. In a Commodus style move, he also worked very hard to associate himself with Alexander the Great. At least he chose an actual mortal to mimic, but it still didn't sound healthy, with him dressing like him and taking the surname Magnus (meaning The Great). As with all these sorts of emperors, there is plenty to talk about, but we have two interesting stories we want to share, which shows how mad Caracalla was.

The first happened on a trip to Alexandria in Egypt. He apparently didn't like the locals there, and Dio reckons that was because they made jokes about the emperor and called him names. Historians tend to assume that there was some sort of disturbance there, rather than it being quite that petty. According to Dio, Caracalla visited the city, pretending that it was a typical imperial visit, gathering people together for a celebration, and then had them all killed. It sounds like it was a proper massacre with Dio saying:

'And, to pass over the details of the calamities that then befell the wretched city, he slaughtered so many persons that he did not even venture to say anything about their number, but wrote to the senate that it was of no interest how many of them or who had died since all had deserved to suffer this fate.'

The second story comes from him attacking the Parthians in 216-17. For a start, the whole campaign against the Persians could have been part of his roleplaying as Alexander the Great, but that's not the mad bit. We have mixed reports on exactly what happened, but the Herodian version is very unpleasant. There was a fight to be the leader of the Parthians, between two brothers; Vologases V and

Artabanus V. Artabanus got the upper hand, and Caracalla took advantage and organised a marriage between himself and Artabanus' daughter. Caracalla entered Parthian territories and headed to meet his new family-in-law. As Herodian tells it, they got there, and the locals were looking forward to a party:

'Abandoning their horses and laying aside their quivers and bows, the whole populace came together to drink and pour libations. A huge mob of barbarians gathered and stood about casually, wherever they happened to be, eager to see the bridegroom and expecting nothing out of the ordinary. Then the signal was given, and Caracalla ordered his army to attack and massacre the spectators. Astounded by this onslaught, the barbarians turned and fled, wounded and bleeding. Artabanus himself, snatched up and placed on a horse by some of his personal bodyguards, barely escaped with a few companions.'

Dio claims that the cause of the fighting between the two empires was that Artabanus had outright refused to let his daughter marry Caracalla. That sounds more likely, we suppose, but the outcome was the same. The Parthians took a beating.

Clearly, Caracalla was a horrible, sneaky lunatic, and he ended just like you would expect. In fact, he was assassinated by Macrinus, a Praetorian Prefect (they are still causing trouble). We are told that this happened while Caracalla was nipping off to have a piss. Which is no way for an emperor to go.

Macrinus: 217-218

There was a slight gap in the Severan family ruling the Roman Empire, when the bloke who had Caracalla killed, Macrinus, took over. He is notable as the first equestrian ever to get the job, even if he only lasted about 14 months.

His reign started badly with the whole world smelling blood and deciding to take the piss out of the Romans. The Parthians, under Artabanus V, wanted revenge for Caracalla's war and attacked. The Romans had a fight with them at Nisibis, and in the following peace treaty, they had to pay through the nose to be able to keep the territory they had in Mesopotamia. There was a similar story with the Dacians and the Armenians, who had attacked. It was a costly fourteen months.

Back in Rome, Macrinus was in trouble as well. The remaining members of the Severus family had banded together and were pushing the 14-year-old Avitus, an illegitimate son of Caracalla's, as an alternative to Macrinus. They got the backing of some of the army, and Macrinus was beaten at Antioch. He was later executed, along with his co-emperor, who was also his ten-year-old son.

Elagabalus: 218-222

So now Rome had a 14-year-old as emperor. Avitus was his name, but he is known as Elagabalus because his family were the priests of a god known over in Syria as Elagabal, which became Elagabalus. The young emperor only lasted four years, but it sounds like a pretty weird reign. The family members who had sorted out him getting the throne were female, including his mother and grandmother. This meant that these imperial women had a lot of control over things, which wouldn't have gone down too well with the macho Romans.

We also have a lot of stories about the young emperor and his sexual exploits, which isn't too surprising if you give a teenager power over a massive empire. What seemed to really upset people is how feminine and eastern the Elagabalus appeared to be. His god of choice, Elagabal, was given a temple in the centre of Rome, and there are claims he wanted to replace Jupiter as the main god in Rome with his god from Syria. He also married a vestal virgin, which as you can assume from the job title, was against the rules.

The theme of Elagabalus rule was one of out-there sexual behaviour, coupled with offending the traditional elements of Rome. He often dressed in both an eastern and a feminine way, with transvestism being the order of the day.

According to Dio, Elagabalus:

'carried his lewdness to such a point that he asked the physicians to contrive a woman's vagina in his body by means of an incision, promising them large sums for doing so'

You have to feel for the kid, that must have been some intense stuff to work through with the eyes of the world watching. However, before you start to feel too sorry for the lad, there are stories of him inviting guests to parties based on their disability. So, he would have eight one-eyed men, or eight deaf men, all in the same room to be laughed at. Even for a Roman emperor, there were some issues there.

Despite all that, in the end, it wasn't the traditionalist senators who got rid of him, but his family members who were split between supporting him or his cousin and heir, Marcus Aurelius Alexander. Elagabalus tried to have Alexander assassinated, but couldn't get anyone to do it, and eventually, the Praetorian Guard had had enough and killed him. Which is a pretty standard end to a non-standard emperor.

Severus Alexander: 222-235

Now Rome had a second teenage emperor, who was dominated by their mother, in a row. Severus Alexander, as he is known, was possibly as young as 12-13. His actual year of birth is a bit hazy, but either way, this was a child.

As an indicator of much his mam might have been in charge, when Alexander got married, his mam, Julia Mamaea, eventually had her banished to Libya. Against Alexander's wishes. If that's not enough how about the titles she was given? She was known as 'the mother of the Augustus, camp, senate and fatherland'. That's actually a reasonably standard title for the mam of an emperor, who was really influential. Later on, it was extended to include 'the mother of the whole human race.' Now, that's a mam on a power trip. It's safe to say that she was the real power behind the throne, which no doubt put some nose out of joint. Officially there was a council of 12 regents, meaning the Senate oversaw the young emperor, but as far as we can see, that was absolute bollocks.

How upset people really were with this is a bit questionable because he did manage to stay emperor for 13 years. During that time there was a major change in the east. The Parthians were done for, and a new power had raised up; The Sassanids. An early play for the Sassanian Empire was to reclaim the lands of their Persian predecessors, which meant taking over the Roman provinces in the east. So, in 230, the Sassanids took the province of Mesopotamia and mooched into Turkey. Before Alexander and Mamaea could do anything, they had to put down a mutiny by one of the legions in Egypt. In the end, by 233, the scrapping in the east was done. Technically the Romans had won because they had kept Mesopotamia. Still, it was a shambles of a victory, and Alexander, in particular, was shown to be rubbish as a military leader. Although, that's probably a bit harsh since he got the job done, especially since he also needed to deal with a mutiny in Egypt at the same time.

In the traditional double whammy, once the east was a bit calmer, the Germanic tribes kicked off as well, and in 234 Alexander went north to fight the Alamanni. While he was there, in 235, the army decided they had had enough, and they declared Maximinus Thrax, the bloke in charge of training new recruits, as emperor. Maximinus accepted and had Alexander and Mamaea killed.

We haven't been complimentary about Alexander, but he managed to rule for thirteen years, and overall, it was quite peaceful. Particularly on the domestic front. That was no mean feat, and both he and his mam should get credit for that. The end of Alexander was the start of an absolute shit show. In fact, what followed was so bad that is known as the Crisis of The Third Century. We are in for a bumpy ride for the next few chapters.

As an endnote that doesn't impact anything much, while Alexander was emperor, Dio, the writer we quoted a lot in the last few chapters, was a consul. Weirdly, he was told by Alexander that he would be best off being consul from outside of Rome, so he didn't get killed. We aren't sure why, but it looks like the historian had upset someone. He must have written something mean.

Nazca

During the end of the BC and the beginning of the AD period, South America didn't have quite the same level of city building as Mesoamerica. Which is a shame because it's the stuff we really like that tends to be in and around cities. And by stuff we mean pyramids. However, there is still plenty to look at, and we did find one South American culture that we thought was very interesting. This was the Nazca culture, which was to be found in Peru, in the Nazca Valley believe it or not, between 200 BC and 600 AD.

The first thing about the Nazca that we want to talk about is the Nazca Lines. These are giant drawings done in the sandy soil in the area. They were made by moving along the ground, removing the top layer of soil, the stones and whatnot, and leaving the different coloured ground underneath showing. They would move along in one line, curving it around to make a shape. They are mostly animals; there are a monkey and a hummingbird and massive cool looking spider. These are really big drawings, with the monkey being made from a line that is 110 meters (360 ft). That means that you can only see some of them from the sky, although a few of them can be seen from nearby hills as well.

Art like this is known as geoglyphs, as in 'ground drawings. The Nazca weren't the only ones doing them, and there are examples in places like Kazakhstan and the USA. We even have them here in Britain. Our best version is White Horse Hill. Unsurprisingly, that is a white horse drawn on a hill, and you can find it in Oxfordshire. Our version is also ludicrously big, stretching to being 110 m (360 ft) long. It is made from chalk filling a shallow trench, contrasting with the grass around it. The Nazca Lines are not that robust and are only still around because of the dry climate in the region. A bit of rain and they would be gone.

We don't know what these Nazca Lines were for, but considering they will have taken a concerted effort of quite a few people to make each one, they must have had a good reason for it. Given that a lot of them could only be seen from the sky, a good guess is that it was for the benefit of a god. They are really very good, and well worth a look at some photos. We like the monkey one.

The second thing about the Nazca that is worth a mention is the Chauchilla Cemetery. This is a burial site used by the Nazca, and it shows their surprising way of burying the dead. Like with the lines, the arid atmosphere means that a lot of the bodies are very well preserved. So well preserved that there is still hair on some of the bodies. It appears that the bodies of the dead were dried, wrapped in cotton, painted with resin, and placed in tombs. They are in an upright seated position, which is really creepy looking, although why that is worse than a dead body lying down, we don't know. The other way they prepared their dead was by drilling a hole through the skull. It used to be assumed that the dead, who were prepared in this way, were some sort of enemies. In that assumption the hole in the forehead was for a string to run through, so the heads could be displayed as a 'trophy.' That's grim. Still, historians don't think that anymore, as the dead appear to be part of the Nazca people and there would be no need to celebrate them being dead. Although we all have family members we don't like.

For a little-known civilisation, compared to headliners like the Aztecs and Incas, they were an interesting group. For a start, they were big into whales, which you don't see very often. One of the Lines is even in the shape of a whale. That alone, we quite enjoyed.

The Gallic Empire

In our last Roman history chapter, we met the rest of the Sevaran Dynasty. This chapter is going to cover from 212, when Severus copped it in York, all the way to the 270s. That takes in the rest of the Severan Dynasty, which ended in 235, and then almost 40 years of an absolute shower of short-lived, terrible emperors. It's a period where the Romans were not focusing much on Britain, hence the extended period for the chapter. In fact, Britain didn't have much to do with the Roman Empire at all for quite a lot of it, which you will see in a bit. We also aren't helped by a few of the histories we have relied on, written by Romans, like Dio and Herodian, ended during this time. Mostly because they died, which is probably fair enough. We have been picking on them for being sketchy and sometimes downright wrong, but they were better than nothing.

In this chapter, we will ask ourselves: What's better than a Roman province in Britain? (the answer is two provinces in Britain). What effect can the Middle East have on Roman Britain? Can Britain leave the Roman Empire?

Two Britannias?

Let's start with everyone's favourite subject. Admin.

Around this time, Britannia was split into two provinces, either towards the end of Severus' reign or under Caracalla. The two provinces were called Britannia Superior and Britannia Inferior, with inferior being the north and Superior being the southern part. The border between the two was roughly the line between Chester and Lincoln, meaning anything above Wales, and below Scotland, was in Britannia Inferior. Tempting as it might be for people from the south to see that as a value judgement, it's better translated as Upper (Superior) and Lower (Inferior) Britannia. It seems odd to us that the south would be upper since we arbitrarily see north as up, and you have to say the north is more mountainous than the south, so there is more up to have in the north. However, this was a naming convention used in different places around the empire, and there is a bit of doubt about what it exactly means. It could be that it was a question of proximity to the sea, or it was based on which way major rivers flow through the province. The explanation that makes the most sense to us is that it's based on proximity to Rome. The 'Superior' part of each province was the bit closest to Rome. It doesn't really matter in any way, but we spent a long time trying to figure that out.

The capital of Britannia Superior was at London and was governed by a consular governor, and the province had two legions in it. Britannia Inferior was based in York and was governed by a praetorian governor, with one legion. This does show the relative importance of the two provinces, regardless of Upper and Lower (pipe down you southerners). A consular governor was a standard governor of a province, whereas a praetorian governor was of lower rank, and was in effect a commander of a legion.

It does seem odd that there would be two legions in the south and one in the north. For more than the last 100 years, all the problems had been in the north. Nevertheless, it's helpful to remember it wasn't exactly a hard border between the two, and there is evidence of attachments from legions in the south heading north to help with building projects. Still, if I were in charge, I would have as many soldiers as I could spare stood on Hadrian's Wall eyeballing any Briton coming down from the north.

So why was the province split into two? The answer to that isn't specific to Britannia. It was more of an imperial policy, that was decided on by Severus and carried on by Caracalla. Severus spotted that if a province that had a lot of legions in it, like Britannia with their three legions, the governor of that province was automatically a threat. Any popular governor with a few legions in his province had access to a ready-made army to try and make himself an emperor with. To be fair, this must have been obvious to Severus since he had become emperor by that exact route. He had used his legions, as governor of Pannonia, to fight the governor of Syria and the governor of Britannia for the imperial throne. He would have looked pretty silly if he had started handing out legions to potential rivals, and Britannia wasn't the only province to get split up.

Incidentally, the reorganisation was good news for York. It had already seen a bit of development when Severus made it his headquarters for the attack on Scotland; a Roman Emperor isn't going to turn up to a place without sufficiently nice places for him to stay. However, it got a bit of a bump with it being a province's main settlement, and the town literally got a promotion at some point after this. Previously, it had been a Municipium, which just means a town, or city, of a certain stature, where the people lived under Roman rule and had specific duties and rights. At some point, after York became the headquarters for Britannia Inferior, it was upgraded to a Colonia. That's the word we get 'colony' from, and it started out meaning what you think it means: when the Romans set up a new town somewhere it had conquered, it was a Colonia. By this point, though, it really just meant 'very important city.' We aren't exactly sure when this happened, but it was done by 238, and the clever money is on Caracalla giving the place the upgrade.

Britannia (both of them) were pretty peaceful, as far as we know, after the invasion of Scotland by Severus and

Caracalla. Severus had organised a lot of building and rebuilding in Southern Scotland, including to Hadrian's Wall. So maybe the quietness was because the Britons in the area knew they were on to a loser and just wanted to keep their head down. Alternatively, Caracalla, for his many, many faults, might have organised a lasting peace with the tribes in Scotland before he went off to Rome to get on with some fratricide. The building works carried on into the 220s, including working on military buildings around the Pennines and along Hadrian's Wall. This time the construction didn't seem to be because the Britons were stirring up trouble, or because they had burnt something down. It looks like they were giving the place a face-lift, which makes sense because a lot of those buildings would have been built a long time before. That said, it does suggest the Romans weren't too sure the place was secure yet, although you already get that impression from the fact that there were still three legions posted there. Despite that, all was quiet on the northern front, so the Romans were doing something right.

One other big change for the people of Britannia, other than lots of different admin, was the granting of citizenship to everyone, who wasn't a slave, in the empire. A bonus which was handed out by Caracalla in 212. Universal citizenship sounds like a massive change but wasn't quite as exciting as it sounds. It's definitely true that Roman citizenship had been an enormous deal in Roman history. A Roman citizen had rights that a non-citizen didn't. They could vote in elections, they could own property, they were allowed to have a legal trial to defend themselves against claims. Citizens were also not allowed to be crucified on a cross. They could still be executed, which is not ideal, but at least they wouldn't be crucified, which is a brutal way to go: every cloud and all that. Citizenship was also a divide in the army: citizens joined the legions, and non-citizens joined the auxiliaries. With the new rule, legions still only took citizens, there were just more of them now. Eventually, this would be scrapped altogether, and the legions would start taking anyone.

The Romans had been using citizenship as a tool to keep people on side for years. In the 1st century BC, the people of Italy who weren't Roman, which was most of what is now Italy since Romans were from Rome, waged war to be given citizenship. That means by the time the Roman Republic was the Roman Empire, citizenship was given to all of Italy below the Po River, which is near enough the northern border of modern Italy. Not that it was just Italians who qualified. Other people, from outside Italy, also had it. People who moved to a Roman colony, say in Africa, were also citizens. Beyond that, it was a handy bribe to give to the leaders of regions that the Romans had just conquered. As in 'keep your people in line, and you can have all these lovely rights.' There is a claim that maybe Boudicca was a Roman citizen since her husband Prasutagus had been so onside with the Romans.

Citizenship was also given to men who served as auxiliaries for a full term, which was 25 years. It was a decent offer for the auxiliaries because, even though they wouldn't get a lot of time to enjoy being a citizen, as they would have to wait for 25 years after they joined up, citizenship was automatically given to the children of citizens. It was a handy bribe for the Romans to have up their sleeves. The Roman army was pretty important - as in entirely indispensable for the empire. As the empire grew, they needed more soldiers to keep control of it, including some bits that didn't want to be in it, like Britain for the last century or so. More importantly, they also needed the army to keep other people out, like the Britons not in Britannia. That would be a big ask if you only got men from Italy to join up and, by the 2nd century, Italy was such a small part of the whole empire. So, they needed men from elsewhere to join up, and citizenship was a handy carrot to dangle.

So why did Caracalla just hand it out to everyone? And what did this granting of citizenship mean for the people of Britannia? In theory, it means a lot to the people in Britannia. They had all these new rights, but it's safe to say these rights were less important than they had been. For a start since Rome wasn't a Republic anymore, the ability to vote didn't mean quite as much. The prestige of citizenship had diminished a bit, and there was more of a focus on wealth to decide who gets to play with the big boys. It seems like, even at the time, people weren't too impressed. For example, Dio doesn't give Caracalla's granting of citizenship the time of day. He didn't like Caracalla, so maybe that didn't help, but Dio claimed it was a move to make more money:

'This was the reason why he made all the people in his empire Roman citizens; nominally he was honouring them, but his real purpose was to increase his revenues by this means, inasmuch as aliens did not have to pay most of these taxes.'

Meaning that if everyone was a citizen, they all had the same tax burdens, meaning more money for Caracalla. Still, there was the not being crucified thing, so swings and roundabouts.

A New Roman Empire

We said at the beginning of this chapter that we don't have a lot of info on Britain during this period, partly because the Romans had other things to worry about. Well, this next bit shows that to be a slight understatement.

There was a new power in the east. The Parthian Empire, who the Romans had been scrapping with for more than 200 years, had collapsed. They had been taken over by the Sasanians, with their new dynasty starting in 224. The Sasanians were a Persian empire, meaning they were based around modern Iran and that region, and their capital was near modern-day Baghdad, in Iraq. They were a big deal. But, as we are about to see, they had an eye on being quite a bit bigger.

The Sasanians had started going at Roman territory from

the 230s and had been more than a touch successful. In the 250s they had another proper go and attacked Roman provinces around Syria and Turkey, which must have ticked off the Romans. As much as we would hate to devalue the anti-Roman efforts of the Britons on Scotland, this doesn't feel the same as the problems the Romans had with the Scottish tribes. Realistically the Britons, even the whole island put together, couldn't have caused much harm to Rome. They were an annoyance that needed to be dealt with or just ignored. The Sasanians, on the other hand, were a rival empire who could cause some severe problems for the Romans.

This attack on Roman provinces was a good example of these severe problems. In 253, at the Battle of Barbalissos, which is in Syria, a full Roman army of 60,000 men was wiped out. The only response to a threat like this was for the Romans to take the fight to them. The emperor of the time, Valerian, left his co-emperor, and son, Gallienus back in Rome and headed off to give some Persians a kicking. It started pretty well, and he had got back Antioch and Syria in 257.

In 260 Valerian was hanging about in Edessa, a city in Southern Turkey, with his army recovering from a plague which had weakened them quite a bit. At this point, the Sasanian king, Shapur I, invaded, and the Romans and Sassanians fought the Battle of Edessa. It did not go well for the Romans. In fact, it was up there with the worst things to happen to the Roman Empire. Not only was it another loss of a massive Roman army, but Valerian was taken captive by the Sasanians.

The taking of an emperor and a massive army would be a setback for anyone. However, there was already a co-emperor back in Rome, and the empire was built out of armies. So, it would all be fine. Well, it might have been fine, if it hadn't been a case of it never rains, it pours. The Romans started taking a beating all over the place, particularly with angry folk crossing the Rhine and Danube to cause trouble. One of the tribes, the Iuthungi, made it into Italy itself, which must have been a bit close for comfort. That might be why Gallienus didn't try to get his dad back, and Valerian died in captivity.

All of this doesn't have much to do with Britain. Yet. In fact, the only thing worth mentioning here is that it was going off in the Middle East, and the Germanic tribes were roaming around Roman provinces, but nobody in Britain was kicking off. Did they just not get the news? For the last 200 hundred years, the Britons had been losing it at every opportunity. Yet now, here were the Romans with a captured Emperor Valerian in the East, and an Emperor Gallienus barely keeping things together in the West. Britain? Nothing. They just didn't fancy it this time.

However, Britain wasn't completely unaffected, and their involvement came from the troubles in Germany. There was a bloke called Postumus, who was a commander of a Roman army on the Rhine (Germany). Emperor Gallienus was focused on stopping the tribes on the Danube and had left his son, Saloninus, with the military commanders, including Postumus, on the Rhine. They did pretty well and beat an Iuthungi army which was travelling back up after running amok in Northern Italy. The Iuthungi had been having a lovely old time in Italy and had nicked themselves a lot of very cool stuff. As is the way with soldiers, when the Romans soldiers beat them in battle, they took all this cool stuff as a lovely bit of second-hand loot.

So far, so Roman, but it all went a bit wrong when Saloninus ordered that the nicked stuff should be collected back in and given to the people it had been taken from in Italy. Unsurprisingly, the soldiers didn't like that, and they did what annoyed Roman soldiers tended to do. They declared their commander, Postumus, emperor. What makes this different to the previous attempts at this was that, not only did Postumus take on the title, but he didn't try to take on the current emperor. Instead, he went independent and set up his own thing called the Gallic Empire. This meant that

Germany, Gaul (mostly France), Spain and Britain were part of a new Gallic Empire and not the Roman Empire. Rome didn't exactly hand over the territories, and never relinquished claims to it all, but in reality, from 360 to 374, Britain was in the Gallic Empire rather than the Roman Empire.

What did this mean for Britain? Actually, less than you would think. It's worth remembering that this wasn't a revolt of an oppressed people trying to leave Roman rule. This was Roman citizens being annoyed at how Rome was being run, so it was more a civil war than a revolt. It was pretty clear that the Romans in Rome weren't able to protect the western provinces from the Germanic tribes that were running around. So, they might have banded together in their own empire, but they were still all Romans. Postumus even set up his new empire as a replica of the Roman Empire. There was an emperor, a senate, Praetorian Guard, legions and the obligatory coins. It had all the things that make the Roman Empire look Roman. Life seemed to go on as it had in Britain, or at least as far as we know. Something we do have from this period is an inscription from Lancaster, in North West England, on a rebuilt bathhouse which had collapsed. The inscription is dedicated to Emperor Postumus, so at least someone was a fan.

It's a big change, swapping empires, but Britain the change didn't alter the fact that Britain was at the edge of an empire, albeit a much smaller one now. The capital of the Gallic Empire was at Cologne (Colonia Agrippina), which is in Western Germany. So, most of Britain was still run by Romans, who were reporting to Romans on the continent. Which would count as a double layer of European management, and that would really upset certain British newspapers.

We don't know what happened to the people in charge of the two Britannia provinces in the transition between one empire and another. The assumption is that Britain was quite happy to be in the new Gallic Empire. Or at least they weren't going to resist it too much. If you look at a map, you can see that the rest of the Gallic Empire was very much between Britain and Rome. So, it's easy to assume that the powers that be in Britain were pretty keen on joining in. If they had tried to fight it off, it doesn't seem likely that Emperor Gallienus was going to ride to their rescue. For a start, he was busy with the bits he could still claim to be in charge of.

In the end, as you can guess, the Gallic Empire, and Britain was eventually folded back into the Roman Empire proper. Emperor Postumus was assassinated, killed by his own soldiers, in 269 after nine years in the job. He was followed by four short-lived emperors before it was all ended by Emperor Aurelian (the Roman emperor, not the Gallic one) There was a battle in northeastern France to finish it all off. We are told that the Gallic Emperor Tetricus I had organised a surrender to the Romans, but the Gallic Empire legions didn't fancy that, and they had to fight it out. Even with the battle it sounds like, the Gallic Empire went out with a whimper, and Britannia was once again actually part of the Roman Empire, rather than just theoretically.

So, what have we learnt? It turns out that the Britons couldn't bring themselves to kick up a fuss during every single period of Roman turmoil. Southern England has had a superiority complex for thousands of years. And Roman citizenship was maybe less exciting than it sounds - except for not being crucified.

The Crisis Of The Third Century

Something called the Crisis of the Third Century is always going to be a winner for us writing this. On the downside of the exciting period, is how confusing the whole thing is. It all kicked off with the death of Severus Alexander in 235, and we are going to run this chapter to 270. It's a bit complicated and involves a lot of people over the next 45 years, but let's have a look.

Maximinus Thrax, a Couple of Senators and A Load of Gordians

Maximinus became emperor in 235, and he qualified for the job because the army had backed him, and because he had organised the death of Alexander. For a 3rd-century emperor, that's about as qualified as it gets. He was the emperor for three years, and he was the absolute opposite of the last couple of teenage emperors. Maximinus was a giant of a man, who, if he were around now, would no doubt include the word 'alpha' in his depressing tinder profile.

He launched into a massive offensive against the Germanic tribes and set himself up in Serbia to keep an eye on them all. He also increased the pay for his army and increased taxes for everyone else to pay for it. No doubt the army was quite pleased with Maixumus, but the senators across the empire were not too into him. For a start, he was basically a barbarian and certainly wasn't of the senatorial class. And posh folk have never been too big into tax increases.

The beginning of the end for Maximinus came in 238. It kicked off in Tunisia, and a bloke named Gordian was declared emperor, and he, in turn, declared his son, also called Gordian, his co-emperor. The Senate saw this as an opportunity and backed them. Unfortunately, the people in the province next door, Numidia, didn't support the Gordians because the governor of Numidia didn't like daddy Gordian. So, he attacked and killed them. The Gordians had lasted three weeks, and now the Senate was left standing there with their dicks out. Their solution was to get the legions in Italy together and declare two of their own, Pupienus and Balbinus as co-emperors. The plebs of Rome didn't like that and kicked up enough of a fuss that they also announced the grandson of daddy Gordian, also creatively called Gordian, as caesar and heir to Pupienus and Balbinus.

Maximinus was killed by his own soldiers after a bit of fighting, which means that Pupienus and Balbinus were now emperors. They concocted a plan to get everything back under control and were soon setting off to beat Rome's enemies. Pupienus was to go and fight the Persians, and Balbinus was off to fight against the Goths and the Dacians. Before they could set off the Praetorian Guard, who presumably had been enjoying being commanded by hard man Maximinus, killed them, leaving Gordian III to take over.

Before we are done with Maximinus, its worth mentioning one of his more aggressive sounding policies. We haven't mentioned the Christians of the empire too much so far. However, they were already a decent sized population by this time. They were certainly big enough to have annoyed Maximinus. His aggressive policy was the offer to grant people immunity from taxes in exchange for them getting involved in some persecution of Christians. We are now getting into the period where the Roman Emperors, on and off, put the boot into the growing Christian population.

Gordian III, who took over in July 238, was yet another teenager. Just. He was 13, which meant that the Senate was able to have a fair bit of control over things, although the power behind the throne was a Praetorian Prefect, Timesitheus.

Gordian lasted nearly six years, which is impressive considering what else was going on. A lot of his reign was spent fighting the Germanic tribes, and the Goths were causing some trouble, but the Romans managed to push them back in 242. Next up was the Sassanids, and Gordian headed east with Timesitheus. They did pretty well, and territory was being taken by the Romans along the Euphrates. Unluckily for Gordian, Timesitheus got ill and died on the campaign, leaving Gordian with a new Praetorian Prefect, Julius Phillipus. A year later Gordian was killed by his soldiers, and he was replaced by Phillipus.

Philip the Arab, Decius, and a Hand Full of Other Blokes

Philip, known as Philip the Arab, was from Syria, and he lasted five years in the top job. He quickly ended the war with the Sassanids, a peace he had to pay for with a massive bribe. The reason Philip was so keen on peace was that he wanted to head back to Europe to stop the Germanic tribes, including those pesky Goths, from heading over the borders into Roman provinces.

It wasn't all work under Philip. While he was emperor, the Romans celebrated 1000 years since the official founding of Rome.

The other feature of Philip's reign was how many usurpers popped up to try and take his place. They were all over the place, but the one Philip really needed to worry about was, Decius. He was the bloke Philip had put in charge of the legions on the Danube, which meant control over a lot of legions. In 249 Decius' men declared him emperor, and it ended with him beating Philp at a battle near Verona, in Italy.

Decius was only emperor for two years, but they sounded like a very unfun couple of years. For a start, there was a plague running across the empire, which puts a dampener on things. During all that, the plebs in Rome decided they would prefer someone else in charge, a senator called Licinianus. His attempt to usurp Decius was feeble and didn't get anywhere, but it must have been a blow to Decius' ego.

Internal Roman strife was the last thing the emperor needed because the Goths were seriously going for it, and in 250 they crossed the Danube and headed into the Roman provinces of the Balkans and down into Greece. Decius clearly needed to solve that, but at the Battle of Abritus, in Romania, his army lost big time, and in the process, he got himself killed, along with his eldest son.

It's worth noting that Decius' reign is known as a period of horrible persecution of Christians, who were taking the blame for all the bad stuff that was happening. It didn't work, and the campaign of persecution was called off before he died, but this was the beginning of a pretty crappy time to be a Christian in the Roman world.

When Decius died, there were a couple of candidates for the job. Valerian had been left behind in Rome to run things while he was campaigning, so he had a good shout. However, in the end, it was one of the generals from the Balkans, Gallus who got the job. Gallus lasted from 251 to 253, and his reign made Decius' look like a walk in the park. The Goths were still running around Greece and into Turkey. The Alamanni and the Franks had crossed the Rhine and headed as far down as into Spain. The plague, known as Plague of Cyprian, that had started in 249, was still causing serious damage. This included killing Gallus' heir, the younger son of Decius, Hostilianus.

Unsurprisingly, what with all that going on, a usurper popped up. Like Gallus, this new emperor wannabe, Aemilian, had been doing good work fighting the Goths over in the Balkans. He was doing so well that his soldiers declared him emperor. Aemilian invaded northern Italy, but Gallus had an ace up his sleeve and ordered the legions from the Rhine, under a man named Valerian, to head down to attack Aemilian. So now we have Aemilian marching to replace Gallus and Valerian following him down to protect Gallus. What eventually happened in this imperial Benny Hill sketch was that Gallus was killed by his own soldiers, Valerian was declared emperor by his legions, and he won by default because Aemilian also got killed by his own troops.

That right there is a lovely bit of snapshot of third-century Rome. Absolute carnage.

Valerian, Gallienus, Gothicus and Quintillus (for a bit)

We have come across Valerian before, in our Roman Britain chapter. He took over in 253 and made his son, Gallienus, his co-emperor. With the empire being so big and in a complete shit state, they split the job into two. Valerian was in charge of the East, and Gallienus was in the West. Gallienus' job was to push back against the Goths, the Franks, the Alamanni, the Saxons, and keep an eye on North Africa. Easy. We are told he did ok, but he did lose a chunk of territory to the Alamanni. The area that he lost was called the Agri Decumates, which was the area between the Rhine and the Danube, where the Black Forest is. A lot of the Roman defences against the Germans used the two rivers, so the triangle of land between them was a pain to keep hold of. More than a century earlier Tacitus had called it 'a remote nook of our empire and a part of a Roman province.' Before that, it was apparently of 'land of questionable ownership.' Which suggests it wasn't a major loss, although the Romans didn't typically like losing anything if they could help it.

Valerian had had less luck in the East, as we mentioned in our Roman Britain chapter. He took a beating from the Sasanian king, Shapur I, and was taken prisoner in 260. Gallienus either decided he had too much on, or he was pleased to get rid of this dad and chose not to try to get him back, leaving Valerian to die in captivity. Luckily, the Sassanid plan was similar to when the Romans pushed over the Euphrates in the other direction. Shapur didn't try to keep all the Roman territories in the East, and mostly just robbed everyone and went home.

One interesting element of father and son splitting the empire was that it meant a different style of ruling in different parts of the empire. A big difference in the way they did things was that Valerian had gone in hard on the persecution of Christians, including the execution of bishops. Whereas, Gallienus was more inclined to leave them alone to worship in the west of the empire. This toing and froing about the Christians would be a feature of Roman rule a long time after this.

Back to how things were falling apart for the Romans, we know what happened in northwest Europe under Gallienus. The Gallic Empire was set up in the same year that Valerian got captured. Which meant that a fair-sized chunk of the empire was out of commission. That wasn't all of it though, there was a second breakaway section of the empire Gallienus had to worry about. Out in the East, there was a local ruler who was doing very well out of being in between the Romans and the Persians. The city of Palmyra, in Syria, was a handy buffer between the empires and a handy spot for trade between the two. When Gallienus took sole control of the Roman Empire, he gave their ruler, Odenathus, the title of dux (duke) and put him in charge of the whole region.

It was a nice arrangement for the Palmyrians and the Romans. Then things took a bit of a turn in 267 when Odenathus and his heir were killed. This left someone called Vaballathus as the new king of Palmyra. Although, he was about eight at the time, so that meant it was his mam, Zenobia, who ran things.

Zenobia was given a Cleopatra style write up by the ancient sources, which probably isn't a coincidence since she claimed to be a descendent of the Egyptian ruler (she wasn't). Palmyra being under new management was a problem for Gallienus because, under Zenobia, the Palmyra started to act more independently of the Romans. Nevertheless, during the end of Gallienus' reign, they were handily keeping a lid on the East, and anyway, he wasn't around for much longer to worry about it.

Gallienus had suffered a lot of usurpers to the emperorship. If you believe the unreliable Historia Augusta, there were more than thirty of them. In reality, there were fewer than ten, which was probably more than enough. The one that eventually got him was a bloke named Aureolus. Gallienus was over in Serbia fighting Goths, when Aureolus, a leader of a unit of cavalry, declared himself emperor. Gallienus turned around to sort that out, but the emperor was assassinated before he could get there. That was convenient for Aureolus, but he still didn't manage to get himself made emperor. The job was grabbed by a scary sounding fellow called Claudius Gothicus.

Claudius Gothicus was from Illyria, which is around Albania, and was a hard as nails general who jumped straight into carrying the fight against the Goths and their mates. He was the only emperor for a year and a bit, but he did have some success against the barbarians. And that explains his name. 'Gothicus' is the title he claimed for beating the tribe. Not that everything went his way. In the East, Zenobia and her newly minted Palmyrene Empire had gone properly rogue and had taken control of Arabia and done straight into North Africa through Egypt. This meant that the Roman Empire had now split into three bits. The Palmyrene Empire in the Middle East & North Africa, the Gallic Empire in Western Europe, and the actual Roman Empire in the middle. And even that was being invaded by Germanic tribes. It had all gone horribly wrong.

Luckily for Gothicus, the pressure was taken off in Europe when the Goths were stopped in their tracks. They were suffering from a plague that went through the tribe. Unluckily for Gothicus, he got it as well and died.

Gothicus' brother, Quintillus picked up their reigns, but he lasted all of five minutes, a few months at most, before the legions on the Danube decided they would prefer the cavalry commander, Domitius Aurelianus. Quintillus committed suicide before Aurelian, as he was known got to him.

This happened in 270, and it would be a few more years and a few more emperors before we can call a proper end of the Crisis of the Third Century.

This whole chapter has pretty much been just a list of emperors, wars, and invasions into Germany. Exciting as that is, it's also worth pointing out that this would have changed a lot of the empire for the worst. Many chapters ago, we laughed at the idea of the Pax Romana (Roman Peace) which started under Augustus. The Romans might always have been fighting, but compared to what was going on here, it was relatively calm back then. All this fighting all over the place would have absolutely hammered the economy and made it a much worse place to be. The Romans in Britain were no doubt quite happy about being on an island, which would have protected them from the marching armies and raiding tribesmen. It was and will carry on being, a complete shitshow, but we can see more of that in the next Roman history chapter.

The Nok Culture

Sub-Saharan Africa, during the centuries we are talking about, is not exactly awash with easily accessible historical records. Nevertheless, we had no worries about figuring out a topic for this part of Africa. We have been loving this topic since we heard about it a few years ago. The Nok Culture is fascinating.

The Nok people were from central Nigeria. They lived from around 1500 BC to 300 AD, and very little is known about them. In fact, they completely fell out of historical records until the 1920s. The re-discovery of them came from the excavation of a tin mine, which was co-owned by a British Colonel. This mine was near the village of Nok, hence the name. Later, in the 40s, another British man, working in Nigeria, which was a British colony, came across some of these terracotta heads because one of them was being used as a scarecrow. Luckily, this man, Bernard Fagg had studied archaeology at Cambridge, so he put a bit more value on these figures than whoever used it as a scarecrow head. He realised that the tin mines in the area were throwing up artefacts from this ancient civilisation.

We should pause now, and you should go away for a sec to search 'Nok culture' and find the pictures of these terracotta figures and heads, they are really cool. You can find our favourite by searching 'Nok rider and horse.'

Now you are back, we should say that these figures are a lot of what we know about this group. Archaeologists are sure that this group, living in central Nigeria, were just a small part of a much wider trade network. It makes sense because we are looking at one very small part of one country in Western Africa. Other discoveries from them include iron tools, so Nok is classed as an Iron Age culture, which makes sense. We know they traded with other cultures, so they would have had decent access to the same technologies as the people living on the Mediterranean. It also means that the Nok culture spanned the end of the Stone Age and the beginning of the Iron Age.

Something we found strange when we were reading about the archaeologists' attempts to find more Nok items, was that they rarely find whole statues. That isn't because they have been broken by being underground for 2000 years, or that ancient Nigerians were surprisingly clumsy. They were intentionally broken up before they were buried. Apparently, this isn't uncommon in prehistoric cultures, and it is presumably part of some sort of ritual. That makes it sound like the archaeologist's job is part historical discovery and part doing massive jigsaws.

So, what happened to the people of the Nok culture? In the first few centuries of the Common Era (AD), the pottery of the culture changed, and then they just disappeared. Historians don't know whether that was a cultural change for the people living in Nigeria, or if there was an invasion/migration of other people into the region. It's a similar question asked about the people of Britain before the Celts. Were they wiped out? Or did they just move on the new (and no doubt less impressive) pottery and ways of living? The work being done to discover more about these people is still relatively new, so hopefully, there is more to learn about them.

A British Empire

The last time we had a Roman Britain chapter, there was a nice bit of admin, with Britain being split into two provinces, and an attempt at a separatist Roman Empire. Hopefully, you enjoyed that because this chapter is going to feel a bit familiar. In this chapter, we ask ourselves: how many emperors is too many? How many provinces are too many? And when shouldn't you give a bloke a navy?

Everybody Is Revolting

The Gallic empire had ended in 274, while Aurelian was emperor. He was killed in 275 and was followed by two very short-lived emperors, Tacitus and Florianus. We don't care about them, but for anyone keeping count, Aurelian was murdered, Tacitus apparently died of an illness, but was maybe murdered, and Florianus was murdered. So far so Roman. However, it's the next bloke, Probus, who we are interested in. He got the job of emperor in 276, and he is a bit more involved in the story of Britain. It seems that Probus wasn't a popular man, and he had some serious rebel problems. Any problems for an emperor at this point would have been very, very worrying since 274-276 had already seen three dead emperors. If he stubbed his toe, he probably assumed he was going to end up dead.

In 280-81 Probus had to deal with three usurpers in quick

succession. Our early favourite was Bonosus, who is at least tangentially related to Britannia, in that his dad was Romano-British. That is just a fancy way of saying he was a Roman born in Britain. Bonosus was in charge of the naval fleet on the Rhine, but in a terrible day at the office, an attack from a Germanic tribe ended with his ships being burnt while they were at anchor. Everybody has messed up at work at some point and considered going big and doubling down to get out of trouble. Bonosus went really, really big. As a naval commander having your ships burnt from under you is a matter for the Human Resources Department - meaning at the very least Bonosus was losing his job (and presumably his bonus - see what we did there). More pressing was that there was a decent chance he would be executed. Oddly, Bonosus didn't fancy that, and his clever solution was to declare himself emperor, along with a bloke called Proculus. They did this in Cologne, which is where Postumus had started off his Gallic Empire not long before. There must be something in the water over there.

Bonosus was put down by Emperor Probus pretty quickly, and Proculus didn't do much better. He had turned to the Franks, a Germanic tribe on the edge of the empire for help, but they just turned him over to Probus. According to the Historia Augusta, the pretenders had claimed Gaul, Britain, and Spain, which makes it seem like they were trying to kick-start the Gallic Empire Part 2.

Probus would have gone for the slap-down-the-pretender hat-trick in 280/81. However, the third usurper, his friend and governor of Syria, Julius Saturninus, got himself killed by his own soldiers before he could get anywhere. Syria comes up a lot in all this, it seems like they were up there with Britain for causing trouble to the empire.

We like to stop every now and again to point out how big the Roman Empire was, and how diverse the people involved were. We have here Emperor Probus, a man who was born in what is now Serbia, having a fight with a bloke who was from Spain but had a dad from Britain.

When Probus was done with Bonosus, another challenger appeared: a bloke stationed in the Middle East, but who was from around Morocco. When you compare that with the much bigger British Empire, it seems mad. In terms of British Prime Ministers, we have had some Irish ones, like Wellington, and Disraeli was Jewish of some Italian descent, but he was born in England, as was his dad. If you are pointing to the island next door and the fact that one of them was Jewish, you are really scraping the bottom of the barrel to have something to compare to the Romans.

Regardless of all that, how did these attempts at becoming emperor impact Britain? It didn't massively, but there was also an attempt at something similar by a governor in Britain. The story of this is painfully vague again. We have it from two Greek authors writing later from Byzantium, Zosimus and Zonaras, but they are mostly just short references. They tell us that a governor in Britannia revolted against the emperor. They don't say which one, or whether they were from Britannia Superior or Britannia Inferior, but it was a governor. That's pretty much all you are getting.

This revolt was clearly a much smaller effort than the big three Probus had put up with. It didn't involve any battles or anything exciting like that. Apparently, the job of fixing it was given to a bloke named Victorinus. It was made his problem because it had been him that had recommended the rebellious governor for the job in the first place. His solution was to head to Britain and pretend he was running away from Probus as well. Once there Victorinus blagged a meeting with the rebellious governor and killed him, before sneaking off back to Rome. Job done. It's all oddly neat for the Romans, but that's how it went down, we are told. Just to add to our general wonder at how diverse this crowd of murderous, disloyal lunatics were, Victorinus was a Moor, like Julius Saturninus. That is what the Romans called North Africans from the province of Mauritania, which was mostly modern Morocco.

Carausius - The More Emperors, The Better

Probus died in 282, and the following few emperors aren't too interesting for Britain. The next emperor we should care about is one you might recognise the name of, Diocletian. He was made emperor in 284, and was a big deal, especially after a really ropey period for the Romans. We said the few emperors after Probus weren't too exciting for Britain, and there were a few. Between autumn 282 and winter 284, there were three emperors, Carus, Carinus, and Numerian. For you emperor death fans, we are looking at respectively: struck by lightning, assassinated and unknown, but probably murdered.

It gives you an insight into how much the Romans had been in a crisis when they were on emperor number five in about two years. In fact, if you go back to Valerian, the one who had been captured by the Sasanians and was emperor until 260, the turnover after that is mad. We count ten emperors in the 14 years between 260 and when Diocletian took over in 284. That's an average of fewer than three years each. In the last 14 years, we have had half that number of Prime Ministers in Britain (Blair, Brown, Cameron, May, and Johnson), and being an emperor is meant to be a job for life. We can get shot of ours every four or five years, if we like, and we still manage to hang onto them for longer.

Diocletian had seen that this turnover of emperors was a problem, and he had concluded that the empire was too big for one bloke to rule over it. So, he got himself a co-emperor. That sort of thing wasn't new for the Romans, but this was a bit more practical than most of the other ones. Most co-emperors before this were just a dad making sure his son would be next in line by giving him the title. Diocletian's approach was a bit more equal, although Diocletian was still very much the daddy. If you will.

Diocletian chose a bloke called Marcus Aurelius Maximian

as his co-emperor. He was initially given the title of caesar, which is in effect a junior emperor. However, he was soon bumped up to augustus, and Diocletian took charge of the eastern bit of the empire and Maximian got the western bit. The 'western bit' was actually pretty big, since it covered Italy, Africa, Gaul (mostly France and nearby countries), Spain, and Britain.

Maximian's first job was to head into Gaul and give a group of bandits, called the Bagaudae, a beating. We don't have details on who they were, or what their problem was, but they aren't important. What is important is that Maximian was helped by one of his commanders, a bloke named Mausaeus Carausius. For this, Carausius was given a sweet new job, fighting Saxons and Franks on the coasts of Gaul and Britannia. Both the Franks and Saxons were Germanic people, but as ever it's not cut and dry on who was who. For example, some Frankish tribes were living in Roman provinces, and some were living outside it. Wherever they were, they were clearly causing some troubles in Gaul and Britannia, raiding and generally acting a bit more piratey then the Romans would like.

Obviously to fight piracy you need a navy, which he was given command of, as well as some land troops. These land troops consisted of men from several legions. When a smaller group of men were temporarily taken from the main legion and sent to do a specific task, they were called a vexillation. Along with the vexillations under his command, Carausius also used some Frankish men to help fight the pirates. Fighting fire with fire. With all this lot, Carausius had some success tackling these raids. If anything, he was too successful. Suspicion was raised at it all, and if the accusations were correct, Carausius was on the take. We are told that he would find out where the pirates would be raiding from his Frankish soldiers. He would then let the raid happen, but then he would catch the pirates on their way home. Crucially, on their way home with their recently acquired loot. Or booty as we are sticking with a pirate theme.

This sounds dodgy, but who cares? The pirates have been stopped. Isn't that the point in Carausius' job? Yes, but the folk who had the booty stolen in the first place were probably half expecting to get some, if not all of it, back. Or maybe they had even hoped against all hope that someone would have fancied stopping them getting robbed in the first place. Carausius didn't like that bit of the job, so he let it happen and kept hold of his booty for himself.

There is a slightly telling quote from a Roman historian called Eutropius, who was writing a little bit later in around the 370s. He said:

'However, though many barbarians were frequently intercepted, their booty was not returned to the provincials in its entirety, nor was it sent to the Emperors.'

Which suggests second-hand booty theft would have been acceptable if Carausius had kicked a taste upstairs to his emperor.

Maximian wasn't a fan of this turn of events, no doubt because of the lack of kickback, and went to intervene. Also, since he had given him the job, it was probably a touch embarrassing that the bloke sent to keep the Roman settlements around the coasts safe, was instead pocketing everyone's stuff. Carausius was sentenced to death, but he decided a holiday in Britain was better than being dead (new tourist slogan for Visit Britain?), so he legged it to hide in Britannia in 286.

By now we should know what that means. When a commander of an army (or navy in this case) has annoyed an emperor and is worried about getting the chop, we get a new emperor and maybe a new empire. An empire set up in Britain. So about thirteen years after the end of the Gallic Empire, we have the Empire of Carausius, a.k.a. The Carausian Revolt. This was much more significant than the revolts against Probus, and Carausius and his mates held out for ten years, until 293. How he held out was mostly due to an error on Maximian's part. Commanders of armies were forever revolting against emperors. Sometimes they managed to fight off the emperor's legions, but mostly they didn't. Carausius had been given soldiers, so he had himself an army, including the legions in Britannia. More worryingly for Maximian was that he also had a navy, and an island to hide on. And since that stolen navy was the one that Maximian would have used to sail over to Britain, it posed a bit of a logistical conundrum for him.

Obviously, the Romans in Britain jumped in support of Carausius, or he wouldn't have been able to set up his little separatist British Roman Empire. They had all recently been in the Gallic empire, so they were somewhat used to not being ruled from Rome. However, it wasn't just a Britain problem Maximian had, because Carausius didn't just hunker down in Britain. Realistically, with the soldiers he had, he couldn't exactly be a proper threat to Rome. Still, he did use his navy to control the English Channel, and had territory in northern France, including the big port at Boulogne and as far inland into France as Rouen. Rouen is only about 60km (37 miles) inland, but that's far enough to be embarrassing for Maximian. Daddy Diocletian was probably looking very disapprovingly over from the east at all this.

While the navy was the real issue, it looks like Carausius' army wasn't to be sniffed at either. Like with all these wannabe emperors, the coins Carausis minted tell us a bit about what was going on. From these coins, it looks like Carausius had vexillations from the armies of Britain, Germany, Moesia (a province around Serbia and Bulgaria) and Italy under his control. Even with that, the odds were in favour of the Romans in Rome rather than the Romans in Britain. Maximian obviously had some attempts at dislodging Carausius, but they weren't particularly successful. We are told of a particular effort, in 288-89, to head over to Britain. The source on it is pretty vague about the exact outcome but blames the bad weather for an apparent loss, and we can only assume it was an absolute shambles. Maximian did a bit better on the Gallic side of the English Channel, though, and he did get back most of the territory in Gaul by 290.

Carausius' coins also show us an attempt from him to either prove his legitimacy to the people in his territory or to get Diocletian and Maximian to leave him alone. He issued coins with profiles of him, Diocletian and Maximian on it, with the phrase 'Carausius et fratres sui.' Which translates as 'Carausius and his brothers.' As in 'Carausius and his fellow emperors.' We can't decide if that was an attempt for the new British emperor to try and be one of the cool kids, or if it was meant for the people in Britain to make Carausius seem fully legitimate. It feels a touch desperate either way.

We quite liked Carausius when we read his story. A bloke from the Menapian tribe of Belgium, taking over an army and navy so he could sack off the Roman Empire. He was a cheeky little chappy, but his coin game was a bit much. He issued other coins including a reference to a poem by Virgil, a 1st century BC Roman poet. Already that sounds pretentious, but the line it refers to is:

'now a new lineage is sent down from high heaven'

This was written pre-Jesus, but it's got a definite second coming vibe to it. That's a bit too messiah complex for our liking. If that isn't smug enough, he also used another Virgil line:

'The Golden Age Returns'

Smug. These lines must have been for the people living under him in Britain because there would have been no point in trying to impress Diocletian and Maximian. What's interesting about that, other than showing how insufferable the man must have been, is that, presumably, people must have been able to understand the reference. Meaning a fair chunk of the people in Britain at the time must have been educated enough to get references from poems that were more than 300 years old. Or maybe it was like when

Tory ministers quote the classics, or Kipling, and expect a massive round of applause from the cheap seats. Maybe Carausius was just out of touch. Or a twat.

As for the man himself, it wasn't Maximian who ended Carausius' reign. He was murdered in 293, by one of his own, Allectus, who is thought to have been Carausius' Praetorian Prefect. Even in a copy of the Roman Empire, the Praetorian Prefects are trouble. In the same year, Maximian successfully took back the last bit of Gaul, the port of Boulogne. Even after that, it took another three years before the Romans could sail an army over to Britain to beat Allectus and get Britannia back. The Romans (the ones still in the Roman Empire) had built themselves a fleet and launched a two-pronged attack. One army marched and beat Allectus in Hampshire, just south of Reading. The other, led by a bloke who would be very important to Britain in a future chapter, called Constantius, marched into London (Londinium) to 'liberate it.' Actually, Constantius ended up arriving in time to stop the army who had just been beaten in Hampshire coming over to sack the city. That was a bit of luck for the ancient Londoners, but we aren't sure why the immediate reaction to being beaten in a battle, was for the defeated army to have a run at London.

What did this change of management, back to the Roman Empire, mean for the people of Britain? For a start, it was another Gallic Empire situation, in that it was a Roman revolt against other Romans. That means things had carried on in much the same Roman way for everyone. As ever, we don't have a lot of information on what Carausius was up to when he was in charge. It does look like the man carried on defending Britain, not just from the other Romans, but also from the pirates he had initially been asked to protect them against. There was a string of defensive forts along the south coast, called the Saxon Shore Forts. These were built over a long period, but it looks like Carausius was part of that building process. Considering how all this started, the locals must have been glad that he was finally doing his job properly. Generally, the whole thing is a relatively small blip in the history of Roman Britain, but, significantly, it was the second time the Romans, or the ones in Rome at least, had lost control of the place for years at a time.

Another Bit of Admin

Diocletian was a proper reformer and considering how mad the Roman Empire had been for ages by this point, you can see why. He wasn't happy with just splitting the job of emperor between two people, in 293 he went further than that and split it into four, called a Tetrarchy. We will go over that properly in the Roman history chapter. Still, for now, it was basically the empire being split into two, east and west, with each half having a senior emperor (Augustus) and a junior emperor (Caesar). Which is why when Britain was taken from Carausius, it wasn't done by Maximian. He delegated that job to his Caesar, Constantius. This is an important change for the history of Rome and the history of Roman Britain, but for now, it was some of Diocletian's other reforms which are a bit more relevant.

Diocletian loved splitting stuff up. Including provinces. So much so that he ended up doubling the number of administrative regions in the empire. That means Britannia went from being split into two provinces, Britannia Superior and Britannia Inferior, to being divided into four provinces. These were called Maxima Caesariensis, Flavia Caesariensis, Britannia Prima and Britannia Secunda. You will be less than surprised to hear we don't know exactly where these were. Historians are comfortable in claiming a proper location for a couple of them. Maxima Caesariensis was South East England, based around London and Britannia Prima was in the west, probably based around Gloucester. However, the best guess for Flavia Caesariensis is that it would be in the east, based around Lincoln and that Britannia Secunda was Northern England.

For anyone wondering what the names mean; 'Caesariensis Maxima', is a way of saying The Caesarian Province of Maxima, so those two provinces were named after prominent Romans and their families. 'Prima' and 'Secunda' are 'first' and 'second.' Later on, there was maybe a fifth province, called Valentia. What that name means is disputed, as is the whereabouts of this province, or if it even existed. Which is a bit annoying even for this period of Roman history.

What does this mean for Britain? The same as it did for the rest of the empire. Loads more bureaucracy. It meant that there were now four people in charge of provinces in Britain. The whole reform seems to have developed over time, but by 312 at least, Roman Britain, with its four provinces, was grouped together and called the Dioceses of Britain. It's worth pointing out the obvious here, the Romans used the term 'diocese' for an administrative unit, just like the Catholic Church and the Church of England. This was the start of the 4th century, so Jesus had done his thing ages before the naming, but who came up with it first? Actually, it was the Church that borrowed it from the Romans. 'Dioceses' comes from the Greek word for administration. For a double weird term theft, the administrators of these dioceses were called 'vicarii' a.k.a. vicars. In a few chapters time, we will see how the Romans got on board with Christianity, so it made sense that the Church would mirror the admin of the empire.

Above the diocese, Britain was grouped into the Gallic Region and controlled by a regional praetorian prefect, but Roman Britain was still treated as a whole. Don't tell the Daily Mail, but that means Britain was managed by a bloke out of the German city of Trier, which is very close to Brussels. What difference did this make? Well, it meant that every part of Britain will have had some attention paid to it by a very local governor. What that translates into is hard to say, and we are sure some bits of Roman Britain were still less looked after than others.

For the Roman emperors, the main benefit of the many

new provinces would be that the angrier provinces, and their governors, would be less able to revolt and set up an empire. It was the same logic as splitting Britain into two. A quarter-sized province is even less likely to revolt than one that is half-sized. Unless loads of Roman governors teamed-up, which as we have seen doesn't seem too likely. Will it work? We'll see.

So, what have we learnt? Setting up your own empire is entirely doable. Vicars used to be a lot more hands-on with the world. And you shouldn't try to beat pirates with more pirates.

From Crisis To Calm

Our last Roman history chapter covered a lot of the Third Century Crisis. And we hope you liked it because it's not over yet. The first half of this chapter will be about the end of that particular clusterfuck, and then we get to have a look at Diocletian and his nice, calming influence.

Aurelian, Some Old Men & Probus

So, we have got to 270, and Emperor Aurelian. He was a soldier who had worked his way up the ranks, which was useful because he had some problems to contend with. The most pressing was the tribes storming down from Eastern Europe. There were the usual problems from the Alamanni, the Iuthungi and the Samaritans, who we have already met. They were joined by newcomers, to us at least, the Vandals, who had moved up to the Danube from Poland. These barbarians got deep into Italy before Aurelian could send them packing. Clearly, this sort of thing was a bit worrying, and the fact that Italy wasn't safe meant that Aurelian channelled his inner Hadrian and built a wall around Rome. It was creatively named the Aurelian Wall, and you can still see it. If you are ever in Rome, you should check a bit of it out. Incidentally, with all the trouble from around the Danube, Aurelian decided to just give up on keeping hold of Dacia, and organised withdrawal from the province and left it to the barbarians. After the last few decades, you can't be too critical of the Romans wanting to turtle up a bit.

Aurelian's second issue was with Zenobia and the Palmyrene Empire, which by this point ran in a crescent around the Mediterranean, from Southern Turkey to Egypt. As far as splinter empires go, that's a big'un. Aurelian went over in 272, and they fought a battle at Antioch, in Southern Turkey. The Romans won and were quite successful in fighting a series of battles until they could besiege the Palmyrene capital of Palmyra, in Syria. Aurelian won the siege, captured Zenobia, and had her taken back to Rome to be paraded at a triumph. There was a smaller revolt soon after in Palmyra when they declared Zenobia's son emperor (we think he was a son anyway). Aurelian, presumably being properly sick of all this now, wasn't having any of it and destroyed the city. While it wasn't wiped off the map, Palmyra was now no longer going to be trying to form another empire.

Interestingly there is a bit of an argument about the aim of the Palmyrene Empire. Was it to be a whole new thing, as a sort of early Arabic nationalist movement, or was it meant to be a part of the Roman Empire, just trying to make a change? Most historians seem to think Zenobia's actual aim was to keep as part of the Roman Empire and take over the running of it for her family. The idea of an emperor coming from a power base of Syria wasn't mental. We have already seen Pernicious Niger try, as well as Philip the Arab. In fact, someone from that direction had been involved in most of the squabbling over the empire. Even if they were just posted there as a governor.

Either way, the Palmyrenes were done, and the next step was the Gallic Empire, which we have already looked at. Once they were back in the fold, the empire was a bit more intact, and Aurelian was looking like a bit of a winner compared to the previous lot. He did, however, have some questionable ideas. He mixed things up in term of religion, replacing the main god of Rome, Jupiter, for Sol Invictus, a sun god, who was a patron god of soldiers. He also made himself a living god, giving himself the title Deus (which just means god). The emperors had been gods for a long time, but they usually waited until being dead before they were deified. Not for Aurelian, he was a literal living god.

Soon though he was a dead god, and the story of his death, as told by Zosimus, is ridiculous. One of his staff, Eros, had made a mistake in some of his work. Aurelian had a reputation for being overly strict with his punishments, and Eros was worried. His solution was to forge a letter with a list of men to be executed. He then showed it to the men at the top of the fake list, who ran off to assassinate Aurelian. It probably wasn't that simple, and there are suggestions the army was upset with him anyway, but it's too mad a story not to include. If that is the case, it was a bad way for a fairly solid emperor to go out. Aurelian was a bit of a bright spot in the 3rd-century.

Unlike a standard assassination of an emperor, it looked like there was no plan for what to do when Aurelian was dead, but the Senate got together and gave the job to Marcus Claudius Tacitus, a 75-year-old. Even that decision took six months to make. You can't keep a 75-year-old bloke waiting for six months, it's not like he had many half-years left in him. There is a suggestion that it was Aurelian's wife, Ulpia Severina, who was in charge for those six months, but that's just a guess, as the sources are quiet on the whole thing.

Either way, Tacitus had a hell of a job on, and he spent his short, less than a year-long reign fighting. The Franks and the Alamanni were at it again, and the Heruli tribe, a group from the Sea of Azov, north of the Black Sea, were running riot through Turkey. Tacitus was actually doing pretty well against the Heruli before he died in mid-276. He was possibly killed by soldiers, which was the traditional 3rd-century Roman emperor's way to go, but he might have just died of disease and being 76.

Tacitus was replaced by his Florianus, Tacitus half-brother. He managed to be emperor from June to September 276, before he was killed. Although he might have committed suicide because it was obvious another bloke was going to get the job soon enough.

The other bloke was Probus, who had been declared emperor by the legions in the East. Probus was a bit like Aurelian, he had shit to deal with all over the place, but he seemed to get it done. The tribes along the Rhine and the Danube were still causing havoc, but by 279 he had that lot calm enough that he could head off east. There was some trouble in Turkey, but this time it wasn't a tribe or the Persians causing trouble. This time it was a group of bandits led by someone called Lydius the Isaurian (Issuria was a region of Turkey). He had been causing grief and was holed up in the city of Cremna (also Turkey), and the Romans were struggling to get him out. In the end, Lydius was killed when he fell out with an expert artilleryman, who then defected to the Romans and offered to snipe at Lydius. Which he did.

From there, Probus headed to Egypt to put down a revolt. After which the empire was relatively calm, although there were some issues from usurpers, like Bonosus, Proculus and Saturninus, who we mentioned in the Roman Britain chapter. One crucial change Probus made to the empire was the inviting in of the tribes from the edges of the empire. He let the lot in, Franks, Vandals, Goths, pretty much all the tribes we have been talking about in this chapter, all of whom had been causing absolute havoc. It was probably a good deal for the tribes, who were moving west in search of money and lands. Being given what they wanted, without having to fight, would have been a winner. For the Romans, it looked a good deal because it meant these tribesmen were not only no longer attacking the Romans. Now they were in Roman territory, and they were going to help repel further invasions from the East - better to have them in the tent pissing out than outside pissing in. It was a solid plan, which would backfire spectacularly later on.

You will be surprised to hear that the end of Probus

came from being killed by someone else who wanted his job. In this case, the usurper was the Praetorian Prefect (surprised?) Marcus Aurelius Carus, in 282. Probus was on his way east to fight the Sassanids when the legions back on the Danube declared for Carus. The soldiers were a bit annoyed with Probus since he had finished a lot of the fighting, he had them working on public projects, like agriculture. There was no loot in that, so we doubt the soldiers were hard to persuade to bump Probus off as soon as it looked like he would lose.

Carus & Co

Carus didn't have long to enjoy being the top dog, but he is notable in that when he was made emperor, he didn't try to get the approval of the Senate. He was the emperor because the army said it was ok, which is normal, but he didn't even pretend to care what the Senate thought. While Carus didn't last long, he did some fighting along the Danube, before setting off to fight the Sassanids. He was over that way when he died suddenly, the next year, in 283. We are told that he was killed by being struck by lightning. That was at least a new one for Roman emperors, but that could easily not be true. Before he went, he did have enough time to make his two sons, Carinus and Numerian, his caesars, and heirs.

He had tasked the oldest son Carus with looking after the West, while he and Numerian headed east. Numerian only lasted until 284, but before we go into that, we should pause for a sec.

The last Roman history chapter, and this one up to this point, has been a whirlwind of emperor names, wars, empires, and slightly funny deaths. If you are going to take some important things from this Third Century Crisis it might as well be these:

The tribes from Eastern Europe were causing all sorts of

problems and didn't seem to be looking like stopping their raids/invasions over the Danube/Rhine borders.

Power had got away from the Senate now. Emperors were not just being made and ended by the army, but they were picking exactly who they liked, and the people they liked were not Italian senators. The trend was now for men being born in or based in the Balkans getting the top job. And a lot of them were of pretty low birth.

It's a bit 'what if', but plenty of historians reckon the whole empire could have disintegrated if there hadn't been a handful of all these emperors and usurpers who knew what they were doing. For most of what we were talking about, it felt like the empire was running away with itself, and nobody was really in control.

Diocletian

Our last few chapters have been awash with a load of emperors, lots of scrapping, and the odd competent leader trying to fix things. What Rome needed now was an emperor who could be around for a long time. Someone who could get down to the business of organising things to stop all this happening over and over again. Enter Diocletian.

The story of how he became emperor is a bit weird. Not struck by lightning, Carus style, but still odd. The co-emperor Numerian was in the East to sort out taking troops out of Sassanid territory and back into the Roman provinces. Everyone was told that he had an eye infection, so he travelled in his litter with the curtains shut. Syria must be dusty, after all. After a while, though, a horrible smell came from the litter, and it turns out he wasn't so much ill as he was dead. His father-in-law was blamed for the dead emperor and was killed on the spot. In all fairness to the quick execution, the father-in-law was a Praetorian Prefect so he could very well have been guilty.

After the death of Numerian, Diocletian was declared emperor by the legions in the East, giving him immediate control over the eastern half of the empire. Note that his becoming emperor had nothing to do with Numerian's brother, and co-emperor, Carinuis, who would have had his own plans. This was in November 284, and a few months later Diocletian met Carinuis, for a winner takes all battle. They met roughly in the middle, around Belgrade in Serbia, and Diocletian won. So, he took it all. Easy.

Diocletian was emperor for 20 years, which is a really long time considering who came before him. We touched on some of the things he did in the Roman Britain chapter, but let's have a proper look.

Diocletian realised that the empire was far too big to manage. To be fair he wasn't the first, and we have seen a few co-emperors splitting responsibilities for east and west before. In 286, Diocletian decided to do a bit of that as well and picked Maximian to be his co-emperor, making him an Augustus. Diocletian stayed in the East, in Nicomedia, a city in Turkey that wasn't far from Istanbul, and Maximian was to look after the West from his base in Milan, Northern Italy.

Six years later, Diocletian gave himself and Maximian an assistant each. Both the East and the West had an augustus (senior emperor), and a caesar (junior emperor), and this system is known as the Tetrarchy. It's a Greek term for being ruled by four leaders, and a handy word to have lying around.

The new caesars of this Tetrarchy were Constantius in the West and Galerius in the East. The split meant that the empire was, in effect, split into four. Diocletian, working from Nicomedia still, ran the Middle East, Egypt, and Turkey, up to Istanbul. Galerius had the rest of Turkey, Greece, and the Balkans up towards Italy. He worked out of Sremska Mitrovica (Sirmium) in Serbia. Maximian, was up in Milan running Italy plus a bit above the Alps, North

Africa, excluding Egypt, and Spain/Portugal. Constantius had Gaul and Britain, based out of Trier (Augusta Treverorum) which is Germany.

What you will notice there is that the main emperor was out in the East. Even the second most important emperor was up in Milan, so Rome wasn't the seat of power for any of them. This was a bit of a trend from now on. The East was often the seat of power, and the emperors spent much less time in Rome. Which is weird for the Roman Empire.

As we covered in the Roman Britain chapter, Diocletian recognised the whole thing. More provinces, and more layers of people running things. We have seen that's the way the running of the empire was going. However, Diocletian made the process of taking power away from the Senate, official, by making a proper bureaucracy to administer things. Bureaucracy gets a bad reputation but considering the empire had spanned from Baghdad to Carlisle, at points, maybe it was a good idea to have people looking after all the bits in between.

The restructuring Diocletian was extensive, it covered everything from administrative to economic to the military. Those economic changes were significant, and they included setting maximum prices for everyday things, like food. He also reorganised and increased taxation, setting up a land tax, including in Italy, who had been exempt from that kind of thing before. However, as much as ancient economics is a laugh a minute, it was the military changes which are the most interesting.

We have been talking about legions for the last 300 odd years of Roman history. By the time the Roman Empire was an empire, the approach to Roman warfare was pretty standardised, with the legions at its centre. Under Diocletian, there was a change of approach, probably because he realised that they had gone from an ever-expanding empire, smashing tribes and smaller kingdoms, to a slowly shrinking empire getting hammered constantly from every which way. The soldiers were now reorganised into two different groups: static border defences and mobile armies. The static border forces were for keeping an eye on borders like the Rhine, Danube, and Hadrian's Wall. They were known as limitanei, named after the limes (limits/borders) they were on. You might also see them called ripenses, which comes from the word from 'riverbank,' as they were guarding the Rhine and the Danube. The mobile armies were stationed within provinces rather than at borders. They were designed to move about and help with any problems which popped up. These armies were called comitatenses, and they were the more elite of the two groups.

Our description of the way this work is how the army would end-up being organised, but it was a process of development. Some of these changes were more firmly put in place later, but Diocletian moved the army a decent way in this direction. It goes to show how sick the Romans were of getting beaten up by everyone, that they would change how they did things in the army. They loved the army.

All this reorganisation and restructure was good stuff, but it didn't solve all their problems. We know that Carausius and the Allectus in Britain caused a bit of trouble, but Constantius, the caesar in the West, had other issues in his corner of the empire. He had to fight those annoying Alamanni as well. Maximian seemed to have a slightly easier time, although he did have to put down a revolt in North Africa in 298. The trip down there might have been the first time he had visited Rome in the twelve years of his reign. Considering he oversaw that part of the empire, that seems very odd to us.

The East was a bit more of an issue for the Romans. There was the standard fighting with the tribes in the Balkans and the surrounding area, but it was the Sassanids that were a bigger problem. Their new king, Narseh, decided he was the new Sharpur and wanted to have a crack at the Romans again. This involved invading Syria and Armenia, and there was some definite toing and froing before the

Romans got the upper hand. They pushed the advantage and drove down to take the city of Ctesiphon, which was the traditional sign of the Romans beating a Persian empire.

It must be said that the Tetrarchy did as well as anyone in the third century. Certainly, in terms of keeping the empire together with the angriest barbarians and Persians on the outside. For anyone missing some good usurper chat, since Carausius and Allectus were in the other chapter, we do have one for you. A bloke named Aurelius Achilleus had Egypt declare themselves as independent in 296, which was before the problems with the Sassanids were really kicking off. Egypt was still an essential part of the empire, so Diocletian himself headed over to besiege the rebels in Alexandria. It took a while, but inevitably Diocletian won. It wasn't a particularly impressive attempt at a new splinter empire or even a good attempt to take over the Roman Empire, but it doesn't feel right to have a few of them per chapter.

Before we leave Diocletian, we should have a look at his (unhealthy) relationship with religion. The things he did generally sound very sensible, but he did stray into mad emperor a bit. He had side-lined the Senate by this point, and while he shared his power with the other three emperors, he was very much in charge. On top of that, he set himself up as a god, which is never a good sign. From 287 he started calling himself Jovus (Jupiter, the main Roman god) and Maximian was Hercules (Jupiter's son). Managing to have himself as a god, and putting Maximian in his place as his less impressive son, was a lovely double megalomaniac whammy. On the subject of religion, it was also a pretty bad time to be a Christian, as Diocletian ran some horrendous sounding persecution of them.

In 305 Diocletian decided to retire and made Maximian go with him at the same time. The process was in place, where the caesars would step up, and a couple of new caesars would be appointed. Nice and tidy. The man himself retired to where he was from, in Croatia, and built himself an absolutely ludicrous palace to live in. That palace eventually became a part of the city of Split, and is still sort of standing, with the whole thing having been incorporated into the city. You should visit, it's so weird sitting and having a pint in a pub built into a wall of a palace built by a Roman emperor.

Diocletian oversaw a very calm period for the empire, at least compared to most of the last century. Don't worry, though, it gets mad again almost as soon as he retires, which is something to look forward to.

The Hopewell Culture

We wanted to include a chapter on something that was going on in North America during our period of Roman Britain. As we are sure everyone is aware, we aren't awash with written records for this period on that side of the Atlantic. North America was going through what is classified as the Woodland Period. This spanned from 1000 BC to 1000 AD, and it was a period that saw an increase in farming crops for food, and bigger advances in pottery.

The temptation is to see the people in North America as very primitive, but that wouldn't be right. They certainly weren't as big into metal making as they were in Europe, but they were relatively sophisticated compared to how you might imagine them. By not being big into metal, we mean the making of alloy metals like iron. However, they certainly did some good stuff with copper. Have a search for 'Hopewell copper falcon' to see one of them which we quite like.

This 'Hopewell' falcon came from the people of the Hopewell culture, which developed around 200 BC to 500 BC, in the east of North America. This wasn't like a kingdom, but more of a shared culture, in the same way that the tribes of Gaul, Britain and Ireland were all Celtic at one point. Unfortunately, the nice-sounding name has a boring back story. It was the name of the farm in Ohio where a group of burials were the first glimpse of the culture was found. These names are always disappointing. It's like the

Nok all over again.

While people were still farming and hunting, the quality of their pottery and metalwork suggests that the settlements that grew up around the lakes and rivers were able to support specialists. The people of the Hopewell culture certainly did a good line in pipes. They also built burial mounds, like what you can see across the rest of the world. Some of them are pretty big, standing at 9 meters (30 ft) tall, so they must have been a community effort, again meaning that the folk there were doing well enough to have big groups of people with the time to be building these mounds.

Not only were they making all the things you would expect a culture at the turn of the first millennium to be making, but they also traded them over serious distances. Discoveries from Hopewell sites have included things that have come from as far away as the Gulf of Mexico (bottom of the US, where Florida is) the Rocky Mountains (North-West US way, around Wyoming). That's not quite a trade route to rival the Silk Road, but the people of North America were still trading goods across 1000 miles, which is no mean feat.

We want to end our bit on North America by talking about Britain because we are nothing if not Anglocentric. Clearly, there are only so many ways you can bury your dead, and not too many ways to do it in a fancy, grand way. You basically have to build something big to put over them, like the Nubian Pyramids (take that Egypt). However, it's impressive how similar the mounds that the society in North America built, are to the barrows you find in the British Isles. Although, ours tend to be longer and thinner, hence the name 'long barrows', where the North American ones look like weird perfectly round hills. It's not important, but we quite like the idea of two separate people on either side of an ocean doing the same thing for the same reason. Add to that other versions, like the Kufun of Japan, which were keyhole-shaped mounds they put their influential dead in, and it's mad how similar we all are.

What A Load Of Cs - Constantius Chlorus and Constantine

We last left Britain, in 296, with the Roman provinces just having been taken back from Allectus, by the proper Roman Empire. This was done by the caesar in the West, Constantius. And considering it had been ten years in the making, with the splinter empire lasting from 286 to 296, in the end, it sounded quite easy to reclaim for the Roman.

You would imagine that an invasion by the official Romans would have meant Allectus had dragged all his soldiers south to fight them. Moving soldiers around our island has often gone badly for the Romans, and if soldiers were taken from Hadrian's Wall, you would assume that the Britons up there would take advantage. What actually happened was nothing. Or at least nothing big enough that it got reported. That means that this chapter is another one that is heavy on Roman politics rather than mad Britons running riot. At least a lot of the politics happened in Britain.

In this chapter, we ask ourselves: is it possible to stop the children of important people getting good jobs? What's going on in Scotland? And what's the best 'fuck you' picture ever sent?

The Empire Comes To Britain

In almost every period previously, as soon as the Romans took one eye of their northern border, they found Britons from the north crawling all over it. Not this time, though, or at least as far as we know. When Constantius took Britannia back, there was some trouble in the south, when some of the defeated soldiers wanted to go souvenir shopping in London. Luckily for the ancient Londoners, Constantius was sailing up the Thames just in time to stop it. Apart from that, it seemed like aneasy win. There are some claims that there were, in fact, some problems in the north, but they seem a bit unfounded. Not that we are above clutching at some of the more exciting looking straws of rebellion. However, in this case, it really did look calm.

For a start, we have the fact that Constantius pretty quickly left our island to head back to the continent, so we assume there wasn't much to do on our side of The Channel. There is also the fact that the coins he had minted to celebrate his jaunt to Britain weren't about beating angry Britons, it was about him saving London from other Romans. This coin had an image of him heroically doing that with the phrase 'Redditor Lucis Aeternae', which means 'Restorer Of The Eternal Light'. If he had slammed some northern Britons, we assume there would be coins with an equally pretentious quote, and a picture of him stood on a pile of dead Britons, or something similarly subtle.

So, Constantius left Britain soon after winning it back and headed back to Gaul to do some rebuilding, not least of the port at Boulogne, which had been under the control of Carausius and Allectus. As we know, Constantius was caesar under his augustus, Maximian. That means he was waiting for a promotion to augustus, which he got in 305 when Diocletian decided to retire and made Maximian go at the same time. Constantius got promoted to augustus in the West, and a bloke named Galerius got the job in the East. Diocletian's plan to spread out the responsibilities was a good one. It meant, in theory, that each quarter of the empire got some imperial attention. In theory, it also meant that there more jobs to go around, which might mean less chance of an assassination of an emperor every five minutes. As you can tell from our liberal use of the phrase 'in theory,' it didn't really work. There was one significant problem with the theory. People. People are horrible.

As newly minted augusti, they needed to find themselves a couple of caesars. What happened next involves a lot of names that are all remarkably similar, so you will need to focus up for a minute. The obvious candidates for the job of caesar in the West were Constantius' son, Constantine, and Maximian's son, Maxentius. If nothing else, that goes to show how the Romans lacked imagination for the naming of their sons. Unfortunately for them, the power was in the east, and Galerius (the augustus over there) had different ideas. The chosen caesar in the West was Severus, who was a friend of Galerius. The chosen caesar in the East was a bloke named Maximinus, and despite the name, he wasn't a relation of Maximian. He was, however, a relation of Galerius.

Constantius' was no doubt annoyed that his son had been passed over for the job in the West, and you can bet your last quid on the fact that it had annoyed Constantine. There was also the added worry that Constantine was in Nicomedia, which was Galerius' headquarters in Turkey when all this was happening. That would have been a dangerous place for him to be since neither Severus nor Maximinus would like a potential rival for power hanging about. You have to assume that Galerius wasn't a massive fan either since he had picked his own men for the jobs in the first place.

Luckily for Constantine, his dad had a plan: Constantius decided he was due a return to Britain for a campaign, and he wanted his son to join him. Which he was allowed to do, sort of. We are told that Galerius was planning to have Constantine assassinated, but, because Galerius liked a drink, Constantine was able to leg it one night, before the augustus sobered up the next day to put his morning assassination order in. The other version of that story is that Constantine waited until Galerius was nice and hammered and just asked him if he could join his dad. Being happy and drunk Galerius forgot he was angry with Constantine and agreed. Either way, this means Galerius and his mates had to go for plan b, which was to just kill Constantine as he travelled from east to west.

A part of the story of Constantine running west to escape assassination involves some very casual animal cruelty. Every time Constantine stopped to get fresh horses; he killed the other horses to stop the people following him getting fresh mounts. That's unbelievably harsh on the horses. Generally, it's thought that all this was a story that was later told to make Galerius and co look like violent arseholes, but it does go to show that everyone wasn't getting on.

However they got there, Constantius and his son Constantine were on a campaign in Britain over 305-06. Why was there a need for a Roman emperor to come to Britannia with an army? We don't exactly know. Although, we do know he was heading north to Scotland. Speaking of the north, it's worth pointing out that the people he was going to campaign against, in the far north, were now referred to as the Picti (Picts). The way the Romans referred to the people of Scotland changed a lot over the time they were on our island. At first, there were different tribes, like with the rest of Britain, such as the Votadini and the Selgovae. Then, by the 3rd-century, there were two broad confederations, the Caledonii and the Maeatae, and later, from the fourth century, we have the Picti. The name Picti apparently comes from the Latin' Painted Ones,' although it could just as easily come from a Latinisation of the term the Picts, or a group of Picts used to refer to themselves. People tend to go for the 'Painted Ones' route, and to be fair, it does give off more of a Braveheart vibe, so why not.

The Picts mostly lived in the northeast of Scotland, above the line between Glasgow and Edinburgh. Who they were is a touch controversial. For example, there is a shout that the language they spoke was different from the Celtic languages that were native to the island before the Romans appeared. It might be that they spoke a language based on what was spoken even before the Celts arrived. Generally, the view is that they were a regional variation of the people we have been meeting so far in our story. More specifically, that they grew out of a closer confederation of the Caledonii and the Maeatae. Whoever they were, they were no friends of the Romans, and they would take over the mantle of 'pain in the arse in the north' for the rest of Roman Britain.

Going back to Constantius, as ever, we don't know much about any of what went on. Or, as we said, why they were even really there. You would have to be tempted to point out that if Constantine was in danger of being assassinated, being on an island on the other edge of the Roman Empire, with the company of an army was a good place for father and son to be. Another logical explanation would be there was trouble in the north of Britannia, presumably from Britons in Scotland. It certainly wouldn't be the first time, and it wouldn't be the last. We are told in a panegyric that the reason for the trip north was so Constantius could:

'gaze upon the Ocean, that father of the gods who restores the fiery stars of heaven, so that as one about to savour endless light he might already see almost continuous day.'

Apparently, he wanted to see the far north, because he knew he was going to die soon. If that sounds too 'fluffy' to be a real reason for marching an army to the edge of an empire, you probably have a point. A panegyric is a declaration about someone full of praise, a bit like a eulogy. We have tried not to include too much from those when talking about emperors. They are about as reliable as listening to a government minister talking about their own department's actions. It's likely to be so full of bullshit it's about to pop, so paying too much attention to them is unhelpful.

Those of you with good memories will remember another

emperor who made it up to towards the top of Scotland. He had enjoyed the scenery as well. That was Emperor Severus, who campaigned in Britain in 208 (not the bloke who was caesar in the West at this point - the Romans really needed a bigger pool of names to work from). In fact, Constantius' whole trip was like an emperor-based tribute. Constantius probably set up his base in York (like Severus), he probably took the east coast route up the island (no doubt dressed as Severus, like a mediocre tribute band). Then you have the seeing the far north thing (what a pathetic fanboy). As with Severus' campaigns, any gains in territory up in Scotland that Constantius made, weren't turned into an expansion of the province. In fact, the whole thing ended with the ultimate homage to the old Emperor Severus, when Constantius went and died in York in 306. Get your own thing Constantius, stop stealing from Severus.

This is where it gets interesting for the Roman Empire. Constantius was dead, so that means Severus was to get promoted to augustus. (The 4th-century caesar of the West, not the 3rd-century one Constantius had an emperor crush on). Unfortunately for Severus, Constantine didn't fancy some other bloke replacing his dad. Constantine's solution to that was to just declare himself as emperor, with the support of the legions in Britannia. This is getting silly now, he might be the son of an emperor, but ten years after the end of the empire started by Carausius, we have someone else standing in Britain declaring himself emperor. Not the emperor of a rival new empire based on Britain. Not a caesar in the West of the Roman Empire, like his dad had started out as. He declared himself as a full augustus, meaning he was looking to directly replace his dad, and skip being a caesar all together.

How this declaration happened is particularly impressive. We are told that Constantine sent Galerius notification of his dad's death, along with a portrait of himself in the robes of an augustus. The brass balls on that one. That's not even a quick, funny snap on your mobile, as a fuck you. Someone had to draw that out. There will have been plenty of time, between it being started and it being sent, to realise that doing it might be taking the mickey.

You should take a minute to imagine Galerius' reaction to hearing the news that Constantine had declared himself augustus. Particularly if he did send a picture of himself doing it. It's an enjoyable thing to imagine, but if there was a toddleresque meltdown of a tantrum, Galerius' eventual decision was actually pretty sensible. It had taken years to winkle Carausius and his mates out of Britain only a decade before. That means a squabble with the newly self-declared augustus would be, at best, a long-term pain in the arse, and at worse a full-blown civil war. To make things even more complicated, the Praetorian Guard in Rome decided to declare Maximian's son, Maxentius, emperor. It was quickly going the way of imperial successions before Diocletian tried to fix it. So instead, Galerius decided to try and make everyone roughly happy. He didn't let Constantine become augustus in the West, and that was given to Severus like it was meant to. However, Constantine was allowed to become caesar in the West, under Severus, instead. You can imagine how awkward that was in the imperial halls of power. We are getting strong The Thick of It associations out of all this. Awkwardness aside, this sounds like a solid plan to stop some brutal Roman on Roman fighting. It didn't, obviously, because nothing would ever stop the Romans going at each other. The full story is so much more mental than we have given it credit there, but we will go over that in a Roman history chapter.

Did Constantine Forget Britain?

It looks like Constantine returned back to Britannia at some point between 307 and 315. Or at least a Roman army did something impressive on our island. We can guess that because he got the title Britannicus Maximus sometime around 315, which is the title emperors gave themselves when they did something exciting in Britain, usually involving killing some Britons, or maybe a usurper. There were a few of them knocking around.

Beyond exciting usurpers and the like, there was a lot of building work done around the late 3rd and early 4th-century, and it's hard to date exactly when it was. One area that was heavily developed was York, and there is a claim that it was Constantine who organised that. It would make sense for him to be interested in that particular city, as it was the place he was declared emperor, and it would reflect poorly on him if it looked a bit scruffy. A lot of these building works were military in nature, defensive walls and whatnot, and this was a bit of a change in policy in Britannia, and around the empire generally. We get this from Zosimus:

'But Constantine destroyed that security by removing the greater part of the soldiers from those barriers of the frontiers and placing them in towns that had no need of defenders'

As in, Constantine moved his legions from the borders, like Hadrian's Wall, and moved them into better-fortified towns. It was something that Diocletian had started doing, and Constantine is getting credit for continuing with that. There are pros to this newer approach, as far as we can see. We know that towards the end of the third-century, Britain was getting trouble from tribes like the Franks. They weren't coming from the north, and they were arriving by sea. Which would make a defensive position like Hadrian's Wall a bit less useful. The con to moving defences into towns would be that it meant anyone could land on a beach or climb over a wall and wonder about the place breaking things, while the soldiers were tucked up in the cities. That's probably a bit unfair, for a start, we imagine the soldiers could leave the towns, but it's safe to say that Zosimus was not a fan, saying:

'To speak in plain terms, he was the first cause of the affairs of the empire declining to their present miserable state.'

Zosimus was writing in the 6th-centauryf, and by then the Roman Empire was not in a good way, and he blamed Constantine for that. Which is a pretty big claim, and certainly not what he is remembered for, which you will see in the next few chapters.

That is the end of that. It wasn't exactly directly about the Romans in Britain or the Britons for that matter. However, when something that big for the whole empire happens, with Britain as a backdrop, it's worth a mention. So, what have we learnt? Well, Britain seems to be a really good place to hide when Romans want to kill you. There is no point in trying to stop Romans killing each other. And a picture tells a thousand words.

Tetrarchy Civil War

We have covered Constantine and his rise to being an emperor in the British history chapter, but it's worth going over properly. Diocletian set up a perfectly reasonable-sounding system of running the empire. The Tetrarchy meant dividing up the empire so four different people could properly run their corner of it. And it took absolutely no time to entirely fall apart, and for it be just as messy as it was before Diocletian got there.

This one is a confusing inception style kaleidoscope of intermingling civil wars, and every bugger has the same bloody name. But here is our summary of what happened between Diocletian setting up his system and Constantine taking sole control of the empire.

Diocletian Retires

In 305 Diocletian had had enough, and he retired, forcing Maximian to go as well. This meant the two caesars got promoted to augustus and two new caesars were appointed. That means a post-Diocletian world had:

- East (augustus) - Galerius

- East (caesar) - Maximinus Daia as his caesar (we will call his Daia for reasons which will become clear)

- West (augustus) - Constantius

- West (caesar) - Severus (don't worry he is not important)

This arrangement upset two people who had wanted to be emperor, Constantine, who was Constantius' son, and Maxentius (Max Junior) the son of Maximian (Max Senior). This was made worse when Constantius died in 306, and Constantine just declared himself augustus in the West, never mind that Severus was next in line. It was a move which was the starting pistol for all sorts of mad shit. Max Junior also decided to declare himself as emperor, and he persuaded Max Senior to come out of retirement as co-emperor with him.

Since the West now had four emperors, and only one of whom had been told he was actually an emperor, Galerius had to do something. His solution was to send Severus to attack Max Junior and Senior in Rome. Unfortunately for Severus, all his soldiers had recently been in Max Senior's army, and they defected back to him. This all ended in 307, with Severus being executed by the Maxes.

Happy Families

In 307 Max Senior reached an agreement with Constantine, meaning when Galerius inevitably came for the Maxes, Constantine wouldn't get involved. They sealed the deal with Constantine marrying Max Senior's daughter/Max Junior's sister.

Galerius did arrive in Italy to try and end the madness, but when he got to Rome he struggled with a siege, and things were made worse when some of his soldiers, again, started defecting to the Maxes side. Nevertheless, it wasn't all plain sailing for the Maxes. In 308, Max Senior decided his son was slowing him down and tried to depose Max Junior.

Unfortunately, this time his pull with the soldiers didn't work, and the army-backed Max Junior, so Max Senior was forced to run off to hide by joining Constantine.

In the same year, Galerius called a meeting chaired by Diocletian to discuss all this. The outcome was that the new official line up was:

- East (augustus) - Galerius
- East (caesar) - Maximinus Daia as his caesar
- West (augustus) - Licinius
- West (caesar) - Constantine

There are two points about this. Firstly, it meant Constantine had got a demotion from his claimed status augustus to a mere caesar. That didn't last long, and he got the augustus title soon after. Daia, the caesar in the East, also didn't like his title, so managed to force himself a title bump as well. So now we have four official augusti in the empire.

Secondly, Licinius was only technically the augustus in the West. In reality, Max Junior was still in control of the Italian and African territories that the augustus of the West was meant to have. So Licinius was augustus in the West in the same way that the person working on a shop's till is the manager, just because they have nicked their name badge. Fake or real, we now have five augusti in the empire.

What has happened to Max Senior? Well, he was working for Constantine now, but in 310 he tried to usurp him as well. Again, the soldiers didn't fancy that, so Constantine caught him, gave him a beating and Max Senior later committed suicide. Which is at least one less Max.

Constantine vs Max Junior and

Licinius vs Daia

In 310 the other big event for the Roman Empire was that Galerius died. What should have happened, according to the rules, was that Daia would be bumped to the senior emperor of the East and there would be a new caesar. What actually happened was that Licinius, who should have been emperor in the West, but had no control, shared the East with Daia. So, the set up was now:

- East (augustus) - Daia and Licinius (although technically not)

- East (caesar) - nobody

- West (augustus) - Licinius (although not at all, because Max Junior was really in control) and Constantine

- West (caesar) - nobody

So far, we have been light on actual wars, but it's about to go off. Nobody liked anybody in this situation, but alliances were formed. Licinius and Constantine teamed up, and Daia and Max Junior formed a partnership.

In 312 Constantine and Max Junior were getting into it and Constantine finally got rid of him. Max Junior's death came at the Battle of the Milvian Bridge, where he had built a collapsing bridge to trick Constantine. Unfortunately, in a classic case of 'hoisted by your own petard,' the bridge collapsed with Max Junior on it, and he drowned.

In 313, it was Licinius and Daia who were scrapping. The fighting went Licinius way, and in an anticlimactic finish, the war ended when Daia died. Possibly of natural causes or suicide. Not a heroic way to go, but at least it's not falling off your own trick bridge.

Constantine vs Licinius

Now we have Constantine in the West and Licinius in the East. Instead of diving straight into a war, they got together and organised a peace. There was a period in 316/17 where there were a couple of battles, where Constantine edged it, but the two men still split the empire. Only Constantine had picked up Pannonia and Moesia in Eastern Europe. It wasn't until 324, when they finally fought properly, that Constantine won and executed Licinius a year later. Obviously, this happened a lot slower than we made it sound, as there were nearly 20 years between Diocletian retiring and Constatine grabbing all the power for himself.

Constantine the Christian

All that is interesting, watching Diocletuians system getting ripped apart. And by now it was fully dead, particularly as Constantine had by now set his sons up as caesars, meaning Rome would be run by a dynasty again. Something which Diocletian specifically didn't want.

However, that's probably not why you have heard of Constantine before. It's also not why he is known as Constantine the Great. The scrap between Constantine and Licinius is the first one which was as much about religion as it was anything else. At least that's how it's often phrased. It's an exaggeration we are sure, as Constantine was probably very, very, keen on being the only augustus in town.

The Christians had been taking a beating from Roman emperors, on and off since Jesus had taken a nap in a cave. Diocletian had been one of those who had stuck the boot in, and he went in for persecution in a massive way. As with all these things, it's hard to know if these persecutions were more to do with: political benefits, a heartfelt religious conviction, scapegoating or a fear of people having loyalty to an outside source.

However, during the resulting fight for control over the empire, Constantine had converted to Christianity. In 313 Constantine and Licinius had got together for the Edict of Milan. This, among other things, gave the Christians the right to worship in the Roman Empire. It also restored some of the stuff that had been nicked from them in recent years. In the end, Licinius didn't really get on with Christians, and he got involved in some persecution in his half of the empire. This means the final battle was between a pagan emperor and the first Christian emperor (as far as we know). Whatever it was, Constantine becoming emperor was a massive step in making the Roman Empire Chrisitan. You can't deny that was a pretty significant thing, considering the next 1700 years or so.

It was under Constantine that the First Council of Nicaea was called. This was a big meeting of bishops from all over the place. They got together to discuss the problems they had been having following the spread of Christianity. It was easy for someone in Britain to come up with a different interpretation of Chrisitan beliefs than someone in Jerusalem. The empire was a very interconnected place, but it's not like they could ring each other up to argue things out. So, the Christian bigwigs had to be a get-together to make sure it was standardised. You don't need to be a historian to have an idea about what can happen when two groups have a different view on their religion, so this sort of thing was a good idea. The First Council of Nicaea council formed a lot of the basis for a lot of how the Christian Churches work even now, with the biggie being the confirmation that Jesus was equal to God.

Constantine The Ruler

We might as well finish up with Constantine. We know he fought to be the sole emperor and that he was a Christian, but what else did he get up to?

One other thing Constantine did which echoed through history, or historical maps at least, was to rename the city of Byzantium. We now know that city as Istanbul, and it sits as a sort of gateway between Europe and Asia (assuming you don't want to go through Russia, which is too big to be a gateway). While he was beating Licinius, he decided to rename the city Constantinople, and he made it his capital in 330. Constantinople basically means Constantine's City, which is a high-rolling move. It is more important than that because, as we have mentioned previously, the power of the empire was moving away from Rome, eastwards. Now the default place the emperor was hanging about was in Turkey, and not Italy.

Clearly, Constantine felt there was some room for improvement in what Diocletian had done, given he tore up the tetrarchy arrangement. However, he did carry on with the general gist of a lot of Diocletian's reforms. As we know, the military was changed to accommodate the two types of armies, the ones on the borders and the more mobile units elsewhere. We have already seen in the Roman Britain chapter that Constantine was blamed for moving soldiers from the borders and into the towns, which some folk reckoned doomed the empire.

Constantine also dove in on the administrative approach. Under his rule, the orders of senators and equestrians, with the plebs below, broke down even further. It was a slow process, but by this point, it was slightly less important who your dad was, and a bit more important what sort of job you had. Not wholly, nepotism is the barnacle on society that will never die, but it was a general trend.

Something we did skip over, while getting excited by civil wars, was the usual external worries the empire had. The Germanic peoples in Eastern Europe hadn't gone away, and there were the typical excursions against the Sassanids during all of this. Just not on the same scale as the civil wars - also we have been writing about them for a while, and there are only so many times the Alamanni can invade before you want to ignore it as attention-seeking. However, it's worth mentioning that Constantine campaigned on the Rhine in 328, against the Goths in 332 and the Sarmatians in 334. It was in that last effort where he reclaimed Dacia as a province. The Romans had been taking, losing, and retaking, that particular province for quite a while by now. So, taking control was a bit of an achievement.

Right at the end of his reign the Sasanian Empire also kicked up a fuss, and when Constantine died, in 337, he was on his way over there to deal with their emperor Shapur II.

Speaking of his death, as Constantine had spent a lot of effort in defeating his rivals, how he organised his succession was crucial. Constantine had a bit of a bumpy ride with his family. Back in 326, he had ordered his oldest son, Crispus, to death. Constantine did that because he was told by his wife, Fausta, who was Crispus' stepmam, that Crispus had tried to sleep with her. After Crispus was dead, Constantine found out that Fausta had lied, and he was understandably upset. Even so, Faustus' punishment of being executed by being locked in an overheated steam room sounds pretty grim.

The rest of his sons fared better. In fact, by the end of Constantine's reign, he had appointed them all as his caesars, along with two of his nephews. They were all given different regions of the empire to control, which isn't too dissimilar to the Tetrarchy arrangement. Except specifically keeping it in the family. For how that went after Constantine's death in 337 (as if you couldn't guess) you will have to wait for the next Roman history chapter.

Christianity

We have mentioned Christianity a bit so far in our story, which makes some sense. The new shiny religion formed and spread within the Roman Empire, and by the end, it would become the state religion. Most people will be aware that Christianity started in the first half of the 1st century - BC means Before Christ and AD is shorthand for 'in the year of the Lord'. What is less obvious is that in the early years, Christians were a Jewish sect. More specifically, they were a Jewish sect who were convinced that the messiah had come and that the end of the world was nigh. They toned down the immediacy of the 'end is nigh' chat, with the focus being the second coming of Jesus later on. However, what they couldn't tone down was the position of Jesus as the messiah. This wouldn't fit in very well with Judaism which is a monotheistic faith, although God and the Son of God as two parts of the same being is a good loophole in that respect. Even so, the two religions quickly began to divert.

Despite the moving apart, the Christians had come from the Jewish faith, and they share quite a few similarities. This was an issue for Christians. The Romans and the Jews did not get on, and there were quite a few very bloody wars between the two groups. As time went on the Christians grew further and further apart from the Jewish faith. Nevertheless, you can easily see a scenario where the Romans are gunning for the Jews, and it was easier to just include the Christians in any persecution. Better safe than sorry, as it were.

Christianity spread from its origins in the Middle East pretty quickly. With the Roman Empire being handy for that. The area around Jerusalem that is featured in the bible had a clear connection between Europe and North Africa, and people were frequently moving between the different regions, for trade, the military and general governance. Early success for Christianity was in the 'Greek' part of the empire, but it went much further than that. For example, one of the apostles, Peter, was executed in Rome itself in the 60s. This was around the time of the early persecution the Christians come under Nero in 64. He managed to blame them for the Great Fire of Rome. Despite that, Christians weren't quite as persecuted as you might imagine. Don't get us wrong, they got enough grief to have a fair few martyrs around the place. However, there weren't many instances of official, full empire, anti-Christian rules. There were just more general instructions to give them a kicking if they were being particularly annoying. Most of the grief the Christians got was localised scrapping.

That's not to say there were zero examples of Roman emperors going out of their way to persecute the Christians. We have already heard about Emperor Maximinius, in the 230s, offering tax breaks to people for sticking it to them. We do have to say, that is a very modern approach to fucking with people a government don't like. Shortly after that, in the 240s, Emperor Decius decreed that everyone in the empire needed to make a sacrifice to the gods - the gods being the Roman ones, rather than an optional pick the god of your choosing scenario. This wasn't necessarily aimed at the Christians, but we doubt many of them would have been comfortable being involved in a ceremony for someone else's gods.

Like any new religion, the Christians didn't need grief from the outside, as they could work up conflict all by themselves. A big feature of the early centuries of Christianity was the in-house fighting. Jesus was around, in person, until the 30s. After that, his apostles were around for most of the rest of the century. Even during that time, there was some divergence on the fundamentals of the new religion. There were all sorts of elements that could cause confusion and arguments. It wasn't until the First Council of Nicaea in 323 that everyone got together, and there were officially rulings on everything, like was Jesus the same as God and when is Easter? Why didn't they just pick a date? Why does it move every year? It didn't stop the arguments, but it meant that the powers that be had an official way it was meant to be, and anyone who disagreed was a heretic.

For the Christian Church to have powers that be it meant a proper organisation for those powers to sit atop of. It was early in the formation of the Church that the system of bishops and priests developed, with Peter being the Bishop of Rome (a.k.a. the Pope) before his death in the 60s. The admin of the church will have got a lot easier when it became the state religion of the Roman Empire. It was Constantine who brought the religion into the mainstream, and it was him that organise the First Council of Nicaea. He had issued the Edict of Milan in 313, which guaranteed that Christians could freely practice their religion. This only gave Christians protections, and it didn't make the empire Christian. In fact, not every Roman emperor after Constantine was a Christian, so there were a few setbacks on that. It wasn't until the Edict of Thessalonica, in 380, when Emperor Theodosius I, made Christianity the religion of the Roman Empire.

In terms of Roman Britain, there weren't many parts of the empire as far away from the origin of Christianity as we are. However, reach us, it did, and it looks like there were Christians here by the end of the 2nd-century. Towards the end of Roman Britain, there would have been plenty more, if only because, as we know, there was a fairly consistent influx of people from the rest of the empire, and they would have brought it with them. However, actual evidence of Christianity in this period is pretty few and far between. You can probably attribute that to the fact that, after the Romans, Britain dumped Christianity for a bit, so everything will have been replaced by other gods.

The Great Barbarian Conspiracy

We last left Britain in 307. Constantine was caesar in the West, but he was working his way up to being promoted to augustus. By 225 he was the only emperor in town, and he ran the whole empire. Which meant, when Constantine died in 337, it kicked off the customary fighting over the succession. It's safe to say that the Roman Empire was living in interesting times. However, while it was going off in the empire, the next big event in Roman Britain was in 343.

In this chapter, we ask ourselves: can the Romans be so obnoxious that it united everyone against them? Have we met the worst person in Roman Britain? How bad does it have to get in Britain before the Romans just give up?

Britannia In Chains

The benefit of Britain being an island on the very edge of the empire was that, by the 4th-century, unless some governor put themselves forward for a fight, it was pretty calm. However, in 343, the island had a visit from Constans. He was one of Constantine's sons that became proper emperors when he died. An emperor turning up in a province like Britain was always a big deal. It usually meant an invasion,

Roman Britain: celts, caesars & catastrophes

or big military campaign was in the offing. Or that we were getting a big wall. Constans had been in the Gaul fighting the Franks, who he beat in 342, and then he headed to Britain. Why? We don't know, as ever, but what we do know is a little bit strange. It happened over winter. As we have said before, marching about in winter wasn't the done thing at the time. It was too cold and too hard to keep everyone fed. Heading to Britain in winter was especially odd because it meant sailing the channel in bad weather, which really isn't a good plan. We know about the timing of the visit from a Roman called Julius Maternus. In a pathetically sycophantic bit of writing he said:

'You have changed and scorned the order of the seasons, trampling underfoot the swelling, raging waves of Ocean in wintertime, a deed unprecedented in the past, and not to be matched in the future. Beneath your oars trembled the waves of a sea still scarcely known to us, and the Briton trembled before the face of an emperor he did not expect.'

That is sickening, but it does suggest that Constans travelled in winter and it was a bit spur of the moment, considering nobody was expecting him to turn up. Predictably the imperial visit is related to trouble in the north, up at Hadrian's Wall and beyond. Constans' jaunt is usually linked to problems with a group of scouts the Romans had set up to work beyond Hadrian's Wall, called the areani. It's generally thought that Constans needed to go up there because the areani were helping the Britons in Scotland, rather than the Romans in Britannia. Which is a bit shifty. Whether the areani had gone native or not, it suggests that the Britons were causing more than the average bit of trouble.

After that short, lacking in detail, imperial visit, all was quiet on the Britain front until the 350s. Constans wasn't a popular man, and when an emperor is annoying people, a usurper pops up. This usurper was called Magnus Magnentius, and he followed the standard procedure by declaring himself emperor and killing Constans. We have to say,

Magnus Magnentius is a top-notch name, and we want him to be a villain living in a volcano lair. Unfortunately, he was just a generic Germanic-Roman general with a grievance. He wasn't in Britannia when he declared himself emperor, so we can't pin this on Britain being mad this time. However, Gaul, where he was based, Britain and Spain all jumped on the Magnentius bandwagon. Magnentius' three-year reign in the West was a solid effort and involved the usual betrayals and fighting you can expect from these things. Eventually, Constantius II, Constans brother, headed over from the East and beat him.

Don't worry if that was too brief, we will be going over it properly in the Roman history chapter. We mainly included that bit of the story here for the cool name, but it was important for Britain because of the aftermath. Constantius II was a touch annoyed about the Magnentius' debacle and wanted to find and punish anyone who had been too pro-Magnentius. He sent one of his men, Paulus, over to Britain to do the job. Now if Magnentius sounded like a supervillain, then Paulus was an actual one. His nickname was Catena, which translates as him being called Paulus the Chain. His time in Britain was described by the Roman historian, Ammianus Marcellinus in a very uncomplimentary manner:

'behind whose face there lurked a serpent, and who was very adroit at sniffing out hidden paths of danger. He was sent to Britain to fetch certain members of the armed forces who had dared to join Magnentius' conspiracy, and when they were unable to offer any resistance, he took it upon himself to exceed his instructions. Like a flood he suddenly overwhelmed the fortunes of many, sweeping forward amidst widespread slaughter and ruin, casting freeborn men into prison and degrading some with fetters, all this by fabricating charges that were far removed from the truth. Thus was perpetrated an impious crime, which branded Constantius' time with an everlasting mark of shame.'

You can see from that long quote that Paulus went in hard

on the locals, violently punishing wrongdoers and making things up when proper accusations couldn't be made. It sounded bad, to the point where the vicarius (vicar) of the Diocese of Britain, Martinus, got involved and tried to stop him. In a classic supervillain move, Paulus just had Martinus arrested. Unlike in the films, it ended with Martinus dying after a failed attempt to attack Paulus. Marvel wouldn't have got very far if they had taken their scriptwriting cues from the Romans. After that, Paulus was recalled and sent to do his things in other provinces around the empire. In the world of the Roman Empire, you really do have to be a disgrace to humanity to stand out as notably bad, but Paulus managed that with room to spare. For fans of horrible justice, Paulus was burnt alive by a future emperor, so there's that at least.

It's worth pointing out that this would have been horrible for the people living in Britannia, but, as you will see in the Roman history chapter, Britain was actually a relatively nice part of the Roman Empire to be in at this point. In fact, Britain was stable enough that it became pretty important to the western part of the empire. There was good farmland in Britain, and they exported food to the continent. However, the Romans in Gaul had been suffering from tribes in the West raiding their provinces. This meant the Rhine was closed off as a way of transporting goods from Britain down to Southern Europe. That was an issue, and the emperors of the time were putting quite a bit of effort into opening up those trade routes again. It's easy to think of Britain as the mad island at the edge of the empire, being backwards and awkward. In reality, during periods of trouble in the western half of the Roman Empire, Britannia was often a steady region. The island was happily separated from the worst of the impact of civil wars and invasions from Germanic tribes. Unless an angry emperor invited a twat like Paulus the Chain to visit.

More Grief From The North

Despite other people having it worse, the 360s weren't particularly pleasant for the people of Britannia, with the problems this time coming from the north. Which is comforting because they had been relatively quiet up there for a while. We have this from Ammianus:

'The Scotti and the Picts, wild tribesmen invaded and broke the peace that had been agreed. They were devastating the places close to the frontier and fear was spreading throughout the provinces, worn out by the previous disasters.'

The first question from that is, who are the Scotti? Like with the Picts, who they were is a bit up in the air. The general view is that they were people from Northern Ireland (Atrium) and South West Scotland (Argyll). In later centuries there would be a kingdom that covered this area, and it looks like the Scotti were the start of that. The rest of the quote shows that the problems came down from the north and that they messed the place up. It suggests the Roman provinces of Britannia were already knackered from previous issues. We assume that the issues were a mixture of getting grief from the north, and Paulus the Chain causing havoc. Which would explain why the legions in Britain would need some extra help.

By this time, the ceasar in charge of north-west Europe was called Julian. His solution to the British problem was to send one of his generals, Lupicinus, to stop the Picts and the Scoti wrecking the place. This was no standard general being posted to Britain. Lupicinus was the Master of The Horse, which made him a right-hand man to an emperor. He was not the sort of bloke you send over to fix a little problem; he would only be dealing with the big stuff. Lupicinus was sent in winter, which, as with Constans, suggests there was a bit of a rush on. We don't have any details on what was going on, but it looks like Britain was in a dangerous state.

As we say, the details are very light, but we do have a source that says he stopped in London to plan his campaign. The same source also makes it clear that Lupicinus was a horrible bloke, but that's not important. We also know that he wasn't given long to get the job done, because Julian recalled him back to the continent, so he could arrest him. It turns out Lupicinus was going to jump into the wrong side of a squabble between the emperors, and Julian couldn't have that.

He might not have had long but seems like Lupicinus would have had a bit of trouble ending the issues altogether anyway. As far as we know, Britain was a bit quieter after he left. Quiet but definitely not silent. There were still raids on the provinces in Britannia and beyond, which culminated in a massive event in 367.

The Great Barbarian Conspiracy

This event is known as The Great Barbarian Conspiracy, although proper historians tend to go with 'the so-called Great Barbarian Conspiracy.' They aren't fans of the term, but since that's how people know it, we are sticking with it. This conspiracy consisted of seemingly coordinated attacks on Britain and Gaul from the Picts, the Scotti, the Attacotti, the Franks and the Saxons. We have met the majority of that lot, but the Attacotti are a group we haven't come across yet. They are generally assumed to be a group from what is now the Republic of Ireland. The sources lack detail, but they do like to call them cannibals, which is a familiar dig at the tribes in the region.

You will be unsurprised to hear that a lot of the problems in the 360s came from the north. We haven't checked in with Scotland for a while, but we do have a quote about them from Ammianus:

'Suffice to say that at the time in question the Picts were

divided into two tribes, the Dicalydones and the Verturiones.'

Who the hell are the Dicalydones and the Verturiones? It feels late in the day to have new players enter the game, but luckily it doesn't look like they have. What we are looking at there is just new terms for the two federations that were in Scotland before the Romans started calling them all Picts. The Dicalydones are probably the Caledonians (Caledonii), from the far north, and the Verturiones are probably the Maeatae, from between Hadrian's Wall and Edinburgh-Glasgow. That's the best guess anyway.

In Britain, the attacks from all these groups, from Scotland, Ireland, and the continent, were pretty effective. The bands of raiders spread themselves out and caused mayhem well south of Hadrian's Wall. This mayhem included the killing of a few influential Romans. One of them was called Nectaridus, and he appeared to be the Count of the Saxon Shore. We have come across the Saxon Shore before briefly. This was the string of defences along the South East Coast, set up to defend against Saxons, and similar folks, who were raiding Britain from the North Sea Coast, around the Netherlands. The man in charge of the land and naval defences involved in this was given the title Count. The second was a bloke named Fullofaudes, who is thought to have been the dux Britanniarum. That's a title given to a commander of soldiers in Britain, dux being the Latin version of Duke. This means that the raiders managed to kill two of the main military leaders in Britain, in fact, they got the two men in charge of both the army and the navy in Britain. If those two were dead, you should assume a lot of ordinary Roman soldiers didn't do much better.

It's hard to know how much of this was a coordinated conspiracy. It could have been a big case of simultaneous opportunism. You have to admit that the odds of these different groups all coordinating an attack feel small. Unlikely as it sounds, that appears to be what happened. Historians generally lean on the side of it not being quite as conspiratorial as all that. It seems to be a few different groups all seeing an opportunity, and to be fair, they all had a common goal. None of them was friends with the Romans, and they all would have fancied nicking some nice Roman stuff.

Not only does that amount of coordination between these separate groups suggest something of a conspiracy, but the fact that it took the Romans completely by surprise means that not everyone who the Romans thought would be on their side were playing by the rules. A good example of that is the areani, who were the scouts in Scotland that Constans came over to sort out. As with when Constans fell out with them, we aren't sure precisely what the areani did wrong. Maybe it was passing along of info, perhaps it was looking the other way as the tribes all stormed past Hadrian's Wall. Or they were just handy scapegoats.

So, what did the Romans do about all this? Well, it took them a while to get going in response. Part of the trouble was that this 'conspiracy' also had the Saxons and Franks attacking Gaul, which made sailing an army across the English Channel a bit difficult. The emperor at the time, Valentinian I, sent his caesar to Britain to sort it out, but he was recalled before he even got out of the port at Boulogne. Instead, a bloke named Jovinus was sent over. Except he did make it either. Valentinian fell ill, and, as a senior general, Jovinus was recalled. So finally, we have the third choice general who actually made it to Britain, Theodosius. He was the new Count of the Saxon Shore.

It's worth pausing here to say that who Theodosius was is important, and it's important because it might colour what we know about all this. He was known as Theodosius the Elder, to distinguish him from his son, Theodosius I, who later the emperor from 379. This is a crucial bit of information because we got a lot of detail about all this from Ammianus Marcellinus, who was writing while Theodosius I was emperor. Generally, it would have been a bad idea to make the emperor's dad look bad. It would have been much safer to make him look like a genius. That means historians are a bit worried about trusting him too much, as it might be that the whole Barbarian Conspiracy was made to seem much worse than it was to make Theodosius the Elder, who was tasked with fixing it in Britain, look better. And we have to say, if Theodosius did what we are told, he was a bit of legend.

With that nepotism in mind, what exactly did Theodosius do? He sailed to Britain with about 2000 men, which, as we know from the past, is not enough men to put down a full-on revolting Britain. Generally, at that point, they needed tens of thousands of soldiers. Theodosius spent the winter in London gathering the soldiers already on the island together, which might have been harder than it sounds. When it had all kicked off, the raiders went through the provinces like a hot knife through unprepared Roman. Quite sensibly, a lot of Roman soldiers had decided to take a little holiday and ran off. These holiday making Romans entertained themselves by forming their own bandit groups to make sure they got something out of the disaster as well. So now, the Roman citizens of Britain, who were already getting killed and robbed by barbarians, were getting done over by their own soldiers. Theodosius persuaded a lot of them to come back, and join him at London, which must have been a relief for everyone involved.

By 368 the Romans had started their fight back, including with the appointment of a new dux Britanniarum to replace the recently killed one. How hard it was to get control back is hard to say. The barbarian raiders were in smaller groups roaming the country, so it might have been quite easy to deal with each individual group once they got caught. We are told that the Romans split up and chase down the tribes, who were slowed by carrying all the stuff they had nicked.

Small bandit bands don't sound too much of a problem for a Roman army, even quite a small one, but Ammianus mentions that a whole province was lost and retaken by Theodosius, and renamed Valentia. This is where the fifth province we mentioned in an earlier chapter comes into play. Where this Valentia was, we don't know, but there are lots of guesses. It could be a bit of land north of Hadrian's Wall, but that seems unlikely since that was pretty much abandoned after this. It was the north that took a lot of the beating, so maybe it was in Cumbria, and Valentia was just a rebrand of an existing province. It's not particularly important, but it does at least suggest that the Romans completely lost control of whole regions of Britain for a while. Obviously, Rome had lost control of Britain loads of times in the last few centuries. This time feels very different, though. The last few times the Romans lost control was when a Roman backed by Roman legions took over as a splinter empire. This time it was non-Romans taking over. If the Scotti or the Franks grabbed an area, then that means absolutely no Roman control. No fake emperor, no fake Praetorian Guard, just barbarians. It was the first time in a while the Romans in Britain were in real trouble from people outside the empire.

The other mystery from Theodosius' time in Britain is about a rebel named Valentinus (which is annoyingly similar to Emperor Valentinian but is a different person). We are told by Ammianus that Valentinus had:

'been banished to Britain for some grave crime, and being a restless and mischievous beast, was eager for any kind of resolution or mischief, began to plot with great insolence against Theodosius, whom he looked upon as the only person with power to resist his wicked enterprise'.

So apparently, while the tribes were running riot, there was a Roman who took advantage and set up his own revolt. Where this was, and how big, it's hard to know, but it must have been really annoying for Theodosius to deal with at the same time. It's also interesting that a criminal, who was from Pannonia, which is over Austria/Hungary way, was exiled to Britain. Cleary, Britain was both far enough away from everyone else, and in a bad enough state, that this counted as a decent punishment. It makes it seem like

Britain was to the Romans what 18th-century Australia was to the British; somewhere handy to send people who you don't like but don't want to execute.

However he did it, Theodosius got everyone to calm down by reclaiming the provinces for Roman rule. He even disbanded the areani, who were those northern scouts who were apparently a bit to blame for the whole thing. Theodosius headed back to Rome in 368, but we are told in the sources that, before he went, he sorted out rebuilding of defences and the proper manning of the frontiers. It does seem a relatively simple end to an event with such a grand title as the Great Barbarian Conspiracy, but that's it. You can see why historians like to downplay all this despite its cool name. A conspiracy from five different tribes across Britain, Ireland and around Gaul, working together to attack the Romans, sounds epic. But how big can it have been if one Roman, even if he does sound impressive, can turn up with 2000 men to solve the attacks and revolts in Britain, in one year? It's sad, but the coolest things about all this is probably the name.

So, what did we learn? Never judge a historical event by its cool name. A visit to Britain from a Roman emperor can be surprisingly boring (you have forgotten that Constans was involved already. Admit it). And Britain still had it in them to be involved in Roman catastrophes.

The Collapsing Empire

Constantine seemed to be a bit of a force of nature. Taking over the whole of the Roman Empire, while keeping the barbarians at bay, was no mean feat. Unfortunately, what followed was less impressive.

The rest of the Constantinian Dynasty

Constantine had set his three sons (Constantine, Constantius and Constans - who doesn't like alliteration) and two nephews (Dalmatius and Hannibalianus) up as caesars. It was very much a case of too many caesars spoiling the empire. What followed his death was a family-based massacre, where the three sons killed off the nephews, and any other member of the extended family old enough to have a claim on a position of power. That what we assume happened anyway, the sources on it are a bit fluffy. The Roman historian, Eutropius, writing just after all this, claimed that one of the nephews, Dalmatius, was killed by soldiers. He reckoned that the murder wasn't ordered by Constantius, but it was 'sanctioned.' Which makes it sounds like in a mafia film where the boss gestures for execution rather than orders it. It's still his fault. Eutropius also calls Dalmatius 'a man of happy genius,' which is a description of someone which we very much enjoy.

The three sons then split the empire into three bits, for

them to control.

- Constantine II got the West - Britain, Gaul, Spain/Portugal.

- Constantius II got the East - Greece, Turkey, Syria, Palestine/Israel, Lebanon, Egypt and Libya.

- Constans got the middle - Italy, the rest of North Africa, and Eastern Europe from Slovenia down to Greece.

After that, they all got on and were just rulers in their part of the empire without any trouble. Except, no, it was an absolute shitshow for the next 20 years. In 340, Constantine II attacked Constans, because he wanted control over Italy and his other territories. In a victory for little brothers everywhere, Constans won, and Constantine II was killed fighting in Italy.

Surprisingly the two remaining brothers didn't launch into a war. That was probably because Constantius II had already inherited his dad's war against the Sassanids. The Persian emperor, Shapur II, had the upper hand, and the war in the 340s was mostly the Romans repulsing Persian attacks. Even so, we imagine it still took up quite a bit of the eastern emperor's time.

In 350, Constantius II needed to leave the East and headed into Europe, leaving behind Gallus, his cousin, to defend the East. The reason for that was that it had all gone wrong for Constans. He had lost the support of his legions, which always means the end of an emperor. This is where the usurper Magnentius pops up, and Constans ends up dead, with Magnentius declared as augustus by the soldiers in the East. Magnentius' power base was Britain, Gaul and Spain/Portugal, which was a fair chunk of the west of the empire. Constantius II couldn't be having that, although it was probably more out of concern for the empire than his brother. He marched westwards, and on the way to see

Magnentius, he beat another usurper, Vatranio, who had been declared emperor by soldiers in Pannonia (Hungary way).

Constantius II and Magnentius finally had a battle in Croatia, in September 351, 21 months after his brother was dead. So, this was all happening much slower than that short paragraph suggested. Even then, it wasn't until August 353 that Magnentius was finally properly beaten in a battle in France, where he committed suicide after losing. To make that happen, Constantius II had needed to call in favours/paid massive bribes to an Alamanni leader, Chnodomar, to help. That makes a bit of a change for the Alamanni, although we are sure as long as they were fighting Romans, they didn't really care which ones it was.

Constantius II was now the only augustus in town, which is no mean feat, but somehow doesn't feel as impressive as his dad. He had picked Gallus, the bloke who had left in the East during all this, as his caesar. It should have calmed down a bit, now one bloke was in charge, but it didn't work out like that. For a start, Gallus only lasted until 354 until Constantine recalled him to Rome and had him beheaded. According to Eutropius:

'Gallus was a man naturally cruel, and too much inclined to tyranny, if he could but have reigned in his own right'

Which means that not only was Gallus an arsehole, but he made the massive error of looking like he would try to take Constantius II's job. That sort of thing rarely ends well.

Gallus was replaced by Julian, Gallus' brother. He turned out to be a much better choice than his brother - and not just because Gallus didn't have a head anymore. It was a good job that Julian was a decent pick because it was all going off. We know from our last Roman Britain chapter, with the Great Barbarian Conspiracy, that it was all kicking off in Europe. The 350s were an absolute nightmare for the Romans. The Alamanni, in particular, were a problem again. They had pushed in from Germany really far into Gaul, taking Cologne (Colonia Agrippina) which was a major city in the province. Unsurprisingly, the Alamanni was led by the same bloke, Chnodomar, who had been helping Constantius II against Magnentius. As we said, they just wanted to be fighting Romans.

In the middle of this, another usurper popped up, Claudius Silvanus, who goes to show how much trouble the Romans were in. Silvanus was the son of a Frankish leader, who had been given important military jobs after helping Constantius beat Magnentius. There were plenty of Franks high-up in the Roman military by this point, and because of some infighting between those Franks, Silvanus ended up declaring himself augustus. The Frank only lasted a few weeks before he was killed by his own soldiers. That's not too unusual, but it shows that barbarians, on the inside and outside, were causing trouble for the Roman Empire. It must have been particularly annoying for Constantius because Silvanus was also the bloke who had been sent to sort out Chnodomar and his Alamanni.

Not that it was just the Alamanni and the Franks who were kicking up a fuss. 355-56 were spent over in Pannonia fighting the Sarmatians and the Quadi. However, it wasn't all bad news for the Romans, in 357 Julian finally beat the Alamanni back, having taken back Cologne, and he dove into the Franks as well, who were asking for it.

While Julian was keeping a lid on the West, Constantius II was back over in the East. In 359 Shapur II launched an attack on Iraq (Mesopotamia) which relaunched the war between the Sassanids and the Romans. It wasn't going particularly well for the Romans, but it was a bit of a stalemate with just some periods of Sassanids gains. In February 260, the Sassanids had picked up enough pace that Constantius ordered a lot of Julian's legions, who were in the West, to head over to support him in the East.

By this point, the pair hadn't been getting on. There was

the usual tension between augustus and caesar, which is always made worse when the caesar does well at something. As you would predict, Julian decided the legions weren't going East, and instead they declared him as augustus.

Two augusti would have usually meant yet another civil war, and if Constantius II hadn't had to stay in the East to keep the Persians from taking even more Roman territory, it would have been. Luckily for the Roman world, Constantius II died in November 361 leaving Julian as sole emperor of Rome, without having to fight about it.

__Julian As Emperor__

Something which makes Julian a bit different to the last few members of the Constantinian Dynasty was that he was a pagan. Once he was in charge, he was able to be open about that, and now suddenly the pagans were back on top. Although he didn't start on with the persecution again, it's just that Christians weren't top of the tree anymore.

In terms of how Julian did as an emperor, he had fixed enough of the problems in the West, that he was able to head east. In 363 he took 65,000 soldiers over to deal with Shapur II. He did pretty well over there as well, getting to Ctesiphon, down in Iraq. Typically, we would say the taking of that city was a sign of the Romans winning a war against the Persian empires. In this case, Julian got there but didn't take it, and the Romans ended up retreating. Eventually, in June 363, he was killed when he got hit by a spear at the Battle of Frygium.

The death of Julian was an issue, as he hadn't appointed a caesar. He was only in his early 30s when he died, so he probably thought he had a while to sort out the admin on that. That was certainly a bold assumption for any emperor to make, and it was a gamble that didn't pay off. Instead of a succession process involving one chosen candidate, the generals of his army got together, and in June 363 they declared a man named Jovian as the new augustus.

Jovian was not the winner's choice. He continued Julian's retreat, but his army got stuck on the River Tigris and had to sue for peace. In this peace, he gave everything east of the Tigris to the Sassanids. As well as handing over the important city of Nisibis, which is in Turkey, and giving up on Armenia. The loss of Armenia must have hurt: the Persians and the Romans had been fighting over that for centuries. This was not well received by the Romans, and it was taken as a bit dishonourable. It certainly seemed quite unRoman to give up like that, but it probably saved his army.

His rule lasted from June 363 to February 364, and there isn't much else to say. He was a Christian so reversed the benefits pagans got under Julian and put Christians back on top. Other than that, the only thing to say about him was that when he was in Turkey, he fell out with the people of Constantinople and burnt down their library. We don't 100% know why he died, but the story goes view is that he died while asleep from the fumes of a nearby fire. He was not a man who cut an impressive figure in the Roman world. And who burns down libraries? Nobhead.

Valentinian & Valens

What happened next was a big moment for the Roman Empire. The next bloke for the hot seat was Valentinian. His credentials were that he was a decent soldier, which was handy for the time. He got the job after a few days of debate from the higher-ups, so he wasn't the obvious choice exactly, but he was conveniently nearby. Straight away he appointed his brother, Valens, as co-emperor (the Romans really did love alliteration).

This is rarely a solid move in Roman history, getting the family involved, and dynasty building is a risky business.

That's not just 20/20m hindsight, and it was something which apparently occurred to people even then. According to Ammianus Marcellinus, a Roman historian who was around at the time, the commander of his cavalry said to Valentinian:

> *"If you love your relatives, most excellent emperor, you have a brother; if it is the state that you love, seek out another man to clothe with the purple."*

This time, though, Valentinian had big plans for his brother, and they literally split the empire into two, east and west. Historians tend to see this as a proper split compared to previous attempts, like with the Tetrarchy or Constantine's kids. Valentinian and Valens are seen as a big step towards there being two empires, working independently from each other.

If it's good enough for Roman emperors, it's good enough for us, so let's see how the brothers got on in their separate halves of the Roman Empire.

Valentinian

Valentinian, the emperor in the West, was seen as the more reasonable of the two brothers. He was a Christian, but he was relatively tolerant of anyone who wasn't, and didn't get too stuck into the factions within Christianity. To be fair, he had a lot else to be focusing on.

He was the emperor while the Great Barbarian Conspiracy was kicking off in Britain, and we know how that went. However, he also had problems from the usual tribes along his other borders. The Alamanni were on the rampage again in 365, and Valentinian had to move up to Paris to keep an eye on everyone.

He also had problems down in Africa, where we don't

hear about problems as often as with Europe. The issue was from the Austoriani tribe. They were attacking around the city of Leptis Magna, which is in Libya. Unfortunately for the Romans in the area, the bloke in charge of the army there decided he needed to be paid for protection. That's a bit much since we assume he was already getting paid for his job - a job which explicitly involved protecting the region from things like the Austoriani attacking. The locals refused to pay, and he left them to it. Doubly unfortunately for the locals was, when they complained to Valentinian, the man he sent down to investigate was bribed to say everything was fine. So nothing got done about it. This is as good an example as anything for how absolutely fucked the Roman Empire was by this point. In fact, Valentinian had a real struggle with the important Romans in his half of the empire, and there was a bit of a return to treason trials and generally fighting with the Senate.

In the end, it was the barbarians, not posh Romans, which finished Valentinian off in 375. He died following a meeting with some members of the Quadi, who were a tribe from around the Czech Republic. They were after a peace deal with the Romans, but their excuses for why they had been fighting the Romans in the first place were so shit that Valentines got overly angry and had a stroke. He died so after, leaving his son and heir, the 16-year-old Gratian, as emperor in the West.

Valens

Valens, the emperor in the East, was the less nice brother, which is probably why the historical view of him is as a half-blind, bow-legged arsehole. He had a less than auspicious start, when, as soon as he headed back east, he had to deal with a usurper. A bloke named Procopius decided he was emperor material, and the city of Constantinople agreed with him. He started picking up a fair bit of territory in Turkey, until, nine months later, when Valens finally beat him and had Procopius executed. All's well that ends well, but it was a bad start for Valens.

After finally beating the usurper, Valens kicked off some brutal revenge against the people who had supported Procopius. Valens also wasn't as religiously tolerant as, and he gave the pagans a really hard time. He also managed to expand this to include the wrong types of Christians. He was an Arian, who thought that God and Jesus were two separate beings, whereas the Nicenes thought God and Jesus were the same thing - one being. We are told that Valens was not nice to Nicenes. It sounds like a bad time to be living in the East.

An external part of Valen's revenge tour included the Goths. Some of the Gothic tribes had backed Procopius, and thousands of Goths had fought against Valens. As part of his victory lap, Valens attacked them. It was a scrap that went ok for the Romans, but in 369 they came to a peace deal. The Goths were to leave the Roman provinces along, and in return, they were allowed more access to trade with the Romans. That certainly makes it sound like Valens had a lot more joy with the barbarians than Valentinian did. Or at least they didn't make him so angry that he had a stroke over it.

Valens was emperor for another few years after Valentinian died. But we shall have a look at the end of his reign, and the madness that follows in the next Roman history chapter.

Huns, Goths & Vandals

We have mentioned the tribes of the Goths and the Huns quite a bit in the latest Roman history chapters, but who exactly were they?

Goths

Where the goths came from is a bit of a mystery. They were a Germanic tribe, and, according to their own legends, they came to mainland Europe across the Baltic Sea from Scandinavia. From there they moved down the Vistula River into Poland. Eventually the Goths carried on south, into the Balkans and across towards Ukraine and the Black Sea. This put them across a long part of the Romans border with Eastern Europe and beyond, which as we know caused some problems. We talk about the Goths as a group, but they were like the Britons, in that they were all one big group, but they were split into smaller units. In fact, there were two big Goth groups, the Visigoths and the Ostrogoths. The Visigoths were based around Romania (Dacia), and the Ostrogoths were based north of the Black Sea in Ukraine. Later on, when the Western Roman Empire collapsed, the Ostrogoths were the tribe that dominated in Italy, while the Visigoths headed to Spain.

Huns

The Huns were from much further east than the Goths. They were a nomadic group, who according to Roman sources weren't big fans of farming and building towns. They did, however, enjoy riding horses and archery. Huns play such a big part in our story because in the 4th-century they started moving west. They had been to the east of the Volga, a Russian river near the border of Kazakhstan. They then moved from the Volga, through to the Don, a river on the western border of Ukraine. By 376 The Huns had beaten the Goths and moved into the Balkans. That put them on the border of the Romans, where they really get involved in our story. You can also blame them for pushing the Goths straight into the Roman provinces. Clearly, the Huns were more of a worry than the Romans for the Goths.

Later on, the Huns would join the Goths in over running the collapsing Western Roman Empire, under their leader Atilla the Hun. Perhaps because we know that the Huns originated in Central Asia, or perhaps because we know that it came towards the end of the Roman Empire in Western Europe, Attila the Hun seems like a very separate figure to Britain. However, in 451 Atilla the Hun fought a battle in Eastern France, possible in Troyes, which is south-east of Paris. That means Attila the Hun was not too far over the English Channel. Maybe it's just us, but it seems to have him so linked to British history.

Vandals

The Vandals are the third tribe that get called out as part of the downfall of the Romans in the West. They are believed to have taken a similar route as the Goths, coming from Scandinavia to Poland. Except they got there first, in the 2nd century BC. They also spread southwards, down towards Dacia, but they were given less room when the

Goths turned up after them, which means they were stuck down in the Balkans. Like the Goths, the Huns forced the Vandals towards Roman territory when they started off their domino effect.

During our story, the Vandals were a bit quieter than a lot of the other tribes, but later on, they got heavily involved. Including, and particularly, during the sacking of Rome in 455. Which is where we get the word vandalism, as in destroying things from. They ended up moving to take over from the Romans in North Africa until they were finally given a kicking by the Eastern Roman Empire in the 530s.

The End Of Roman Britain

We have had the Great Barbarian Conspiracy, and the Roman of Britain came through it, not unscathed but still on top. Nevertheless, we hate to break it to anyone who's been enjoying themselves, but we are in the home stretch for Roman Britain now.

Magnus Maximus

We are starting the end of Roman Britain with something you will be familiar with by now. A usurper came out of Britain called Magnus Maximus. With a name like that, how could he be anything other than a charismatic force of nature? He was a general in Britain, and in 282-3 he had beaten the Scotti and Picts, who were presumably having a bit of a raid.

The emperor in the West at this time was a bloke called Gratian, with this little brother as his caesar. We say, bloke, Gratian was only 16 when he was promoted to augustus when his dad Valentinian I died in 375. As with pretty much all the Roman emperors in the West at this time, he was not a popular man/child. It didn't help that Theodosius I, who was emperor in the East was doing a bang-up job. You can't really trust the names given to rulers, but there must be something in the fact that he is known as Theodosius the Great.

This is particularly relevant to Magnus Maximus, as he had first come to Britain with Theodosius the Elder, who you will remember as the Count of the Saxon Shore who had fought in the Great Barbarian Conspiracy. He was also Theodosius the Great's dad. There is a chance Magnus was related to the Theodosius family, but even if he wasn't, Magnus and Theodosius knew each other. In 383 Magnus was a commander in Britannia, and, as we say, he had been doing well against the Picts and their friends. The classic combination of impressive general and unpopular emperor resulted in a predictable manoeuvre from soldiers in Britain; they proclaimed their commander, Magnus, emperor.

Magnus thought that was a good idea, and he was pretty successful with it. He left Britain and went off marching south, and he was fairly well supported around the western part of the empire. When Gratian was killed by people loyal to Magnus, he became Augustus in the West. To show how weird the Roman Empire had got, the other emperor in the West was Valentinian II. He was Gratian's younger brother, and we mean younger. In 384, when all this was happening, Valentinian was 9.

The power was still in the East, but Theodosius tolerated this usurper for a while. However, in 388, while Magnus was invading Italy, kicking Valentinian out of Milan, Theodosius beat Magnus, and that was the end of him. This was an example of yet another Roman usurper coming out of Britain and doing surprisingly well. Apart from the whole being executed after four years thing.

Magnus has some significance beyond him being a general in Britain who went on to be an emperor for a bit. In an unexpected turn of events, he became a bit of a feature in Welsh folklore. There is a medieval Welsh story where Macsen Wledig (that's Magnus) goes to Wales, finds himself a fair Welsh maiden, and sets up some Welshmen as kings in Britain and a bit of France. It's more involved than that, but that's the gist of it. It's mad that a 4th-century Roman usurper, who was originally from Spain, was a feature of a 12th-century Welsh myth.

Really Near The End For Roman Britain

Theodosius died in 395, and after him, the whole Roman Empire went a bit mad again. If it ever stopped in the first place. He left the East to his eldest son, Arcadius and the West to his other son Honorius. However, it seems Honorius didn't have all that keen a grasp on the goings-on. It looks like the power was actually with the top general in the West, Flavius Stilicho. We are used to the idea that 'Roman' didn't mean from Rome or even Italian, and it hadn't for a very long time at this point. However, Stilicho was half Vandal, a group from Eastern Europe. The empire had become very reliant on friendly barbarian people in their army to keep out the unfriendly barbarians. Stilicho was a big wig in the empire, but more importantly for us, he also oversaw the last known campaign from Roman soldiers in Britain. Obviously, there were Roman soldiers in the provinces of Britannia after it, but this was the Romans sending extra soldiers specifically to campaign against an enemy in Britain. It may have even been that Stilicho went there in person. This campaign was in 396-8 and was against the Picts and Scotti, which will have surprised nobody.

The Roman Empire was in an absolute state for the whole of the 5th-century. In 406 the West of the empire had the double whammy of being overrun by the Franks coming over the Rhine and dealing with a revolt in Britain. This will sound oh-so-familiar, but the soldiers of Britain, seeing the

Roman Empire crumbling around them, decided that they would stick the boot in and declared one of their own as emperor. In fact, they declared three of their own as emperors. The first one, Marcus, was unsatisfactory and got killed, the second one, Gratian (not the child emperor), was found equally wanting, so the Romans in Britain went for third times the charm, and declared a bloke called Constantine as emperor. This really was a winner, and he did so well that by 409 Honorius was sick of him running all over Gaul, causing trouble. Constantine III, as he became, only lasted until 411, until he died of unnatural causes (execution), but that's not too bad going.

We should pause here and just marvel in how our little island was the stage for so many of these usurpers. Generally, there was a lot of it in Roman History, and Britain was part of that for hundreds of years, but the amount of them is still mad. We count: Clodius Albinus, Carausius, Allectus, Magnus Maximus, Marcus, Gratian, and Constantine III. That doesn't include Constantine who proclaimed himself emperor when he really shouldn't have, or indeed the period that Britain was part of the Gallic Empire. There definitely was something in the water. That or the constant drizzle drove them all insane.

Constantine III was massive for Roman Britain, not his death obviously, but his bid for the emperorship. When he ran off to the continent, he would have taken any available armies with him. How many men did he take, and how many Roman soldiers were left? We have seen estimates of Britain having about 17,000 men stationed there around this time, which would be about a third of the forces the Romans used to have in Britain. It does make some sense that soldiers would have been taken from the island. It was going off on the continent, and it's not as if the Romans had spare armies to put into Britain. The whole western half of the empire was in a state, with the Romans fighting among themselves, and the tribes were running all over the Roman provinces.

The Roman empire had been struggling under assaults from the Germanic tribes for a very long time by this point. Frequently, part of their solution was to allow settlement in Roman territory in exchange for service in the Roman armies, the Romans called these people laeti. Using barbarians to fight barbarians is a good short-term solution, but it starts being a bit iffy long term. Some of these Germanic folks started to do quite well for themselves with the Roman army, and we have already met Stilicho, who was the half Vandal, who was basically running the place for a while. It wasn't just the lands along the Rhine that were becoming a bit more Germanic. The Romans had long had a habit of sending members of beaten tribes to Britain, and this continued in the 3rd-century. We have seen Carausius and his Franks, but there are also suggestions of Burgundians and Vandals being sent over much earlier than all this, in the 270s. A hundred years later, in the 370s and Emperor Valentinian moved a group of Alamanni over, with one of their kings being given a high status. There is also the possibility that some Attacotti, from Ireland, were allowed to settle in Wales. All that means there would have been plenty of pockets of non-Romans living in the Roman provinces of Britain.

You would have to question how loyal these groups would be to the Romans, particularly during a time when their own tribes from outside the empire seemed to be winning. A good example of how wrong it could go is the Goths. More specifically a group of Visigoths from around the Danube. They had been migrating west through the Balkans and surrounding area for a while, causing all sorts of problems for the Romans. As was their style, the Romans made friends with a group of them and one of their leaders, a bloke named Alaric, acted as a general in the Roman army. However, it was a bit of an on-off relationship, and he ended up sacking the city of Rome in 410. Which isn't what you want from someone who used to work for you. You have to wonder how much more loyal the laeti in Britain were?

What we are saying is that the Romans had lost a tight

control over the whole place, so how could they possibly be any use to an island right on the edge of their empire? Britain was being hammered by the Saxons, and Constantine, or any Roman emperor, was in no position to help. In fact, the declaration of Constantine as emperor, and his running off with soldiers in tow, leaving Britain at the mercy of more attacks from Saxons, was a big enough event that 409 is traditionally listed as the end of Roman rule in Britain.

This is the quote from Zosimus about the state of Britain in around 409:

'[The] situation in Britain made it necessary for the inhabitants of Britain and some of the Celtic nations to revolt from Roman rule and live on their own, and to obey Roman laws no longer. The Britons took up arms, and braving danger because they were now independent, they freed themselves from the barbarians who were threatening them.'

As in, 'lads forget about us, you are on your own.'

How the Roman provinces transitioned from Roman rule to self-rule is a bit unclear. It's worth remembering at this point that everyone in the provinces of Britannia had been under Roman rule for centuries by now. So, in reality, this wasn't the Britons, as they were when Claudius and Plautius arrived, throwing off rule from Rome. This was people who would have seen themselves, to a greater or lesser extent, as part of the Roman Empire. And now they had to set something up to replace the Romans and all their systems of running things. Presumably, a lot of them wanted to keep something close to the status quo, except with less being hammered by Saxons and the like. However, this wasn't like Carausius or the Gallic Empire. This was a proper divorce, the Britons might have got to keep some stuff, like DVDs or cool buildings, but it was over.

The split from Rome was anarchic, and the Roman system of government and economy appeared to almost immediately collapse. As usual, it is the coins which tell the story. Coins from the continent stopped being imported around 409, and no local versions were being minted. No coins means no taxation and no system of administration. It sounds like a libertarian's dream. Although libertarians' wildest dreams don't usually include an end to manufacturing, which seems to be what happened to goods like pottery making. Libertarians also hardly ever imagine being stabbed and robbed by someone from Scotland. They would not have enjoyed the end of Roman rule in Britain.

In terms of administration, Constantine's governors were kicked out, but they weren't directly replaced. So, unlike under Carausius, a mirror image of a Roman administration wasn't kept up, which might have kept the Roman style economy going a bit longer.

Generally, we have even less info on all this than we have ever had under the Romans, as there were fewer Romans around to keep records. The general story is one of the collapse of Roman rule in the provinces, with people breaking up into much smaller regions being run by warlords. Which would be not that different to the system of tribes that were around the place before the Romans appeared. However, this collapse and rebuilding of our island isn't the story of Roman Britain, so we will have to leave that for when we have a look at Saxon Britain.

And that's it, the Romans were gone. What have we learnt? Considering most people don't know much about the period, Roman Britain was pretty cool. You can't turn your back on the folk of Britain for one minute. And it's best not to romanticise the Romans, even if you like the classics, because they were fucking mental.

The End Of The Roman Empire (Sort Of)

We left the Romans in the last Roman history chapter in the 370s, with the West under Gratian and the East still being held by Valens. So how did the Romans get from that state of affairs to having lost Britain by 410?

There are shelves and shelves of books on how and why the Roman Empire collapsed. However, for anyone following along, the journey from here to 410 is not a surprising one. It's been a mess for a century or so at this point.

A huge event which kicked off while Valens was still emperor was the war with the Goths. In 376 they turned up in numbers on the Danube. This time they weren't there to invade, in the traditional sense. Instead, they were looking for somewhere to escape to. They had been forced west by the Huns who were migrating into Europe. The Huns were from Central Asia, but before this, they had migrated west towards the Volga, around Kazakhstan. They started moving further west and were giving the tribes between the Volga and the Romans a beating. Bearing in mind some of these tribes had been causing the Romans themselves some trouble for ages, not least the Goths, this was something for everyone to worry about.

The Goths sent a delegation to Valens and asked for

permission to move into Roman provinces. There may have been up to 20,000 people who were asking to move in. If they were being pushed over by the Huns, you have to assume that is that if their request wasn't granted there would have been a fight. We have mentioned a few times so far, just how often the Romans allowed people from outside the empire to move in. Usually in exchange for them getting involved in the Roman army. Valens took this approach again because at the time he was building up for an offensive against the Sassanids. He could be back in control of Armenia, and that not only meant there were fewer men available to force the Goths back where they had come from, but a few extra thousand Goths in the army would have come in handy.

From this, you will be expecting the story to go in a very specific direction, and you would be right. Except it was so much more stupid than you thought. Valens allowed the Goths into Thrace, which is basically the European side of Turkey. Once they were there, safe from the Huns, the Romans treated them horribly, and when they ran out of food, a localised famine started. The Romans refused to help, and things were made worse when another group of Goths arrived in the region, without being allowed in by the Romans. There is a fact that is usually quoted to show how bad this got, and it's absolutely devastating. We are told that the Goths were able to buy a dead dog to eat in exchange for one Goth to be taken as a slave.

The spark that lit the inevitable fire was a dinner organised by the two Roman commanders, Lupicinius and Maximus, at Marcianopolis (in Bulgaria). They had invited the two leaders of the group of Goths who had been allowed into Thrace, Fritigern and Alavivus, but made sure the general mass of Goths couldn't come into the city to get food. The Goths outside didn't like that and kicked off. The response from the Romans was to attack the Goths. We assume this led to the death of one of the Gothic leaders, Alavivus, because we don't hear from him again. Fritigern was taken hostage, but he was allowed to go free if he promised to head out and calm the Goths down. He didn't do that, and instead, he went off with his fellow tribesmen and set the world alight.

Fritigern and his mates were joined by the other Goths in the region. Not only that but they attracted support from some units of Goths who were in the Roman army. That feels inevitable, but it must have been terrifying for the Romans, to have bits of their own army disappear to join the other side. Lupicinius followed the new Goth army, but he got beaten in a battle, and the Goths proceeded to roam around the Balkans absolutely wrecking everything. Not only were the Goths kicking up a fuss, but they were actually joined by some Huns and Alans. The latter, who had the best name for a tribe ever, were from north of the Black Sea. They had been caught up in the Hun's migration west as well. The initial explosion of violence was in 377, and in 378 Valens ordered Gratian, the emperor in the West, to head over and stop them. The problem was that Gratian was busy, because the Alamanni were back at it, and had crossed the Rhine.

Gratian's delay meant that when Valens arrived on the scene, from the East where he had been having trouble with the Sassanids, he arrived before Gratian's army. Instead of waiting he just dove right in. By this point, the Goths had calmed down a bit and had offered peace in exchange for lands in Thrace. The Goths just wanted somewhere to live. Valens had none of it, and instead, he fought a rubbish battle where the Roman army got so battered, and so many of them died, Valen's body wasn't even found after.

According to Ammianus Marcellinus:

'The annals record no such massacre of a battle except the one at Cannae'

Cannae was a battle where the Carthaginians, under Hannibal, wiped out a roman army in 216 BC. So, this was the worst thing to happen to Romans in 594 years, and as many as 20,000 Romans died. Although as ever, it was probably a bit less than that.

Theodosius and Gratian

Valens was followed by Theodosius as the new emperor in the East, and he and Gratian did a bit better against the tribes. By 382 they had done well enough that everyone was able to get together and come up with a sort of peace. The Goths were given the option to settle inside the Roman Empire in Thrace and Dacia, which is all they had been asking for to start with. Luckily for the Romans, it was quiet in the East as well, because, in 379 Shapur II of the Sassanid dynasty died, and tensions died down a bit. In 386, they even signed a treaty which meant both empires could split the control over Armenia, just like they had back in the day.

We haven't mentioned Gratian a lot in all this, we have also been quiet on the Roman on Roman violence, but don't worry it was still there. We just wanted to give the Goths a bit of stage time. In fact, we have missed out mentioning a whole new Roman emperor. When Valentinian died, the empire was split between Valens in the East and Gratian in the West. There were a couple of generals who didn't fancy that, called Merobaudes and Equitius. Instead, they declared Gratin's half-brother, and Valentinian's son, emperor, making him Valentinian II. Neither Gratian nor Valens had any say in that, and there wasn't much they could do about it. Which meant that four-year-old Valentinian II was an augustus in charge of Italy, North Africa and a bit of Eastern Europe. Because what this situation really called for the intervention of an infant. It goes to show how much control the generals of the armies had at this point. The power behind the throne seemed to be Merobaudes, a bloke of Frankish birth who was confident he had the backing of the old armies of Valentinian I.

So, Gratian was now sharing power with Valentinian II.

Gratian was a bit of a weird one. He did surprisingly well against the barbarian tribes and managed to keep the job of the emperor from 367 to 383. Considering all that was going on, this was good going. So, he must have known what he was doing, to some extent. Gratian didn't seem very popular, however. The story that gets told in every book about the man is a tale of one of the most inadvisable cosplays in history. Just after Valens got killed by the Goths, along with tens of thousands of Romans, Gratian dressed as a Germanic warrior and paraded around. We assume that's the ancient equivalent of an aspiring Tory minister or member of the royal family dressing up as a nazi for banter.

His unpopularity hit its peak, when Magnus Maximus, who we have met, decided to make himself emperor from Britain. Gratian went to stop him but was abandoned by his own soldiers, and he was executed by Andragathius, the Goth who Maximus had made his Master of the Horse. It's worth noting that Merobaudes had supported Maximus as well. Which makes a lot of not very Roman people, at the top of Roman politics, making some serious decisions for the Roman Empire. Even for a notoriously and long-standing diverse empire, it was clear that the Roman Empire was losing control of itself.

All But Over

This left the now eight-year-old Valentinian II as a co-emperor in the West with Magnus Maximus. In the end, Magnus Maximus was defeated in 388, and Valentinian II died in 392 when he was found having hanged himself. There is a fair chance he was actually killed by one of his generals, Arbogast. Arbogast was a pretty influential bloke, who was also a barbarian, very probably a Frank. He was so important, in fact, that he chose the next emperor in the West, Eugenius.

Theodosius wasn't on board with this, and while he

initially officially accepted Eugenius as his co-emperor, six months later Theodosius declared his eight-year-old son Honorius as emperor in the West. In September 394 Eugenius fought Theodosius in Slovenia and was beaten and executed.

Theodosius died in 395, which left his son Arcadius as the emperor in the East, and Honorius as the emperor in the West. Although they were both too young to actually rule. Arcadius was about seventeen, so he wasn't far off but still needed a regent, called Rufinus. Honorius was only nine, so really the power in the West was with the regent and general Flavius Stilicho. Stilicho was a half Vandal, continuing the run of people of varying levels of barbarian birth running the place.

This is fully the home straight for the Roman Empire as we know it. We said before that the empire had been divided into two between Valentinian I and Valens, east and west. That was true, but as we have seen, it re-joined to a certain extent after that, like when they were fighting off the Goths. Now, with Theodosius dead, the empire was properly split into two. And the split was partly because of the two regents, Rufinus in the East, and Stilicho in the West. They did not get on. In 395, shortly after Theodosius died, Rufinus requested that some soldiers were returned to the East. They had recently been posted to the West because they were in more trouble over there. Now the East needed them to fight off some Goths being led by a bloke named Alaric. Stilicho agreed to give the soldiers back, and he sent the army over. Only when they arrived in Constantinople, where Rufinus was, they killed him. Which we assume they were told to do by Stilicho. We said they didn't get on.

This kicked off a power shift, but the man to fill the vacuum was a eunuch called Eutropius. Alaric was still rampaging about and attacked Greece, so Eutropius decided to buy him off. He gave the Goth an official title, as a general, which gave him the run of Illyricum (Croatia). Eutropius also bought the loyalty of the leader of the army that had killed Rufinus, Gainas, by putting him in charge of Thrace. Gainas was also a Goth.

In a manoeuvre that can't help but remind us of Varys in Game of Thrones (for obvious reasons, if you have read/seen it) Eutropius also teamed up with a general in North Africa, Gildo. This resulted in food from Africa being diverted to Constantinople in the East rather than Rome in the West. This kerfuffle ended when Stilicho sent Gildo's brother, Mascazel, to stop him from doing that. Mascazel did his job, but Stilicho still had him drowned to draw a line under it. Even for the Romans, this was getting nasty.

This was in 398, which was the same year that Stilicho organised the defence of Britain against the sea-raids that were going on. Him managing to do that suggests there was a semblance of control in the empire. A year later a general called Tribigild (a Goth) rebelled against the Romans. Gainas (a Goth) was sent to put the rebellion down, but instead teamed up with Tribigild (Double Goth) and got Emperor Arcadius to get rid of Eutropius. This was a bit of a turning in the tide of the Roman opinion of the goths, and the Romans started fighting back. Although it was still Arcadius' solution to use another general Fravitta (a Goth) to get rid of Gainas.

The culmination of this Goth on Goth violence was when Alaric, who was out on a bit of a limb now his fellow Goth commanders were dropping away, launched an invasion into Italy in 401. By 402 Stilicho had beaten and captured him, although he was let go to return to the Goths. Not that Alaric was Stilicho's only problem. Another Gothic leader, this time without a Roman military title, called Radagaisus was attacking the province of Raetia (Austria/Switzerland). Radagaisus carried on being a threat until a massive battle between him and Stilicho in 406.

By this point, Gaul and Eastern Europe were crawling with Goths, Vandals, Alans and a full array of barbarian tribes. Made worse by 408, when the usurper Constantine III, coming out of Britain, claimed the emperorship. Alaric, who was still knocking about, took advantage of this and was now in the Province of Noricum (Austria). He demanded 4000 pounds of gold, apparently in as payment for his past work (which often involved attacking Romans) but was really as a payment to leave the Romans alone for a bit.

In the East, Arcadius died leaving Theodosius II, a seven-year-old in charge. This was also the year that Stilicho was killed after being accused of trying to replace Theodosius II with his own son.

The result of this was a reign of terror, where anyone associated with Stilicho was tortured and killed. More importantly, it also led to the armies of eastern Rome running through Italy killing any barbarians they could find, men, women, and children. The barbarian survivors of this were understandably nervous and looking for revenge. They turned to Alaric, who hadn't got his 4000 pounds of gold, and was basically surrounding Rome, grabbing the crucial ports and cutting them off. He offered to go away for even more gold and a homeland for his people in the empire. Relations between Alaric and emperor Honorius were bad, which is understandable what with the siege and blackmail. Alaric was threatening Rome, and Honorius from his base in Ravena in Northern Italy was playing silly buggers.

In the end, Alaric got sick of Honorius being a twat and headed to Rome, where he met with the Senate and laid out an agreement. He wouldn't carry on attacking, but he would pick the next emperor in the West, a bloke named Priscus Attalus. So now the West had two emperors, Honorius in Ravena and the Goth backed Priscus Attalus in Rome. Not to mention Constantine III, who was still around the place.

Unfortunately, Honorius now controlled the food supply for Rome, so the people in the city were seriously struggling. We are told that it got so bad some people were advocating the legalisation and regulation of cannibalism. Alaric blamed Attalus for losing the North African food supply to

Rome. Apparently, Attalus had misunderstood just how much of a puppet he was, and when it came to the food supply, he had formulated his own plan, rather than doing what he was told. His plan had not worked.

This led to a falling out between Alaric and Priscus Attalus, and the start of peace talks between Alaric and Honorius. Unfortunately for everyone involved, there was a Gothic leader on Honorius' side who really hated Alaric. He attacked Alaric's people at the talks, and Alaric assumed it was on Honorius orders. This ended all options for peace, and Alaric marched on Rome. In August 410 they reached the city and sacked it. Even with everything going on, it must have been unimaginable for the people of Rome. They were surrounded by all these massive buildings and hundreds and hundreds of years of history of ruling the world. Now here they were, starving and having the city being destroyed by Barbarians.

Luckily for the city, there was still no food, so Alaric and his mates left fairly quickly to head to Africa to get some. Although, that has to be the shittiest definition of luck we have heard.

So, you can see why in 410, Rome wasn't able to keep control over Britain. We have been selling this as the end of the Roman Empire, but it's important to point out that it wasn't. It's just the end of the Roman Empire as far as Britain is concerned. The last emperor in the West is usually seen as Romulus Augustus, which is an apt name, being called for the founder of the whole thing. He was kicked out by a Germanic leader, who made himself the King of Rome. That was in 476. A barbarian king in Rome meant no more empire. Except not really. Or at all. The Roman Empire continued to exist in the East, although it's usually called the Byzantine Empire, after the capital city - Byzantium, which was actually Constantinople and is now Istanbul. The last emperor there was Constantine XI who was kicked off his throne in 1453 by the Ottoman Empire.

That's a lot more Romans, but as everyone knows after it lost half of a small island on the edge of its territories, it ceased to become important. So, goodbye Romans as far as Britain was concerned. It's been one hell of a story, and we hope you enjoyed hearing about that bunch of megalomaniac, family killing, empire building, wall erecting, lunatics.

That's your lot.